GEOGRA
ALTERNATIVE

Diverse learning spaces for children and young people

Peter Kraftl

First published in Great Britain in 2015 by

Policy Press
University of Bristol
1-9 Old Park Hill
Bristol BS2 8BB
UK
t: +44 (0)117 954 5940
pp-info@bristol.ac.uk
www.policypress.co.uk

North America office:
Policy Press
c/o The University of Chicago Press
1427 East 60th Street
Chicago, IL 60637, USA
t: +1 773 702 7700
f: +1 773-702-9756
sales@press.uchicago.edu
www.press.uchicago.edu

British Library Cataloguing in Publication Data
A catalogue record for this book is available from the British Library.

Library of Congress Cataloging-in-Publication Data
A catalog record for this book has been requested.

ISBN 978 1 44730 050 2 Paperback

Cover design by Qube Design Associates.
Front cover: A forest school in Cornwall. (Photo taken by author)
Printed and bound in Great Britain by CMP, Poole
The Policy Press uses environmentally responsible print partners

For Juliet and Emily

Contents

List of figures

Notes on author

Peter Kraftl is a Reader in Human Geography at the University of Leicester. He has researched and published widely on the geographies of childhood, education and architecture. With John Horton and Faith Tucker he is the co-editor of *Critical geographies of childhood and youth: Contemporary policy and practice* (The Policy Press, 2012). He is currently co-editing a volume on *Geographies of informal education* with Sarah Mills for Palgrave. He is co-editor of the journal *Children's Geographies*.

Acknowledgments

I would like to thank several people who read and (critically) commented on earlier drafts of this book and related articles. First, I would like to thank the anonymous reviewers for their constructive, generous and helpful comments on the original proposal and draft manuscript. Second, I would like to thank the editorial team at Policy Press, and especially Emily Watt, for their support, advice and guidance. Third, I would like to thank John Horton (as always), Jenny Pickerill, Gavin Brown and Sarah Mills.

This book would not have been possible without the incredible generosity of educators, learners and parents at over 50 learning spaces around the UK. For ethical reasons as well as space, I cannot name all those who spared time and energy to accommodate my visits and my questions. However, going back in time, I would like to thank the community at Nant-y-Cwm Steiner School in Pembrokeshire, who allowed me to spend several months during 2003 working and researching at the school, and especially Christopher Day and Phil Forder. The homeschooling community responded fantastically to a request to take part in my research: I would like to thank all of the parents who invited me to their homes or spoke to me on the telephone, but especially Leslie Barson and Gina Purrmann, who facilitated many of my visits. At Kilquhanity Children's Village, I would like to thank Andrew Pyle and Gavin Aitkenhead for their time, generosity and hospitality during my visit. Thanks also to Paul Hooper, at Green Learning, and Trythall Primary School, West Cornwall, for extending an invitation to take part in a forest school day – a photograph from which is included on the front cover of this book, with kind consent of the school. At Findhorn, thanks to Lianne Milligan for accommodating my unexpected visit and dealing with my questions with generosity and care. Beyond that, I extend my sincere gratitude to all those at every learning site who took part in my research, in however small a way.

I am very grateful to Sophie Hadfield-Hill, who undertook an interview on my behalf in the US, and who provided several photographs for this book. I also acknowledge the support of the University of Leicester, who allowed me to take a sabbatical from January to June 2011, when some of the research visits for this book took place.

Finally, I would like to thank my family. I am indebted to my parents, my brother, Lyn and Grantie (who passed away while I was writing this book) for their continuing love and support. This book is dedicated to my wife, Juliet, and my beautiful daughter, Emily, for their support, belief and time spent living, learning and loving together.

ONE

Introduction

Many educators prioritise learning processes over learning spaces. In whatever setting, a 'good education' is most often underpinned by the attributes of the teacher, the willingness of the learners, the appropriateness of the curriculum and the quality of the relationship between teachers and learners. In undertaking the primary research for this book, I have been told – sometimes forcefully – that excellent learning experiences can take place in what appear to be the direst, barest and most impoverished physical surroundings. Indeed, in several of the examples included in this book, learning takes place in run-down portable cabins, simple patches of woodland, condemned buildings and on free buses to the supermarket. As it happens, I am convinced that these educators are correct to prioritise 'social' learning processes over learning spaces in this way.

This may seem a strange way for someone who writes as a 'geographer' to begin a book about 'geographies' of alternative education in the UK. Yet it is prompted by a far stronger conviction that space does matter, in all manner of ways, to practices of alternative education. However, this assertion is based upon a very different theorisation of 'space'. While some sections of the book do look at such things as the design of school buildings or the layout of classrooms, I aim to demonstrate that geographies of alternative education go far beyond this. Inspired by a rich vein of work in human geography, I begin from the premise that it is impossible to divorce social processes from spatial processes. The reason that most educators prioritise learning processes over learning spaces is that they – like most geographers – recognise that the physical, material elements of a learning environment can tell us very little when viewed in isolation. The question that then emerges is how all of the other, 'social' processes that characterise a 'good education' might be understood in spatial terms.

This book therefore asks fundamental questions about what happens when we understand those social and spatial processes to be productive of one another. In doing so, I attune to some of the *spatialities* that characterise alternative education in the UK. Pile and Keith (1993, p 6) use the term spatiality to 'capture the ways in which the social and spatial are inextricably realized in one another; to conjure up the circumstances in which society and space are simultaneously realized by thinking, feeling, doing individuals and [...] the many different conditions in which such realizations are experienced'. The substantive, empirical chapters of this book (Chapters Four to Eight) explore manifold examples of spatiality – from understandings of spatial scale, to connections and disconnections with local communities, and from the potential of material mess to the importance of bodily movements in learning. Thus, the overriding aim of this book is to look across a range of alternative learning spaces in the UK in order to uncover and contrast some of their spatialities. This is a task that, as far as I am aware, has never been undertaken before, and I expand on why this is such an important aim later in this introductory chapter.

The second main aim of this book is entwined with the first. I aim to analyse exactly what is 'alternative' about alternative learning spaces in the UK. My working definition is that 'alternative' educational approaches are those that are not administered, controlled and/or predominantly funded through the state-sanctioned educational programmes assumed to be the 'mainstream' in countries where education is an assumed, universal right for children (as it is in the UK). Narrowing this definition somewhat, this book focuses upon a range of UK-based alternatives that provide for children and young people aged two to 18, in a way that somehow supplements or (in many cases) replaces their engagement with mainstream education. I recognise that this in itself is a very broad age range but, as I argue in Chapter Seven, this is part of the point. For, if one looks across homeschooling groups, human scale or democratic schools it soon becomes apparent that they offer an alternative space in which the intentional mixing of younger and older children more or less replaces the incremental, age-based segregation assumed in most mainstream schools. Bearing in mind this working definition, I look at a range of alternative learning spaces, all of which have been the location for my own primary research, including Steiner schools, Montessori schools, human scale schools, democratic schools, forest schools, care farms, homeschooling and a spiritual community.

The question of what makes a particular learning practice 'alternative' is not one that can be answered with a few lines of definition. Rather, this is a task for which a whole book (at least) is required, and which I tackle from different directions in each chapter, before pulling together these disparate strands in the conclusion. As I detail in Chapter Three, it is also the case that many previous studies have grappled with this question, especially in terms of the theoretical, theological and/or pedagogical principles that underpin such alternatives (for example Sliwka, 2008; Woods and Woods, 2009). Yet my approach in this book offers some novel perspectives on this question. A key contribution is the comparative element: simply put, most academic research on alternative education focuses upon a particular learning approach or philosophy, rather than looking across a range of approaches for congruencies and disjunctures (one notable, but far shorter, exception being Ferguson and Seddon, 2007). The organisation of this book – arranged according to theme, not educational type – reflects this. Other than the contextual descriptions in Chapter Three, readers should not expect to find systematic analysis of each approach in turn. Rather, this book will provide a broader picture of the face of alternative education in the UK at the beginning of the 21st century, and will theorise the multiple, complex and sometimes contradictory ways in which educational 'alternatives' intersect with the educational 'mainstream' in the UK.

This book will argue that a focus upon a broadly-conceived notion of spatiality is key to a comparative theorisation of alternative learning spaces. But this is not intended solely as a book for geographers – although I hope that it will offer a substantial contribution to nascent research on geographies of education (Chapter Two). Rather, drawing on theoretical perspectives from human geography, sociology, education studies and philosophy, it is meant to have wide appeal. The diversity of disciplinary influences is intentional. Inspired in part by J.K. Gibson-Graham's (2006, 2008) work on diverse economic practices (on which more below), I demonstrate how the *multiple* spatialities of alternative education dismantle further than previous work any sense of a simple binary between 'alternative' and 'mainstream' education, even though most of the examples I cite expressly position themselves as 'alternative'. Paralleling Gibson-Graham's theorisation of global capitalism, this will show that I am not positing mainstream education, educators or educational spaces as a monolithic, impenetrable entity, nor as a universal force for bad. Indeed, as I am not a teacher or student of education studies by training, I avoid any such evaluative judgments. Rather, I am interested in what a comparative perspective can tell us about the multiple intersections – connections *and* disconnections – between what appear to be 'mainstream' and 'alternative' educational practices (Chapter Four). These intersections are very often spatial – from flows of children between learning sites as they are referred by local authorities, to the operation of particular learning spaces as experimental focal points for local, national or even global change (Chapter Eight).

In order to take account of the fact that alternative learning spaces are connected *and* disconnected from the 'mainstream', I gradually build an argument that most alternative learning spaces can be viewed as *autonomous learning spaces*. I understand the term 'autonomy' to include a range of political and philosophical convictions that have gained increasing currency, especially within anti-capitalist movements, intentional communities, squatter camps and local community economies. Autonomous groups try to do things differently: they are frequently self-reliant (at a collective rather than individual level); they employ flattened hierarchies of power and collective decision-making; they emphasise the primacy of human relations and empathy; and, they attempt to abolish fixed divisions of labour (whether paid or unpaid). At the same time, autonomous social groups attempt to *engage* with mainstream, capitalist societies rather than divorce themselves from them (Pickerill and Chatterton, 2006; Chapter Two provides a fuller definition). At a very general level, it is this mixture of 'doing things differently', engagement, self-organisation and the 'human-scale' that has prompted me to ask whether alternative learning spaces too can be understood as autonomous. As far as I know, other than in discussions of individual autonomy (Curren, 2007), alternative education has never been theorised in this way. Given that *some* alternative learning spaces have common roots with autonomous social and economic practices, I ask what might be gained by viewing those learning spaces as 'autonomous'. However, I also recognise that alternative learning spaces are nothing but diverse, and that some may be built upon very different political foundations than, for instance, the autonomous social movements of Argentina (Sitrin, 2006). I therefore expand and experiment with common uses of the term 'autonomy' throughout the book. I never argue that *all* alternative learning spaces are also *autonomous* learning spaces (or are autonomous *rather* than alternative). Indeed, some learning spaces may exhibit few features of autonomy, at least as it is commonly understood. However, based on my empirical research, it is my contention that an expanded understanding of autonomy can, at least, help us to understand the many connections and disconnections between alternative learning spaces and multiple 'mainstreams'. Chapter Four provides the most detailed examination of these connections and disconnections, while Chapter Nine summarises the expanded theorisation of autonomy that I argue for throughout the book. There, I also argue that this book expands and raises questions about previous theorisations of autonomy, which have tended to emerge from studies of activism, intentional communities and solidarity movements. Specifically, this means that in some cases I am arguing for notions of autonomy that do not necessarily seek to exceed (or even radically change) the dominance of mainstream, neoliberal orders.

This move – from 'alternative' to 'autonomous' learning spaces – is also a significant one if we turn the lens back onto education studies for a moment. Many studies tend to reinforce a binary between 'alternative' and 'mainstream' education, albeit tacitly. In geographical research, for instance, this binary is implicitly reinforced by the fact that very few studies even consider alternative forms of education. Indeed, a similar point can be made (although with more exceptions) for education studies, where studies of alternative education are confined to specialist texts and journals. At the same time, there is very much a sense that, while the educational 'mainstream' may look very different in different places, it is characterised by a set of increasingly homogeneous tendencies that are becoming globalised – neoliberal governance and financing, responsibilisation, flexibility, standardised testing, and so on (Gatto, 2009). Again, by implication, alternative education is pitched as a binarised 'other' to these tendencies. Thus, some scholars and, especially, practitioners outline a series of (ironically often similarly homogenous) impulses that position alternative education somehow outside or beyond these tendencies – including democracy, the human scale, and non-linear learning models (for example Sliwka, 2008). At the same time, I am inspired by two trends in thinking and doing education that challenge and even dismantle this binary, and indeed it would be utterly remiss to claim that this book is the first to do so. First, my concept of autonomy is an extension and refinement of previous scholarly work on alternative education that has questioned the ways in which alternative learning practices relate to the mainstream (for example Woods and Woods, 2009). Thus, in Chapter Two I examine a particular subset of work on alternative education that has examined, for instance, how some alternative educators work with or offer resources for mainstream educators, and which has successfully sought to move beyond the alternative/mainstream binary. Yet, as I argue in Chapter Four, this book challenges this binary even further, and specifically through a concept of *autonomy* inspired less by educational deployments of the term (for example Biesta, 2005; Curren, 2007) and more by those from social movement studies (briefly outlined above and discussed in Chapter Two). Second, I am fully aware of a range of recent curriculum innovations in the UK and elsewhere that have themselves drawn inspiration from alternative pedagogies (notably from Steiner and Montessori approaches). I discuss some of these innovations in the conclusion to this book, but note for now that these vary enormously – from teaching particular 'habits' and competencies, to personalised learning, to programmes like 'Opening Minds' (http://www.rsaopeningminds.org.uk/) and 'Enquiring Minds' (http://www.

enquiringminds.org.uk/). Equally, a range of institutional innovations in the UK, for instance, means that 'mainstream' education is arguably more diverse than ever. However, I note here that a range of other examples exists. Often drawing on alternative educational approaches, these innovations include academies, faith schools and specialist schools. Again, I discuss a particular subset of these innovations in the book's conclusion, focusing on so-called 'free schools' because (as I detail there), some of the most diverse, mainstream-funded schools in the UK are emerging out of this particular programme (accompanied by a series of critical debates about their relative merits).

Building on the above points, the final contribution of this book is that it is intended to be simultaneously outward looking and forward looking. The book is outward looking in three ways. First, in a conceptual sense, while this is a book that focuses on education and learning spaces, much of the discussion develops contemporary theorising in other spheres – around, for instance, affect, life-itself, materiality and inter-generational relations – ideas that have taken hold in different social-scientific disciplines (Chapter Two). Second, while focused upon the UK, I examine connections beyond the UK – from the international influences upon almost every approach I cite (Chapter Three) to the particular relations that connect people 'beyond' local places (Massey, 2005). Third, this book adopts a different 'take' on Hanson Thiem's (2009) argument that social scientists should not simply see educational processes as the *result* of (especially) neoliberal restructuring. Hanson Thiem shows how mainstream education spaces sit at the nexus of production and social reproduction, and may actually produce or resist neoliberal regimes. However, like Gibson-Graham's work, this book begins from a series of examples that explicitly situate themselves outside of, or seek to change, what they see as the insidious outcomes of neoliberalism upon children. I agree with Hanson Thiem but, empirically, start from a very different place. I therefore pose and *begin* to answer the question of what some avowed alternatives might do to challenge ongoing processes of neoliberalism in contemporary mainstream education systems. In a more explicit way than Gibson-Graham, I focus upon an increasing recognition that neoliberalism is premised upon the governance of life-itself, but that alternative ways of ordering life are possible. As I detail in Chapter Two, I follow scholars like Nikolas Rose (2007), who argue that, more than ever, western societies are characterised by intense scrutiny of and attempts to control life processes – from the use of biometric testing at national borders to the possibilities of genetic manipulation. The book is therefore forward looking in the sense that it speaks to contemporary academic interest in dispositions to the future and how future lives and spaces are governed (for example Anderson, 2010). For instance, the book traces how educators try to attune to the different rhythms and materials of mess (Chapter Five) and bodily movement (Chapter Six). In each case, differently-scaled dispositions to the future emerge: it could be that an informal learning activity provides a more hopeful outlook on life in the local, immediate term; or, it could be that homeschoolers view themselves as part of a collective social movement for change (for example Collom and Mitchell, 2005). Thus, in the fullest sense of the term 'spatiality', the book culminates in an attention not only to the socio-spatial processes that constitute alternative learning practices, but also to the ways in which spaces and (future) times are co-implicated. This also helps to build a more fulsome picture that some alternative learning spaces are autonomous – this time because they produce versions and visions of life-itself that go beyond mainstreams, although they are not usually isolated from them (Chapter Eight). Crucially, I will show that these visions are collaborative – not merely geared to the autonomy of individual or collective *human* learners, but to the production of a sense of interdependent freedom among human and non-human communities that may span the entire globe.

This book therefore has two principal aims. The first aim is to compare a range of alternative approaches to learning in the UK, in order to uncover and contrast some of their rich and diverse spatialities. It will explore some of the many ways in which social and spatial processes are co-implicated in the constitution of those approaches. The second aim is to consider what an understanding of such spatialities can tell us about what makes alternative approaches 'alternative'. This task is both outward-looking and forward-looking and will lead to an argument that alternative learning spaces be considered 'autonomous', in multiple, complex and shifting ways.

Introducing alternative education in the UK

Comparatively speaking, the UK exhibits considerable diversity in terms of the number and range of alternative spaces in which children may be educated. While the UK is famous for being one of the first countries to introduce compulsory schooling (formalised, for instance, in the Education Act 1870), British educational law also includes an important clause. Section 19(1) of the Education Act 1996 identifies that

> [e]ach local education authority shall make arrangements
> for the provision of suitable education at school *or otherwise*

than at school for those children of compulsory school age who, by reason of illness, exclusion from school *or otherwise*, may not for any period receive suitable education unless such arrangements are made for them.

The implication of this and other related sections of the Education Act is that it is *parents*, not the state, who are ultimately responsible for ensuring that their children receive a 'suitable' education. In practice, however, few parents exercise their right to educate their children outside of the mainstream sector. This means that the majority of children (around 90%) of school age attend a mainstream school, funded and controlled by the state, and following the National Curriculum. Most of the remaining children (around 6.5% of the total number of school-age children in the UK) attend independent schools – around 625,000 children (Independent Schools Council, 2012). Notably, virtually all of these 2,600 independent schools are fee-paying schools that also follow the National Curriculum. These schools are not the focus for this book because, other than in their financing and administration, they do not conform to the broad definition of 'alternative education' that I outline below. Rather, my focus is upon *alternative* schools and other non-mainstream learning spaces. At the beginning of the 21st century, Carnie (2003) suggested that there were over 70 alternative schools in the UK, educating over 20,000 young people. Most of these schools do classify as 'independent', because they charge some level of fees to some parents. These institutions encompass some of the more 'school-like' spaces included in this book – especially Steiner, Montessori and human scale schools. Thus, a small proportion of the 6.5% of all UK school-age children attending independent schools are represented by those attending alternative schools. My online surveys of each approach (Chapter Three) indicate that this figure has probably increased to over 100 schools since 2003.

However, as I have indicated, this book is not only concerned with school-like alternatives to mainstream schools – it also examines care farms, homeschooling, forest schools, spiritual communities and other examples that include some measure of 'learning'. Understood in this way, a far greater proportion of young people experience some kind of alternative education that *replaces* (not only supplements) *some* of their mainstream schooling. For example, recent estimates indicate that at least 50,000 children (and probably 150,000) alone are being homeeducated (Conroy, 2010). Elsewhere, the number of forest schools in the UK has increased considerably (from a handful in 1995 to 120 in 2006) and the number of farms joining the national network Care

Farming UK has quickly exceeded 100. I explore the detailed figures as far as is practicable in Chapter Three, but it is worth noting here that it is very difficult to provide a precise figure on the number of children receiving some kind of alternative education. For instance, since homeschoolers do not have to register with a local authority if their children never go to school, there is no 'official' count. All of this means that the proportion of children involved in alternative education – at least part-time – probably sits between 5% and 10% of the population (around 300,000 to 600,000 children).

Compared with many other countries, the proportion of children being educated in alternative educational settings is quite high. Certainly, alternative education is relatively prominent in countries like Australia (Ferguson and Seddon, 2007), the US (NCACS, 2012) and in Latin America (Sliwka, 2008). It is worth noting that in the US, it is estimated that over 2 million children are home educated (HSLDA, 2012) and there is a burgeoning movement for alternative schools (www.learningalternatives.net). Moreover, the rise of education in alternative settings in the UK in recent decades is paralleled by gathering global networks that support alternative education (www. educationrevolution.net). But by contrast, other countries have illegalised many or all forms of alternative education: for instance, aside from a few 'free' schools, alternative schools are very rare in Japan, and homeschooling is illegal in many countries like Brazil and Germany (Kunzman, 2009). I will say a little more about alternative education in other countries when I introduce my case studies in Chapter Three.

While it is difficult to be precise about the numbers, therefore, the UK is nevertheless an important context in which to study alternative education. This is also because there is enormous diversity both in the kinds of educational alternatives on offer and the ways in which those alternatives interact with the mainstream. In some countries, educational alternatives exist but may not be so diverse: for instance, Steiner schooling is relatively common in Germany (in fact often being state funded), but homeschooling is illegal; in the Netherlands it is possible but very difficult to homeschool, but care farming is very popular and arguably originated there. This is not to say that the UK is uniquely diverse, but that it is nevertheless an important context in which to study educational alternatives using the comparative approach I advocate in this book. In addition, as I detail in Chapter Four, there are some significant connections *between* different alternative approaches – for instance between care farms and spiritual communities – that make the UK a worthy case study.

A final reason for studying alternative education in the UK in the early 21st century is that mainstream educational policy has undergone some important changes in the past 30 years. Following the Education Reform Act 1988 a National Curriculum was introduced in England, Wales and Northern Ireland (but not Scotland, on which more in a moment). The National Curriculum has undergone some significant revisions since 1988, but the experience of mainstream schooling has been characterised by greater standardisation in terms of curriculum content and assessment since that time. In parallel, successive national governments have introduced various measures to evaluate the quality of schools – from school inspections by an independent body (Ofsted) to standard assessments throughout the school years, to league tables of exam results published each year. After 1997, the New Labour government introduced a series of curriculum reforms and embarked on an ambitious series of school-building programmes that were intended to transform education and schools for generations to come (for example DfES, 2003; see Kraftl, 2012). The difficulty for many critical commentators has been that each successive government has repeated and in many ways exacerbated the kinds of problems with mainstream schooling first identified by critical scholars like John Holt (2004 [1976]) and Ivan Illich (2002 [1970]), and, more recently, Ken Robinson (for example: www.thersa.org/events/video/archive/sir-ken-robinson). That is, that schools are dehumanising and anti-democratic, that they obstruct creativity in favour of learning knowledge by rote, and that they simply institutionalise children to become good, neoliberal workers and consumers – flexible, responsible labourers who can contribute to a country's global economic competitiveness (Mizen, 2003; Fielding and Moss, 2011). In this context, at the end of the first decade of the 20th century, the status of educational alternatives was therefore a little hazy. On the one hand, in a climate of ever-increasing regulation, a review of elective home education (the Badman Review of 2009) recommended far greater scrutiny of homeschooling families amidst fears both about child abuse and the quality of children's learning (HMSO, 2009). While the Badman Review was sidelined by the Conservative-Liberal Democrat coalition government that came into power in 2010, its ramifications for scrutiny of *all* alternative learning spaces could have been profound. On the other hand, the 'free schools' policy – realised by the coalition government – has sought to introduce greater freedoms into state-sponsored education by allowing local groups to set up schools in areas where a specific 'need' is identified (for more, see Hatcher, 2011). The free schools policy has been but one facet of the neoliberal imperative that citizens should become responsible for their own lives in a form of what Beck and Beck-Gernsheim (2002) term 'institutionalised individualism'. At the same time, curriculum reforms proposed for 2014 by the Conservative-Liberal Democrat government have promised greater freedom for teachers (DfE, 2012). In all, for some commentators, the combination of increased surveillance with increased (seeming) freedom can be characterised as a 'schizophrenic' approach, not only to education policy but to the governance of life-itself (Conroy, 2010; see also Chapter Two). To add greater complexity to this picture, Scotland has a separate curriculum from England but introduced a new curriculum – the *Curriculum for Excellence*– in 2010 (Allison et al, 2012), during the period when the research for this book was taking place.

It is the case, therefore, that this book is concerned with a place and a period of history wherein the status of alternative education is not so much in danger, but, rather, undergoing a series of potential challenges and opportunities. Some of these challenges and opportunities stretch back to older debates about state institutions of education; others, like the Badman Review and free schools policy, are much newer. It is also the case that many of these challenges and opportunities – neoliberal trends in education being a key one – are affecting young people in many other countries besides the UK. Therefore, I hope that the choice of the UK will constitute a point of departure from which critical, comparative studies of the geographies of alternative education might proceed.

Researching alternative education in the UK: a note on methodology and terminology

This book is the result of research endeavours stretching back to 2003. It is based upon a variety of funded projects, a period of sustained fieldwork in 2010–11, and a reading of research about alternative approaches to education. My earliest research on education spaces took place at a Steiner school in Pembrokeshire (Wales), where I spent several months undertaking participant observation as a classroom assistant, and undertook in-depth, qualitative interviews with teachers, parents, children and the school's architect. While much of this material has been published elsewhere (Kraftl, 2006a, 2006b, 2008), I do draw on empirical material from that study in this book.

Between 2004 and 2009 I was involved in several research and consultancy projects that took place in schools, youth work settings and other educational spaces. Several projects explored children's play, health (Kraftl and Horton, 2007) and self-esteem, and were undertaken with colleagues at the Centre for Children and Youth at The University of Northampton. I have also undertaken significant research in mainstream school settings, including a two-year Research Council UK-funded project that looked at children's participation in school design, and especially at the *Building Schools for the Future* programme (see Den Besten et al, 2011; Kraftl, 2012, for details). I do not draw directly on empirical material from these studies but use my experience of research in the mainstream sector as context, especially for my conceptual passion that we always view alternative educational spaces *in relation* to the mainstream, not in isolation. This is a key reason for my interest in 'autonomy' throughout the book.

In 2010 I embarked upon a more explicit period of empirical research for this book. I undertook over 70 interviews at over 50 learning 'sites', which varied from homeschoolers' homes and parent groups, to nurseries, to remote forests, to purpose-built and little-known schools. My interviews were in the main with learning facilitators – sometimes called 'teachers', sometimes not. To a lesser extent, I also undertook interviews with current learners (young people) and former learners, although I recognise from my experience as a childhood researcher that I have not been able to engage with young people as much as I would have liked, and there remains scope for further studies to do so. However, this book does at least constitute a start, given that young people's voices are seldom present in previous studies of alternative education. Formal interviews were semi-structured and, where possible, tape-recorded and transcribed. Interviews took a 'life history' approach (Andrews et al, 2006), where I asked interviewees to recount their story of the learning space in which they were situated, with some accompanying prompts intended to tease out the kinds of spatialities as previously discussed. Interviews lasted between 20 minutes and five hours, but the majority lasted between one and two hours. All of the research (especially interviews and observations with young people) adhered to strict ethical codes of conduct, such as those now commonly accepted by childhood researchers (for example Matthews, 1998). A further consideration relevant to the book is that the default ethical position, agreed with participants, has been *not* to name the individual case studies and/or personnel; every effort has been made to withhold identifying information. In some places – with explicit permission – I name case studies and individual people, especially in respect of some photographs, which would have been impossible to anonymise. I make this clear when those examples first appear in the book. Otherwise, I use pseudonyms for both people and places, as is standard practice in social science research.

My analysis of interview quotations attempts to provide some kind of a balance between the inevitable fact that most educators and facilitators do try to justify what they are doing, and the need as an academic researcher to take a critical, analytical stance. The overall effect is that the majority of quotations in this book are positive about alternative learning spaces. In some parts of the book I do focus on more negative experiences – homeschooling children talking about friends who choose not to learn, fights and disagreements in various settings, parents who found that particular alternative approaches did not work for their children, or the fact that several alternative learning spaces have been negatively stereotyped by outsiders. In several other places I offer critical analysis – whether it be teasing out the broader spatialities at play across alternative learning spaces, highlighting the gendered nature of much homeschooling (also Kraftl, in press, 2013a), cautioning that notions of mindfulness and habit must be deployed carefully, and, throughout the book, remaining cognisant that the differences between 'alternative' and 'mainstream' education may not be as great as these two terms imply. However, this book is not critical of alternative education in the sense of that work that does *criticise* alternative approaches (see Chapters Two and Three). The difference is that, in my view, critique must be as much affirmative as it is negative (see also Kraftl, 2012). Several scholars (including Gibson-Graham, 2006; Connolly, 2008; Bennett, 2010; Braidotti, 2011) press for mappings of alternative ways of doing that must to some extent cast those practices in a positive light. That is, the *critique* lies – as is the case for much utopian thought – with showing that other ways of thinking and doing the world are possible, beyond those of contemporary neoliberal/global mainstreams. I am not saying that everything in the alternative education world is rosy. As I point out in this book, many of my respondents themselves picked holes in what they were doing, and talked in depth about their struggles (moral and practical) – ranging from the sacrifices made by home-educating families to the increasing need for some care farms and forest schools to operate using financial business models, which their originators opposed in principle. But, in some cases, I have resisted the urge to take easy pot-shots – I have, if you like, suspended my disbelief – but only to give a more general impression of how alternative learning spaces offer visions and versions of life-itself (Chapter Eight) that may provide philosophical, political and pragmatic lessons for mainstream learning spaces (Chapter Nine).

In addition to formal interviews, I undertook observations (in some cases, as a visiting participant) at the 59 learning sites I visited (Table 1.1). These sites were chosen to represent some of the diversity of alternative education in the UK at the time of the research. Since I undertook a qualitative study, the final sample is not representative either of the full diversity of those approaches, nor of the total number of organisations or groups involved therein. The case studies were chosen and contacted in one of two ways: through initial communication followed by snowballing (homeschooling participants); through publicly available websites dedicated to each approach (for example, for Steiner schools, www.steinerwaldorf.org). The following criteria were used for the selection of case studies, with the first being the main criterion:

- learning does not follow the English/Welsh or Scottish National Curriculum;
- and/or learning is explicitly conceived as 'alternative' to what happens in mainstream schools;
- and/or learning is not principally funded by mainstream education budgets (although there may be some funding from local authority referrals), relying instead upon grants, fees or voluntary labour;
- cases should represent a broad geographical spread over the UK mainland (case studies are located in south-west, south, east and north England and the English Midlands, and in south, north-west and north-east Scotland; there is also a mix of urban- and rural-based case studies).

At this point, many readers will observe that I have missed some obvious kinds of learning space – especially, for instance, informal education, arts-based learning programmes, museums and libraries. These were explicitly not included in my study for three reasons. First, in general, libraries and museums are not principally viewed as 'alternative' learning spaces – they do not tend to be represented as spaces that offer an alternative to mainstream modes of organising learning (for example in Carnie, 2003). Thus, libraries and museums rarely *replace* all or part of that aspect of a child's learning that in the majority of cases takes place in school. Second, it is the case that there exists a large extant body of research on learning in museum studies (for example Golding, 2009) and, to a lesser extent, library studies (for example Koontz et al, 2009), and that the kinds of educational alternatives considered in this book therefore require more pressing attention. Third, in terms of informal education, I have chosen to use this as a theoretical frame for this book rather than an explicit 'case study' (Chapter Two). While informal education entails some important spatial considerations, especially when it takes place in schools through formally sanctioned youth work (Cartwright, 2012), it is also the case

Table 1.1: Sample of learning spaces included in the primary research for this book

Broad approach to learning[1]	Examples included in this book	Interviews with educators	Interviews with learners	Informal discussions with learners[3]
Care farm	10	14	5	2
Forest school	5	9	0	5
Homeschooling	30 families/ groups[2]	35	10	5
Democratic/ human scale school[4]	6	7	0	0
Steiner school	5	11	20	1
Montessori school	3	3	0	1
Total	**59**	**79**	**35**	**14**

[1]There is considerable variety within each approach and overlap between approaches (see Chapter Two): for instance, there is enormous variety between different democratic and human scale schools, and some care farms share forest school principles.

[2]I interviewed the majority of families in their homes or by telephone, but also visited several homeschooling 'clubs' and social gatherings, some on multiple occasions.

[3]This figure refers to the number of learning sites at which discussions took place with individuals or groups – usually during my involvement in learning activities.

[4]Although not strictly a school, I include Findhorn (real name) in this category because it provides several kinds of learning experiences that resonate with human scale and democratic values (details in Chapter Three).

that informal education takes place across a whole range of settings, including those not usually conceived as 'educational' (www.infed.org; Falk et al, 2009). Practically and conceptually it is hard to tell where informal education begins and ends, because it is something that is emergent from social relations: as I put it in Chapter Five, informal kinds of learning are both imminent and immanent to everyday life. It is for this reason that I attend to various forms of informal education *in* alternative learning spaces but do not isolate any settings *as* providers of 'informal education'.

Aside from the Steiner school in Wales, I spent between half a day and three full days at each research site. In the majority of cases I was an observer, usually taken on a tour (with some informal conversation), and sometimes sitting in a corner of a room watching. In other cases, I was involved as a more active participant, especially in forest schools, where I took part in activities such as fire-lighting, den-building and mountain biking with groups of children. It is not the case that one could view these visits as educational ethnographies, as most social scientists would understand the term (Hammersely, 2006). One could, though, loosely term my approach a 'multi-sited ethnography' (Cook, 2004; Pierides, 2010, p 179) as I used ethnographic observation and interviewing techniques on relatively short-term visits to a large number of different sites. Following Marcus (1995), Pierides argues that, in a world characterised by rapid transformations and connections at different spatial scales, 'this mode of ethnography "moves out from single sites and local situations of conventional ethnographic research [...] to examine the circulation of cultural meanings, objects and identities in diffuse time-space"' via a series of 'mapping strategies' through which the relationships forged through such circulations may be charted (Marcus, 1995, p 96; cited in Pierides, 2010, p 185). Pierides (2010, p 186) claims that '[t]he strength of these cases is that they allow the [researcher] to make connections between sites that do not have any "obvious" or known association'.

There are obvious question marks here about the time that one should spend in each study location (especially when visiting as many sites as I did in preparation for this book), and on this point, Pierides is not particularly clear. Yet multi-sited studies of education are becoming increasingly popular — a rough parallel to the present study being Ferguson and Seddon's (2007) research on educational alternatives in Australia. For the purposes of this book, a multi-sited approach had two clear advantages. First, empirically, it offered an opportunity to effect a comparative approach to alternative educational spaces. I did not want to tell a story of isolated case studies but take a thematic approach to asking what similarities and differences exist across a range of learning spaces. I also wanted to chart the different ways in which those learning spaces are positioned in respect of the mainstream, in order to ask what more general lessons — applied as well as theoretical — might be learned from doing so. Second, theoretically, I am influenced by a central assumption among contemporary human geographers that it is not sufficient to look in detail at the internal dynamics of one or two local places, but at the processes that connect places at various scales (Massey, 2005). This assumption chimes with the theoretical basis for this book (Chapter Two) — that, in order to understand how diverse or autonomous educational practices (rather than economic practices) might offer dissonant versions of educational futures, it is important to chart and critically compare a variety of case studies. As stated by Gibson-Graham (2006, pp 167, 195, original emphasis) in relation to post-capitalist economic alternatives: an 'eclectic selection of stories demonstrates that we can start [… at] *any site* [… to] bring into visibility a great variety of economic sites and practices in any particular location, [positing] a challenge to the dominance of any one set of organizing principles'. This is why analysis of all of my primary research was undertaken thematically, and why the emergent themes inform the organisation of this book.

I will repeatedly stress in Chapter Three – where I introduce my case study 'types' in turn – that this book says relatively little about the outcomes of alternative education for young people, especially in terms of their measurable achievements. There are three reasons for this. The first, and the most important, is that this book is intended to foreground the importance of a *geographical* approach to why and how alternative learning spaces look the way they do. Its uniqueness lies in understanding how concepts like place, space, scale and materiality are (in my view significant) constituents in the construction and experience of alternative learning practices. Second, and more pragmatically, there already exist several excellent studies pertaining to the outcomes of alternative education in terms of children's attainment, creativity and wellbeing. I review the most relevant literatures in Chapter Two. Moreover, as I am not a trained teacher or school inspector (although I am an educator in higher education), I choose to leave such judgements to the experts! Finally, as will also become clear in Chapter Three, most alternative educators eschew to some extent the concept of 'learning outcomes'. I therefore focus largely on the kinds of 'outcomes', if we can call them that, which are privileged by educators (and to some degree learners). This is why I analyse a range of themes that may be unfamiliar to some readers with a background in education (like 'life-itself', in Chapter Eight), and offer a different approach to slightly more familiar themes (like 'habit', in Chapter Six).

The qualitative primary research for this book is also underpinned by a detailed review of extant research about alternative learning spaces in the UK and elsewhere. Some of the most important research about each learning space in Table 1.1 is considered in Chapter Three. In later chapters I draw upon these and more general, conceptual writings on alternative, radical and informal education (Chapter Two) in order to tease out points of conceptual argument and international comparison. Of course, even within the confines of a book-length text, these can only ever be partial, and I encourage readers to draw their own conclusions and comparisons where appropriate. Given the relative paucity of comparative studies such as this, I intend for this book to start a dialogue with other academics and, I hope, practitioners – not to somehow have the definitive final word.

The terms used in this book

Bearing in mind the complexities involved in defining 'alternative education' spaces, for the sake of simplicity I use some more limited terms in this book. I refer to 'alternative learning spaces' to describe both my case study sites (see Table 1.1) and, more generally, the settings in which alternative education takes place. I use the term 'alternative (educational) approaches' to refer to the pedagogical, political and philosophical principles underpinning what happens at alternative learning spaces. In order to describe the different agents involved in delivering education, I refer to 'teachers' (at schools), 'practitioners' (at care farms and forest schools) and 'educators' (as a generic term for all such agents). I use the terms 'learning' and 'education' somewhat interchangeably, although usually in the context of the particular example I am discussing. I am well aware of the differences between the terms and tend to refer to education with respect to formalised 'schools', systems and policies, as well as to mirror the use of the term in disciplinary geography (that is, to appeal to the study of 'geographies of education'). I tend to refer to learning with respect to the diverse processes, practices and spatialities I identify in each chapter, but always where it is assumed that some measure of 'progress', skills acquisition and/or knowledge formation takes place.

Structure of the book

As previously discussed, this book has two principal aims. The first aim is to compare a range of alternative approaches to learning in the UK, in order to contrast some of their diverse spatialities. The second aim is to consider what an understanding of such spatialities can tell us about what makes alternative approaches 'alternative'. In order to achieve these aims, I have organised the book thematically rather than according to case-study type (see Table 1.1). The book's major themes divert somewhat from previous research on alternative education. This is in part because I use the findings of previous work as an assumed starting point – and especially their foregrounding of pedagogic and spiritual principles such as freedom, democracy, smallness of scale and learning from everyday life (see, for instance, Sliwka, 2008). It also reflects what I found during my research visits, as well as my conviction that alternative education should be interrogated via a geographical frame. Therefore, before broaching the book's five major themes, I map out two contexts. Chapter Two outlines the conceptual context for the book. I begin by framing my later analysis within nascent but rapidly growing geographies of education, where I suggest that this book makes a particularly important contribution. I then explore three overlapping sources of theoretical inspiration for my work that, when taken together, offer a critical framework for understanding some of the spatialities of alternative education. The three strands of work can loosely be characterised as: 'radical' theories of education, informal education and alternative education; diverse economic and autonomous practices; non-representational geographies and the politics of life-itself. Critically, I highlight areas where my later analysis will deploy, challenge and extend those theories. Since the subsequent chapters proceed thematically, Chapter Three provides a systematic overview of the different 'types' of learning space listed in Table 1.1. It provides a relatively brief introduction to the conceptual and practical roots of each approach, and acknowledges some of the considerable diversity therein, as well as key 'moments' where relevant case studies appear in the rest of the book. It also reviews some of the key academic research pertinent to each approach, with reference to some of the ideas in Chapter Two.

Chapter Four constitutes the first thematic chapter and is meant as a jumping-off point for the remaining chapters. Since I have chosen case studies on the basis that they somehow offer an 'alternative', I offer a relatively straightforward analysis of the ways in which educators explicitly articulate the difference between what they do and mainstream education. But, in the first step towards a theory of *autonomous* learning spaces, the chapter explores some of the diverse and shifting points of connection *and* disconnection between alternative learning spaces and the mainstream – from referrals by local authorities to the kinds of 'remedial' or 'therapeutic' support that practitioners feel they can provide. It also charts some of the connections between different learning spaces. The remaining chapters develop this analysis in a number of different but related directions.

Exemplifying the significance of 'spatiality', Chapter Five combines an analysis of space with one of time, to examine how educators negotiate senses of 'mess' and 'order'. Deploying Actor-Network Theory and non-representational theories of affect, I explore the crucial role of mess. In several learning spaces, material and temporal disorder is viewed as a resource for creating affective 'atmospheres' from which non-linear, creative forms of learning may flow. At the same time, however, many educators have extremely clear senses of the spatial and temporal boundaries necessary for these kinds of learning – which may appear surprisingly ordered, even in comparison with mainstream schooling. I argue that many alternative approaches play with the mess/order dualism in order to create particular learning 'atmospheres' wherein learning is both imminent and immanent to everyday life. In different ways, this experimentation extends the modes of operation of autonomous learning spaces (Chapter Four).

Chapter Six evokes another key geographical theme that has resonance across the social sciences: mobility. It is an exploration of the variegated styles of bodily movement that constitute alternative learning spaces. It considers movement/mobility as a way of engaging with the world: from learning while walking (in forest schools) to learning in the car (homeschooling). In doing so, the chapter leads towards a discussion of *habit*, which is picked up in later chapters. It accounts for how, in some instances, specific kinds of embodied habits are meant to be fostered or 'channelled', via particular bodily movements, in order to achieve particular goals. Given that these goals often entail some notion of individual autonomy, I develop the work of Félix Ravaisson (2008) to open up discussion about the ethical imperatives entailed in such learning habits.

The movements and habits discussed in Chapter Six also entail particular kinds of interpersonal relationship – between educators and learners and between learners and other learners. These are the subject of Chapter Seven, which looks at various styles of interpersonal relationships – including friendships and what I call 'family-like' relations. Herein, I consider the emotional geographies that constitute alternative learning spaces, and especially the role of love. That discussion paves the way for a broader conception of love and related emotions in alternative learning spaces. Extending the work of Ravaisson, I return to the formation of learning habits, this time as more collective, rather than individual endeavours. I explore how the materialities, temporalities and embodied movements discussed in previous chapters combine with notions of love, such that we can speak of how the *force* of habit may create particular affects that may change individuals' habits, and vice versa. This, I argue, is a key spatiality of alternative education: it entails the 'scaling-up' of individual habits into more outward-looking, future-looking and collaborative conceptions of autonomy.

Chapter Eight builds on the arguments of previous chapters towards an argument that alternative learning spaces posit versions and visions of *life-itself* that are *collaboratively* autonomous. That is, autonomous in a sense that is more than social, making room for collaborations with non-human materials, flows and processes. Inspired by the work of Rosi Braidotti (2011) and Jane Bennett (2010), it argues that what sets many alternative spaces apart from, but always in relation to, mainstream education, is a *dissonant* understanding of life-itself that somehow *endures*. I argue for an expanded vitalist materialism that recognises how non-human matter/energy flow through learning – from the neurological bases of attachment, to the flows of food and animal mess through learning spaces, to the simple observation made by one of my interviewees that "without learning, you're dead".

Thus, I argue in Chapter Nine (the book's conclusion) for an expanded notion of autonomy that comes as close in this book as anything to a 'model' of alternative learning spaces. I reflect upon what has been learned – empirically and conceptually – from charting diverse educational practices in a manner inspired by J.K.Gibson-Graham's work on diverse economies. Finally, because in all of my work I try not to divorce theoretical from applied questions, I use my concluding discussion as an opportunity to outline some possible applied lessons for practitioners or policy-makers wanting to learn what the role of alternative – and, quite often, autonomous – learning spaces might be in ongoing attempts to re-imagine the role of children's education within contemporary societies.

TWO

Conceptual frameworks: towards geographies of alternative education

Contemporary research on education is enormously broad, rich and intense, and spans several academic disciplines. It would be inappropriate to try to review these bodies of work in this chapter, and I would therefore direct interested readers to authoritative reviews by disciplinary specialists (Ball, 2004; Moore, 2004; Curren, 2007). Moreover, writing as a geographer – where studies of education are relatively nascent – it is inevitable that this book will omit reference to research that readers from other disciplines may deem important, because I want to interrogate the *spatialities* of alternative education. However, at the same time, I hope that this book will present an opportunity to open up more vibrant cross-disciplinary debate about what a geographical analysis of alternative education might offer. In this chapter I seek to combine a range of theoretical writings that, when read via a geographical 'lens', will offer something new to readers from different backgrounds. In so doing I cover a fair amount of ground, but develop each strand of thinking through the thematic chapters that follow. I begin by situating the book within recent geographies of education and childhood, sub-disciplinary concerns that form the immediate context for this book and my own research. I then highlight three theoretical strands that inform my analysis and which each defy simple labels: 'radical' theories of education, informal education, and alternative education; diverse economic and autonomous practices; non-representational geographies and the politics of life-itself.

Geographies of education and childhood

A critical starting point for this book is that the study of education is less well developed in human geography than other social-scientific disciplines (Gulson and Symes, 2007). At the time of researching and writing this book, several papers in geographical journals reviewed and prospected the development of 'geographies of education' as a possible sub-discipline (Collins and Coleman, 2008; Hanson Thiem, 2009;

Holloway et al, 2010; Cook and Hemming, 2011). These papers outlined a series of overlapping frameworks (such as scale and boundary making) for how a geographical perspective could supplement and challenge analyses of education in other disciplines. Significantly, as Gulson and Symes (2007, p 3) argue, it is important not merely to see spatiality as an alternative 'metaphor' for analysis of educational processes that are somehow more 'real'. Rather, they view spatiality as integral to 'complex theorizations of material and symbolic life' in which educational and spatial processes are entwined. These kinds of analyses are perhaps most obvious when it comes to questions about unequal access to schools or the role of education in urban restructuring, but may also more subtly inflect studies of identity, emotion or power that have for decades been the realm of other disciplines. Broadly speaking – and to some extent following Collins and Coleman's (2008) lead – it is possible to distinguish two strands of work by geographers of education: studies within educational spaces, and especially individual schools; studies of educational systems, and especially the neoliberal restructuring of education. It is important to highlight immediately that there are very few studies of alternative education by geographers (studies by 'non-geographers' are reviewed in a subsequent section).

Despite the relatively recent appearance of the term 'geographies of education', geographers have been undertaking research *within* educational spaces, and particularly within individual schools, since the mid-1990s. This research, paralleling the so-called 'New Social Studies of Childhood' (James and James, 2004), has traditionally been understood as part of a related sub-discipline: 'children's geographies' (Matthews and Limb, 1999; Holloway and Valentine, 2000; Horton and Kraftl, 2005; Evans, 2008; Kraftl et al, 2012). While foregrounding children's experiences of and participation within everyday spaces (notably, playgrounds and urban neighbourhoods), a significant proportion of this research – my own included – has taken place in schools. Seminal work by Valentine (2000), for instance, analyses the ways in which teenagers narrate their identities. She argues that teenagers' identities are produced not only by social categories like age and gender, but the limited, often hidden spaces in a school where they can negotiate those identities. In this sense, schools are important spaces where children have limited freedom to congregate and express their evolving identities in relation to others (for other examples, see Thomas, 2005; Hemming, 2007). While children may express some agency in schools, many studies examine schools as the site of power relations wherein 'young people are both controlled and disciplined by adults, and within which distinct [usually pre-existing] identities are (re)produced' (Collins and Coleman, 2008, p 285). Hence, the micro-geographies of the classroom are scaled-down versions of wider socio-spatial relations and social constructions of childhood – whether in terms of assumptions about gendered usage of information technology (Holloway and Valentine, 2001), the exclusion of dis/abled children from playground spaces (Holt, 2007) or the seating of children in dining halls according to whether they have brought lunch from home (Pike, 2008). Several geographers have also shown how political imperatives – notably around nation-building and national identity – are located in educational spaces. Here, historical geographers have shown how, for instance, in US cities, the playground reform movement of the early 20th century instilled 'American' ideals in immigrant children through their design and planned use (Gagen, 2004; for other examples see Ploszajska, 1996; Mills, 2013). As Holloway et al (2010, p 594) argue in their review, inspired by work in children's geographies, an underlying tenet of all of this work is to move 'the subjects of education – the children, young people and adults involved in learning and teaching – into the foreground'. While this may not be a wholly surprising move for sociologists of childhood (for example James and James, 2004) or education (for example Young, 1971; Willis, 1977), this work provides two key contributions. First, it draws attention to the complicity of the design, organisation and maintenance of internal school spaces in, for instance, the negotiation of identities. And second, it highlights how the school as a space is a significant locus for the construction and contestation of (power) relations between adults and children in ways that reproduce social norms outside the school walls (Jeffrey, 2010). As Ansell (2002, p 180) puts it: schools can be viewed as 'spaces distinct from, but embedded within, the contexts of everyday life'. I explore several of these issues with respect to alternative education, especially in Chapters Five, Six and Seven.

Concurrent to research inside schools, a rich body of work has explored the relationships between schools and their constitutive '*outsides*': with their wider communities, and with broader social, economic and political processes. Although rarely labelled 'geographies of education', several studies have inquired into the relationships between educational policies, school distribution and racial segregation (Bondi, 1991; Johnston et al, 2008), class-based inequality (Erikson and Goldthorpe, 1993) and gender inequalities (Moore, 1996; Arnot, 2002). Clearly, these fields of inquiry are hugely significant but not of direct relevance to this book. Few of these studies relate to non-mainstream education, and the approach advocated by Holloway et al (2010) is the one I favour in this book. However, Hansom Thiem (2009) levels an important critique of geographical studies of education provision and distribution that has import for this book. She argues that many studies of education have

> made valuable contributions, either to the study of educational inequality or to narratives of reform in the sector. But by positioning the spaces of education as derivative (as in most geographers' work on distribution), or rehearsing familiar arguments about the 'difference that spaces makes' (the primary claim advanced by educationalists), they do not convey the full potential of education-geographic research. Most significantly, they neglect education's constitutive properties – that is, how educational systems, institutions, and practices (and the political struggles that surround them) effect change *beyond* the sector. (Hansom Thiem, 2009, p 157, original emphasis)

The implication is, then, that no matter whether one is interested in what happens inside a school or outside, few geographical studies of education have been what Hansom Thiem terms outward *looking*. That is, one could equally criticise children's geographers for viewing identity formation and power relations in schools as largely a matter of the reproduction of dominant socio-spatial assumptions outside schools. Indeed, arguably, the implication of Ansell's (2002) quotation, cited earlier, is that schools are somehow nested within 'larger' structures than more powerfully constitutive *of* those structures. Thus, such studies acknowledge what Hansom Thiem (2009, p 157) calls the 'derivative' or determining impact of (for instance) neoliberalism upon schools, but not the reverse. Hansom Thiem's understanding of a more 'outward-looking' geography of education is, then, one which pursues this reverse: she seeks to afford more constitutive power to education spaces *over* the modes of governance and socio-economic structures that seem simply to produce them. This is a point to which I return in the chapter's conclusion.

While there is relatively little cross-referencing between the two strands of work cited above, there is some overlap – for instance between studies that examine the externally facing relationship between schools and their communities (for example Witten et al, 2003; Holloway and Pimlott-Wilson, 2011), and studies that explore the relationship between circuits of school choice and (sub)urban housing markets (Ball, 2003; Butler, 2003). Indeed, while most of the research inspired by children's geographers takes place in schools or other educational institutions, many geographers do account for how those local, bounded places are cross-cut by national or even global imperatives. These imperatives may include education for citizenship (Turner, 1993; Pykett, 2012) or the production of neoliberal subjects who are mobile, flexible, culturally aware and entrepreneurial (Mizen, 2003; Waters, 2007; Hanson Thiem, 2009; Kraftl, 2012). Such work displays notable resonances with earlier, classical sociological studies of social reproduction in schools (for example Bourdieu and Passeron, 1977). Two other important examples are provided by two journal special issues. In the first, on educational aspirations (edited by Holloway et al, 2011), the editors acknowledge (p 3) how 'developments in neoliberal discourse filter down' into the everyday lives of schools, but also demonstrates how the aspirations of young people may exceed, challenge or subvert those discourses in ways that extend beyond the concerns of education into children's home lives. In the second (edited by Kenway and Youdell, 2011), the editors seek to account for the multiple ways in which emotions are implicated in and productive of educational concerns, identities and practices that may cut across several spatial scales. In other words, the emotional geographies of education are not merely located 'in' individuals or schools but cut across more broadly scaled concerns about citizenship, neoliberalism and activism. I return to Kenway and Youdell's (2011) arguments at various points in this book (for example in Chapter Five).

Notwithstanding the above research, it is notable that there exist very few geographical studies of alternative education. Aside from my own work on Steiner schooling (Kraftl, 2006a, 2006b) and homeschooling (Kraftl, in press 2012a), virtually every study – especially those taking a 'children's geographies' approach – is located within mainstream schooling contexts. Hanson Thiem's earlier (2007) study of homeschooling is an exception, although it is ostensibly a review and (albeit effective) re-theorisation of previous research. Laura Cameron's (2006) wonderful geography of the short-lived, experimental Malting House School in Cambridge is also instructive, but, located in the 1920s, is a historical geography rather than a contemporary example. Studies of home-based learning by Holloway and Pimlott-Wilson (2011) and Wainwright and Marandet (2011) break new ground because they are examples of contemporary education taking place outside of the school. However, they are situated within mainstream, state-sanctioned educational policies aimed to foster lifelong and flexible learning (Extended Services and Wider Family Learning, respectively). Thus, while some of the examples in this book also sit alongside or support mainstream education, and while I want to blur the boundaries between 'alternative' and 'mainstream' education, my starting point is those educational approaches that see themselves as offering some kind of *alternative to* attendance at mainstream, state-funded educational institutions (usually, schools). In the context of disciplinary human geography, a key contribution of this book is to explore the spatialities of a far greater *range* of educational alternatives than has hitherto been the case in geographical research. As I discuss in this chapter's conclusion, this also enables me to ask (and begin to answer) some questions about the constitutive relationship between education spaces and neoliberal versions of life-itself.

'Radical' theories of education, informal education, and alternative education

A major source of inspiration for this book comes from what are sometimes termed 'radical' theories of education (for an excellent discussion, see Fielding and Moss, 2011). The texts that have informed my thinking are too disparate to be considered part of a coherent school of thought. As readers familiar with these texts will quickly see, my selection marks a very particular take on a sub-set of educational theories. Yet these theorists have been chosen carefully – because of the ways they might (or do) speak to alternative education in the UK, and because of their resonance with the conceptual approaches outlined in the other sections of this chapter. I begin with some 'classic' texts on pedagogy, freedom and democracy that will be familiar to many readers. I then discuss two overlapping 'kinds' of education wherein these classic approaches have been refined. First, I explore some of the advances to be made from research on informal education, especially in terms of spatiality, scale and the immanence of learning within everyday life. Second, I introduce studies that have explicitly sought to critically compare and theorise different kinds of alternative education, often inspired by radical pedagogies.

I begin with what have become seminal, classic texts on pedagogic theory. Some of the best-known radical or democratic theories are found in the work of John Holt (2004 [1976]) and Paulo Freire (2008 [1974]). While there are several other influential theorists in this regard (such as Dewey and Illich), I focus upon Holt and Freire because their work is exemplary of theories of learning that are embedded in and intended to be transformative of everyday life. Beginning with John Holt, it is notable in the context of the case studies for this book that Holt's work has been particularly inspirational for a strand of homeschoolers – particularly prevalent in the UK – who favour so-called autonomous or child-led approaches to learning. Holt (2004) was suspicious of both the words 'education' and 'learning'. Rather, he emphasised that learning was indistinguishable from 'doing'; he argued that human beings only engaged in particular tasks (and only became more adept at them) if those tasks helped them to achieve a particular purpose. Thus, on the child 'learning' to read, Holt (2004, p 15) comments:

> [r]eading is not a skill but an act. The child sees written words all around him [sic.]; he sees that [...] words make things happen. One day (if we give him a chance) he decides that he wants to find out what those words say and means, and that he can and will find out. *At that instant [...] he begins to read*. Not to 'learn to read'.

Holt's is a stinging critique not so much of the existence of schools per se, but rather of their modern incarnation – from league tables to testing, from peer pressure to the micro-management and disciplining of intimate bodily functions (see also Illich, 2002 [1970]; Gatto, 2009; Conroy, 2010; Fielding and Moss, 2011). He advocates the creation of learning opportunities outside of established educational organisations and curricula, and especially forms of self-directed learning that follow a child's interests and needs. This is why his ideas have been especially popular among autonomous homeschoolers although, as will become evident in Chapters Four and Five, they suffuse other approaches too.

Holt begins with the individual – with *self*-directed learning – although is directed towards a belief that more autonomous individuals could create a fairer, more vibrant society at large. This is akin to an ethic of 'self-cultivation' (Gibson-Graham, 2006, p 154), posited by various philosophers, that will play a significant role later in the book (Chapters Six to Eight). Paolo Freire (2008), however, begins with a theorisation of both individual and collective autonomy more rooted in Marxist, community-based notions of emancipation. Unlike Holt, Freire's theory of learning is rooted more in talk than action (Jeffs and Smith, 2005; Cartwright, 2012). In forging a pedagogy of hope, Freire seeks to enable dispossessed social groups to overcome the dehumanising power relations that oppressed them (Halpin, 2003). Only through learning – from life – can those power structures be overcome. Education is a form of consciousness-raising (*conscientização*) – fomented not out of a 'teacher-pupil' relationship but out of 'culture circles' that aims at fostering group debate around problems arising from the everyday lives of group members (Freire, 2008, p 38). Freire provides a 'matrix' for that dialogue: a 'relation of "empathy" between two poles who are engaged in a joint search', a relation characterised by being 'loving, humble, hopeful, trusting [and] critical' (Freire, 2008, p 40). From this process, group members are encouraged to emerge as critically-aware subjects, to decodify the structures governing their oppression and, thereby, to creatively re-codify and then act out the conditions for the transcendence of their oppression. In this latter sense, Freire's work exhibits some notable resonances with later theories of autonomy, which I discuss later in this chapter.

The influences of Freire and Holt are found in many critiques of state-controlled education (see Suissa, 2010 for one overview). In many places their work continues to inspire radical and alternative educators, as the subsequent sections on informal and alternative education will demonstrate. Echoes of their work will appear several times across this book, most obviously in my discussions of homeschooling, Human-Scale schools, Forest Schools and Care Farms. On the one hand, Freire and Holt offer important intellectual resources for those who seek to privilege learning as embedded in everyday life, and who seek to multiply the registers in which learning can take place. For instance, Fielding and Moss (2011, p 6) cite Vecchi's (2010) 'hundred languages' model of democracy – a theory that for democracy to truly flourish, learning places should take account of the many styles in which children understand and represent the world – from prose, to poetry, to dance, to music, to painting. On the other hand, Holt and Freire (in particular) have also influenced critical theorists who seek to reframe what learning should *feel* like, not just the practices through which it takes place. For instance, in the rather different context of mixed-race public schooling in the US, Freire's work has inspired bell hooks (2003) to seek spaces in which empathetic, respectful dialogue between students of different ethnicities can take place. She (hooks, 2003, p 41) also envisages democratic education as 'always a part of our real world experience' and a critical immersion in the social relations that make up the present – what she terms 'learning to be fully present in the now' (p 43). But, as I discuss in Chapter Seven, the undoubted power of hooks' work is that she is seeking to foster a kind of intimacy and *love* between apparently antagonistic groups (in this case, white and black students). She uses Freire's notions of empathy and trust to argue for the power of respectful learning atmospheres that 'forge a learning community that values wholeness over division [... working] to create closeness' across differences that seem insurmountable – through, for instance, knowing when to withhold an opinion (hooks, 2003, p 49). hooks' pedagogy is, then, one of hope based in everyday, empathetic talk *across* difference, taking a brave but necessary step not only to work with communities (as does Freire) but to open out the possibilities for creating new and unheralded communities across difference. I argue in Chapter Seven that hooks' call for the (re-)placing of love in learning is a key component of interpersonal relationships through which autonomous, collaborative learning spaces might be fostered.

Informal education

The influence of Freire's work is particularly evident in concepts of informal education. Some of the tenets of informal education appear regularly throughout this book (if not always in name), and so its conceptual underpinnings require some introduction here. Informal education refers to forms of learning that sit between education, social care, play and, sometimes, health service provision. As Cartwright (2012) shows, informal education with the young has existed as long as professionals have engaged with young people in order to support or help them – and certainly since the rise of philanthropic organisations such as the YMCA, in the 19th century. During the mid-20th century, it was recognised that informal education – 'the personal and social development of young people' – was a core component of youth work (Merton et al, 2004, p 5) and to differing degrees this impulse continues in British youth work today. Thus, in addition to providing support for young people, youth workers view themselves as facilitators: they attempt to create spaces wherein young people can reflect upon their lives and feel empowered (Young, 2006; Cartwright, 2012).

Of importance to this book is that – following Freire – informal education is most commonly theorised as a process based upon dialogue, and into which the 'learner' enters voluntarily (Richardson and Wolfe, 2001). It involves mutual learning through conversation and reflection about everyday situations, interests and experiences (Jeffs and Smith, 2005). Informal education is meant to extend more or less naturally from the process of engaging young people – it is imminent to the rhythms of everyday life (Chapter Five). It tends rarely to be a named 'activity' with particular outcomes but something that *may* happen at a point in the relationship between a youth worker and young person (or group of young people) when that young person has gained the confidence, trust, care or even love in their relationship to engage in processes of dialogue and reflection about their lives (Chapter Seven). Indeed, it may be that informal education may not ever happen in the course of that relationship, for whatever reason.

The *spatialities* of informal education are also particularly important for any conceptualisation of alternative education. I want to point out three notable features, which I pick up again later in the book. The first feature of informal education is the emphasis upon 'up-scaling' from the personal to the social (Chapter Seven). Thus, Cartwright (2012, p 161) provides the example of a collaborative project by a group of young people in London that, starting from the disruption to young people's bus routes caused by an international arms fair, led to an after-school documentary project linking 'issues of local concern, such as asylum seekers [...] with the global implications of the arms trade'. As with Montessori, Steiner and Democratic forms of education, the 'educator's' role is one of starting a conversation from whatever matters to young people at a *particular* place in their lives, and letting that flow into matters that maybe of *global* concern.

A second notable feature is that informal educators do not require the same level of control over the physical layout or social organisation of a learning environment as in formal settings. Thus, they instigate very few rules, they do not require a 'classroom' as such and tend to require few learning materials because the everyday environment is seen as one overflowing with immanent learning potential (Chapter Five). Since they seek to foster learning through conversation, learning can simply happen spontaneously, as it would in a homeschooling setting (Falk et al, 2009). It may, indeed, be similarly mobile, taking place on a walk in a corridor or on a street corner (Cartwright, 2012; see also Chapter Six). This is complicated further where, as Falk et al (2009) argue, 'free choice learning' can occur in many everyday settings that may not be explicitly categorised as 'education' (surfing the internet, visiting a museum, walking in a forest). In this book, however, the point will be that many alternative educators somehow promote specific elements of informal education in the constitution of the kind of 'alternative' that they provide. Hence, my specific take on Falk et al's observation will be to turn their observation back on itself. I will suggest that their argument allows us to critically interrogate not only the relationship between learning and everyday life, but the role of practices that *are* categorised as 'education' (in some sense) in the constitution of *life-itself*. I introduce theorisations of 'life-itself' later in this chapter, and return to this proposition about learning and life in Chapter Eight.

A final notable feature of informal education is its shifting position in respect of mainstream education. Historically, many informal educators working with young people operated under a 'detached' model of street-based youth work. Today, rather than working on the street, youth workers are increasingly being called upon to provide supplementary or 'alternative', positive activities *within* schools for young people excluded from lessons (Jeffs and Smith, 2005; Davies, 2012). As both Davies (2012) and Cartwright (2012) show, informal education is so interesting because youth workers have constantly to negotiate their beliefs about informal education's original aims (rooted in Freire), their new physical and metaphorical position in schools *and* the increasingly target-driven nature of contemporary youth work in the UK. They must, in several ways, try to make space for themselves and for informal learning within the mainstream school setting. As I argue in Chapter Four, an understanding of these challenges is not only important to an analysis of informal education: rather, the experiences of youth workers provide a touchstone for understanding some of the *spatialities* of connection and disconnection between different kinds of alternative and mainstream education. As I will show, those dis/connections are multiple, shifting and complex, often requiring the careful kinds of negotiation that informal educators must perform when working in mainstream schools.

Theories of alternative education

Despite an enormous amount of work inspired by Holt, Freire and other 'radical' pedagogues, there are relatively few *comparative* theorisations of alternative education. Simply put, most studies tend to focus on individual approaches, often for good reasons. I examine these studies as part of my 'type-by-type' introduction to my case studies, in Chapter Three, where I also examine studies that critique those approaches. However, in very different contexts, some scholars have begun to look across alternative educational approaches to begin theorising what is meant by the 'alternative' in alternative education. Notably, most studies find a series of general traits that resonate with 'radical' educational theories and, in many ways (although this is rarely acknowledged), with the autonomous theories and politics that I discuss in the next section. Thus, Sliwka's (2008) wide-ranging but brief survey finds a series of familiar tenets: an emphasis upon the small-scale; an innovative and flexible curriculum; a focus on personalised and/or informal learning, relevant to the learner's everyday life; principles of democracy, often geared around notions of community participation and non-hierarchical, inclusive decision-making. Given that further discussion of these themes will risk repetition and overlap with material in Chapter Three, I confine myself here to exploring in detail four recent theorisations of alternative learning that I have found particularly instructive for my own work.

The first example is taken from the Australian context, where Ferguson and Seddon (2007) undertook a multi-site study not dissimilar from my own. They mapped what they term 'new learning spaces' (Ferguson and Seddon, 2007, p 113) – community education initiatives, youth services, employers, health programmes and other spaces. Often, these spaces could be viewed as networks or overlapping 'bubbles' that, taken together, offered a landscape of learning provision, particularly for young people disenfranchised by secondary school. While very different from the kinds of case studies explored in this book (see Table 1.1), their impetus to 'decentre' but not displace mainstream kinds of education resonates with my own. That is, they seek to move away from the idea of 'borders' or 'margins' (Ferguson and Seddon, 2007, p 124). Doing so means that the mainstream no longer seems an impenetrable, monolithic entity and that 'alternatives' seem possible because they are distinct from but somehow connected *to* the mainstream. Thus, 'the idea of learning bubbles suggests that it is their points of connection with other social spaces [...] that anchor learning' (Ferguson and Seddon, 2007, p 125). Their theory of learning bubbles also makes some brief but tantalising assertions about some of the kinds of spatiality attended to in this book: they ponder the role of everyday social practices, material environments, and embodied practices in theorising new learning spaces. While I take great inspiration from their approach, Ferguson and Seddon do not really add flesh to these claims, as they seek to sketch out a possible framework for research on 'new learning spaces'. Thus, the present volume provides in part an opportunity to add empirical and conceptual weight to their framework. Moreover, my discussions of dis/connection, habit, affect and materiality take their work in some different and very much more specific directions, in order to posit a theory of *autonomous* learning spaces (rather than 'new' learning spaces or 'bubbles').

The second example builds on radical and democratic theories of education (mentioned earlier). In Fielding and Moss's (2011) passionate argument for radical education in common schools (schools open to a whole community, children and adults), a two-fold schematisation of the role of alternative *schools*, specifically, is apparent. Most significantly, they begin their 'exploration of social alternatives in the field of education' with a clarion call to 'overthrow the dictatorship of no alternatives' (Fielding and Moss, 2011, p 1). Theirs is, then, a critique of neoliberal modes of governance that have asserted that alternative worldviews are neither possible nor desirable. In this sense, the (re)turn to alternatives is a conduit for a powerfully utopian impulse: alternative ways of doing education are afforded a social and political role in resisting, shaping or even overthrowing the neoliberal mainstream. From this vision, Fielding and Moss (2011, p 15) imagine a two-fold role for common schools: on the one hand, to figure as prefigurative or micro-scale experiments from which might flow larger movements for social change; on the other hand, to present a series of characteristics that would represent the common school and its relevance for a better society – such as 'cooperation', 'solidarity', 'collaboration', 'democracy' and the 'small-scale'. Interestingly, Fielding and Moss present (although not in such terms) a specific take on the notions of connection and disconnection I discuss in Chapter Four. For, in a sympathetic but insightful review, Tannock (2011, p 944) argues that Fielding and Moss ultimately instil an 'either/or' decision – between common schools, mainstream schools, or those who would support the abolition of schools altogether. He specifically argues that Fielding and Moss ignore the possibility that different forms of education may work better in a combination of different institutions – community groups, trades unions, religious organisations, as well as formal, mainstream educational establishments (compare Ferguson and Seddon, 2007). Thus, for him, they do not adequately answer the question – which is in part a geographical one – of how 'the common school [should] build on and relate to those other [...] educational agencies (Tannock, 2011, p 944). In Chapter Four, with a focus on connection and disconnection, I begin the task of tracing some of these possible relations across a more diverse range of learning spaces than do Fielding and Moss. But I also seek to retain the hopeful, utopian element of their work in thinking through versions and visions of life-itself at alternative learning spaces (Chapters Seven and Eight).

My third example comes from a Canadian context. In her study of small, 'rogue' private schools in Toronto, Quirke (2009) provides a very different theorisation of educational alternatives. Her focus is upon the ways in which private schools articulate their *legitimacy*. She argues that mainstream schools prove their legitimacy on the basis of the professionalism of their teachers – that is, on the assumption that teachers will be certified through formal, state-sanctioned training. She argues, however, that rogue schools tend to employ fewer certified teachers and that many teachers who have been formally trained actually downplay their training as part of their 'alternative' approach. Indeed, she argues that rogue schools have alternative ways of proving their legitimacy, based predominantly upon a 'caring consumer ethos' *rather than* training (Quirke, 2009, p 627). This ethos has several features, which resonate strongly with the approaches to learning and child development discussed earlier. For instance, there is a heavy emphasis on the personality of the teachers – whether they will 'fit in' with the school's ethos, whether they 'like kids' and have a 'nurturing approach' (Quirke, 2009, p 626). Many schools foreground the importance of personal attention, smallness of scale and treating children as unique – forging emotional, if not spiritual, interpersonal connections that are characteristic of many approaches to alternative education, and which I discuss in Chapter Seven.

The final touchstone for this book – and the most important – is Woods and Woods' (2009) edited collection of essays about examples of alternative education around the world. Some of the examples in their book overlap with those in this book (notably Steiner, Montessori and Democratic schools). Reflecting on the diverse contributions to their book, Woods and Woods provide an authoritative theorisation of the meaning and potential role of alternative educational practices. Prompting reflection by practitioners as well as academics, they argue that educational alternatives can play many roles. They may stimulate discussion and challenge mainstream practitioners to reflect on their assumptions. Taken together, they may foster a 'large and diverse', international and intercultural, democratic learning community (Woods and Woods, 2009, p 3) that, I want to suggest from this chapter onwards, may represent an educational take on Gibson-Graham's (2006) diverse economies. They may stimulate discussion *across* mainstream and alternative settings about the purpose of education beyond contemporary (neoliberal) concerns for school improvement, testing and accountability. Woods and Woods therefore share the commitment to the connectedness of alternative educational spaces with other alternatives and the mainstream. At the same time, they offer a three-fold theorisation of educational alternatives that is worth repeating (Woods and Woods, 2009, pp 228-9): those that attempt to *separate* themselves from the mainstream and from other educational systems; those that attempt to *engage* with others – and especially in practical terms, with governments and/or funding agencies; and those that hold an *activist* impulse – which somehow promotes wider social change, perhaps through protest or education courses aimed at local communities. Woods and Woods recognise that few examples of alternative education can be classified in one of these three categories; but I agree with them that these are useful starting points for understanding the kinds of alternatives presented by the examples in their book and in the present volume. But, in each of the thematic chapters of this book, I also seek to add nuance to these categories and extend beyond them, as I build a theory of autonomous learning spaces. I begin this task in

Chapter Four, where I chart the multiple, complex and shifting ways in which alternative learning spaces dis/connect with the mainstream.

Critiques of alternative and radical education

It is also worth acknowledging that several scholars have been critical of alternative approaches to education. I detail some specific criticisms of each approach in Chapter Three. However, I want to acknowledge four key criticisms in closing this section. The first is that alternative education has been viewed as a tacit form of privatisation. That is, many alternative learning spaces – especially schools – charge some level of fees to families for children's learning. On the one hand, this means that alternative education may be largely a preserve of the better-off, as Seo (2009, p 409) argues in the case of homeschooling: 'a profitable adventure of threatened middle-class families'. Understood as an (albeit relatively small-scale) component in the privatisation of education, alternative education might reinforce ongoing inequalities in education that still have as much to do with class as they do with ethnicity, gender or any other social differences (Johnston et al, 2008; Andersen, 2011). On the other hand, as I show in this book, alternative education (perhaps unlike independent, fee-paying schools in the UK at least) is more diverse than this: several schools do not charge fees to parents on low incomes; some Forest Schools do not charge at the point of demand (funded for instance through local authority referrals); and several homeschooling families I spoke with comprised one parent living on a relatively low income.

The second series of critiques is characterised by a complex series of political, moral and legal debates around whether children *should* go to school, and whether education (in the form of compulsory attendance, state-sponsored schools) *should* be enforced by law. Again, homeschooling has attracted the most attention in this regard. Some commentators insist that compulsory, state-sponsored schooling should be enforced by law, in part because it is a critical path through which children learn to become citizens and enter into a contract of rights and responsibilities with the state (for example Kunzman, 2009). Others resist this position, contesting that the state only intervenes into the care and education of children in order to allay its fears about what happens in the private sphere of the family – and that there is little evidence that children educated at state-sponsored schools are any 'better' citizens than those educated elsewhere (for example Conroy, 2010). These debates are not the focus of this book, however, and I have glossed considerably over their multiple nuances (for more detail, see Kunzman, 2009; Conroy, 2010; Suissa, 2010; Kraftl, in press, 2013b).

A third charge levelled at alternative education – although not one about which I can find significant published research – is that it is both harmful in terms of children's socialisation, and that it is no better in terms of educational and social outcomes for children than mainstream education. These arguments rest on the one hand on the idea that children educated outside mainstream schools are somehow 'missing out' on the common experience of attending school that is shared by 90% of the UK populace. Interestingly, as I show in this book, teachers and parents at Human–Scale Schools and in homeschooling families are only too aware of this fear, and actively try to mitigate against it. On the other hand, the evidence about children's educational and social outcomes remains a little sketchy. As I detail in Chapter Three, most research shows that children in the most common alternative schools (Steiner and Montessori schools) fare no worse than their mainstream counterparts, but that they also perform better in certain subjects and skills, especially those relating to art and creativity. Similarly, there are several misconceptions about alternative education that should be dispelled: for instance, homeschooling parents rarely sit at home educating their children on their own, and often attend 'classes' that are taught by specialist teachers. Again, as I detailed in Chapter One, this book is less concerned with the outcomes of alternative education than a critical analysis of their multiple spatialities.

A fourth and final charge is that some of the philosophical and political bases of alternative education are fundamentally, logically flawed. Perhaps the best-known argument in this regard is Robin Barrow's (2012 [1978]) book, which patiently dismantles the arguments of Rousseau, Neill, Illich and Postman, all of whom argue for de-schooling and some degree of freedom or individual autonomy in some way. Barrow (2012, p 2) argues that their arguments are flawed because they are overly emotive, they 'overstate, generalise and personalise', and are frequently based less on 'hard facts' than on the supportive claims of friends. In particular, he argues that several of these authors privilege a sense of what is 'useful' learning over institutionalised, compulsory 'book-learning' (Barrow, 2012, p 2), when there is little agreement in contemporary societies over what is 'useful' and what is not. On this latter point I wholeheartedly agree, having myself written a stinging critique of how academics claim 'usefulness' (Horton and Kraftl, 2005). As I discuss in the next section, I am also persuaded by Barrow's arguments about the fallacy of individual autonomy (see also Walkerdine, 1988), since my notion of 'collaborative autonomy'

(Chapter Eight) differs substantially from those of Holt, Illich and others. While my intention in this book is not to argue *for* radical (or, more broadly, alternative) education, I disagree, however, that the logical and empirical failings of these texts would preclude them from having some contemporary relevance. For, on the one hand, there is a gathering sense (among teachers, parents, policy makers and others) in *both* the mainstream and alternative educational sectors that the institutionalisation and standardisation of education in the UK at least has gone too far. On the other hand, many alternative educators whom I have met in the course of writing this book do not simply take the ideas of Illich, Holt or others and implement them in their practical work (and let me be clear that Barrow does not say that alternative educators do this). Indeed, their ideas have often been adopted carefully and critically into situated learning spaces that *also* – as I show in Chapter Four – draw on mainstream, non-'radical' training, policies, funding mechanisms and pedagogies (including book learning, rule-setting and school-like environments). In other words, there is a difference between Barrow's critique of radical education per se (with which I am broadly sympathetic) and the more connective, local implementation of such ideas through *connectedness* with multiple mainstreams. It is also important to recognise that in some situations a short-term break *from* school-like settings can be highly successful in terms of a young person's behaviour or learning. I provide some concrete examples of this in Chapter Six, where I explore how young people's habits can be shifted in the 'naturalistic' environments about which Barrow is quite cynical – *but* with the crucial caveat that the intention of these short-term 'breaks' is very often to *return* young people to an engagement with mainstream school. Once again, then, I do not disagree with Barrow's argument, but seek to qualify it through an empirical examination of how radical educative pedagogies travel and intersect with other (broadly, non-'radical' or 'alternative') approaches. In Chapter Eight I also qualify Barrow's critique through a very different interpretation of the 'natures' of learning – romantic (and Romantic) interpretations of which Barrow is again rightly critical.

I want to reflect upon these critiques in two ways. It is important, first, to note that these critiques of alternative education exist. And second, and more significantly, I deal with these critiques in a rather more oblique way, by thinking less about what might be wrong with alternative education and more about potential interactions with the mainstream – which may be both negative and positive. In other words, it is through the concept of autonomy (which I turn to in the next section) that I stress a series of dis/connections between 'alternative' and 'mainstream' learning practices that are spaced and timed in multiple, complex and subtle ways. I develop a theory of autonomy that is in part grounded in the (largely individual-focused) notions of autonomy that are the target of some of the above critiques. But I also (quite deliberately) focus upon autonomy as a socio-spatial, *not* simply an individual trait that is the feature of learning spaces so 'radically' other from the mainstream that they turn away from that mainstream (compare Barrow, 2012). In the vast majority of cases, they simply do not turn away like this – they are not, actually, *that radical.* This does not mean that the critiques go away: instead, they form part of the ongoing discussion about what makes alternative learning spaces 'alternative' (or not), and about the ways that they (may) interact with the mainstream in the production of what I believe are potentially creative, dissonant, autonomous versions of life-itself (Chapter Eight; see also Braidotti, 2011).

Theorising alternatives: diverse economic and autonomous practices

While the previous section outlined theorisations of educational alternatives, this section explores a very different, but no less important starting point for this book. It examines just two examples of a range of contemporary theorising about alternatives to global capitalism, and to the seemingly inexorable rise of neoliberal modes of governance. I focus upon studies of diverse economic practices and autonomous spaces – not, principally, because they happen to have been produced by geographers, but because they offer an important entry point to the theorisation of alternatives that is thoroughly suffused with the kind of comparative, multi-sited ethnographic approach to empirics that I take in this book (Chapter One).

I begin with J.K. Gibson-Graham's (2006, 2008) work on diverse economies, which has been an important source of inspiration for scholars of queer theory (Brown, 2009), environmental politics (Fournier, 2008), development (Escobar, 2010) and, in isolated examples, education (Fielding and Moss, 2011). Gibson-Graham (1996) begin by re-theorising capitalism, dominant representations of which figure it ('it' being the operative word) as an obdurate, immovable, inexorable, inescapable, face-less and place-less system. They argue that such representations are merely that – an imagined economy (Leyshon et al, 2003), over which individuals and organisations seem to have little control, and in the face of which any alternatives are deemed impossible, implausible, or utopian in the pejorative sense (see also Jacques, 2002). Instead, they review capitalism as but one way of ordering the economy and, by extension, of ordering social spaces. Seen as simply another (albeit pervasive) mode of economic ordering, set alongside feudalism or communism,

> capitalism became slightly less formidable. Without its systemic embodiment, it appeared more like its less well-known siblings, as a set of practices scattered over a landscape – in families, neighbourhoods, households, organizations, state, and private, public and social enterprises. Its dominance in any time or place became an open question rather than an initial presumption. (Gibson-Graham, 2008, p 615)

This refreshed view of capitalism saw it as a process, less than an obdurate thing. Once viewed as such, capitalism appears fallible because it is reduced to a network of people, things, places and ideas that, as Actor-Network theorists would have it, holds firm only as long as its constitutive relations can cohere (Latour, 2005). Thus, faults may already exist somewhere in the system – becoming especially apparent at times of economic crisis, for instance. Gibson-Graham then place this refreshed view of capitalism alongside a comparative reading of Marxism, feminism and poststructuralism, which each contain the seeds of potential alternatives to capitalism – of what they term a 'new economic politics' (Gibson-Graham, 2006, p 6). For instance, feminist analyses have uncovered vast reserves of unpaid, non-market transactions in household labour and parenting cultures (for example Holloway, 1998), while more recent work on children's caring roles in Africa highlights the enormous economic burden lifted from already struggling nation states by that informal work (Evans, 2010). Moving from a critique of capitalism, Gibson-Graham engage in a form of affirmative critique wherein they map (figuratively and literally) a diverse array of alternative economic practices in terms of what they *offer*, not what 'deficits' they have that would need to be addressed by conventional models of capitalist economic development. They open out a vast range of spaces – not all of which may necessarily be compatible with a progressive politics – in which individuals and groups try to do things differently. Their examples include worker cooperatives, local exchange and currency schemes, hunting, poaching and theft, social enterprise, Community Supported Agriculture, voluntary labour, indentured labour and informal international financial networks, and much else besides (for a brief summary see Gibson-Graham, 2008, pp 616-17).

Thus, their work is an affirmative mode of critique because it not only dismantles the seeming obduracy of capitalism but *shows* that alternatives are possible – in all kinds of places, from all kinds of starting points. But it is most powerful because, in the act of mapping diverse economies, possible points of connection, arching across time and space, can be found. Gibson-Graham's work 'offers a vision of global transformation through the accretion and interaction of small changes in place […] a landscape of potentially articulated projects and practices, connect[ed] imaginatively as well as practically' (Gibson-Graham, 2006, p 196). Practical constraints prevented me from visiting the sheer range of geographical contexts covered by Gibson-Graham. However, the current volume asks in a similar vein what might be gained – conceptually as well as practically – from mapping the versions and visions of habit, love and life-itself posited by alternative learning spaces.

Importantly, Gibson-Graham (2008) critique earlier ideas that such experiments, communities and economic collaborations can be branded 'alternative' to neoliberal and/or global capitalist mainstreams (compare Leyshon et al, 2003). Rather, in deploying the concept of 'diversity' (in 'diverse economic practices'), they are keen to chart the many overlaps, connections and resonances between what appear to be 'alternative' and 'mainstream' formations. This book is an attempt to chart such diversity in terms of alternative learning spaces. For instance, in Chapter Four, like Gibson-Graham, I tease out some of the connections and disconnections between 'alternative' and 'mainstream' learning practices. This means that neither category can be seen as singular or immutable, but rather multiple, complex and constituted in all kinds of changing ways. Similarly, it means recognising that some alternative education practitioners must draw on mainstream knowledges (such as teacher training), financial practices (becoming privately owned businesses) and organisations (taking local authority referrals). At times, however, because of these connections, I do not want to see these practices only as 'diverse'. Rather, I want to view them as 'autonomous', albeit taking a particular and more extended definition of that term. I turn to the notion of autonomy in the next section.

Autonomous geographies

The inclusion of 'non-capitalist' experiments in the diverse economies project (Gibson-Graham, 2006, p 616) resonates especially with other attempts to document and theorise alternatives to capitalism. I am thinking here of those alternatives that may take the form of intentional communities and activist/solidarity movements, wherein special interest groups invest in spaces, lifestyles, modes of social organisation and belief systems that somehow set them apart from the mainstream. Often associated with utopian experimentation, intentional communities may be co-housing projects, ecological or low-impact communities, spiritual communities and much more besides (Sargisson, 2000; Pickerill and Maxey, 2009; see www.diggersanddreamers.org.uk for an up-to-date list of UK examples).

Alongside Gibson-Graham's work, of interest to me is a framing of *some* such diverse formations as constitutive of '*autonomous*' rather than straightforwardly 'alternative' spaces (Pickerill and Chatterton, 2006). The difference is more than semantic, and therefore Pickerill and Chatterton's usage of the term is important to this book. While often anti-capitalist in nature, Pickerill and Chatterton argue that autonomous collectives are rarely inward-looking, isolated or escapist communities of interest. Rather, they seek communal alternatives that stitch together diverse interest groups and identity groups, across time and spatial scale. Autonomous practices may therefore include the global networks of activists that took up hundreds of urban sites in the 2011 'Occupy' movement, or urban-based 'social centres' that form often temporary connections with other, variegated traveller, squatter and direct-action groups. But autonomous practices do not merely 'jump scales' and connect diversity. Rather, they have two further, notable features. First, they constitute a 'praxis, [concerned] with the revolution of the everyday' (Pickerill and Chatterton, 2006, p 3). They are concerned with living alternatives – sharing resources and skills, experimenting with new lifestyles in small and temporary ways, and, of significance to this book, engaging in collective learning and critical reflection through the course of these everyday experimentations. These are lively, fleshy, engaged spaces that begin less with a grand utopian vision than in the *process* of living differently. Second, autonomous spaces differ from many earlier communes and cooperatives because they do not aim for complete isolation from mainstream modes of governance, policing or everyday life. As Pickerill and Chatterton (2006, p 3) put it, 'the nature of autonomy means the lack of an "out there" from which to build autonomy, hence creating a constant interplay between autonomy and non-autonomy'. While far from perfect, autonomous groups exhibit an acute awareness of their public face and a desire – not always successful – to make connections with diverse public groups, near or far, radical or not. They do not merely attempt to connect with other autonomous spaces, but with mainstream groups, however (and wherever) conceived. Thus, much like Gibson-Graham, Pickerill and Chatterton engage in a process of charting, theorising and urging academics to work with a diverse range of autonomous groups.

Beyond Pickerill and Chatterton's work, the concept of autonomy has been interpreted in other, often overlapping ways (Brown, 2007). For instance, an important book by Sitrin (2006) identifies several features of autonomous movements in Argentina (called *Horizontalidad*). These include 'democratic communication', 'collective practice', a striving for 'non-hierarchical and anti-authoritarian creation rather than reaction', 'autogestion' – or 'self-management', where 'the relationships among people create a particular type of project, not simply the project itself' (Sitrin, 2006, pp vii, 3). As I do in this book (Chapters Five, Six, and Seven), Sitrin also emphasises the significance of emotion – the 'affective politics' in which 'creating affection, creating a base that is loving and supportive, [is] the only base from which one can create politics' (Sitrin, 2006, p vii). Like Holloway (2010), this is a theorisation of power and efficacy that comes from doing, from experimenting, and from engaging in relationships. Sharing (for instance with Freire and many other democratic educators) roots in Marxism, these notions of autonomy are less about revolution and the seizing of state power than demonstrating the power of everyday actions and emotions to enact change, however small scale.

Arguably, this theory of autonomy gains even greater purchase when read alongside Gibson-Graham's work on diverse economic practices. Both approaches are grounded in empirical and political engagement; they are also theoretically rich and emphasise – via an attention to spatiality – the complex and multiple ways in which alternative and mainstream practices intersect. However, they both raise a number of considerations (potentially positive and negative) for a consideration of alternative *learning* spaces. The first is whether and how as an academic one seeks to valorise any diverse or autonomous practice simply because it constitutes an alternative to the mainstream. Talking to colleagues engaged with radical, activist or critical politics, many are slightly suspicious that certain forms of alternative education (notably homeschooling and the fee-paying schools included in this book) might actually represent further forms of privatisation that reinforce the neoliberalisation of education (see also Seo, 2009). Certainly, as Gibson-Graham (2006, p 615) acknowledge, some alternatives may be 'unsavory'. Yet, second, it is curious that it is *assumed* that educational alternatives are considered forms of privatisation, whereas economic or environmental alternatives are branded 'autonomous'. For, as we will see, virtually all of the examples I cite are intimately connected with mainstream processes, and several share political or conceptual roots with autonomous social movements – from the interaction of some Forest Schools with statutory service provision for young people, to the active roles played by Care Farms in addressing the relative socioeconomic disadvantage of the 'publics' living in communities nearby. Clearly, other organisations (like Montessori and Steiner schools) cannot interact in these ways but, as I show, just because they charge fees to (some) parents, this does not mean that they are reticent to engage issues of broader social or economic import. Third, it is for this reason that in this book I do not want to view educational alternatives as somehow existing in a bubble, set apart from other kinds of diverse economic or autonomous practices. In reality, they are very much entwined: for example, in Chapter Eight I discuss examples of Homeschoolers involved in local food growing and eco-housing cooperatives, and Care Farmers who position themselves as a resource for diverse 'alternative' and 'mainstream' groups seeking to live very different versions of the 'good life'.

Finally, it is the case that autonomy cannot be understood in a single or simple way. This section has highlighted a series of characteristics that appear in many, but not all 'autonomous' spaces – ways of relating within a community, ways of connecting to others 'outside', ways of feeling, and more besides. I will not be arguing that all alternative learning spaces are autonomous – at least not in the ways described above. Rather, I will highlight that *some* alternative learning approaches do share a common interest, not only in notions of individual autonomy, which are familiar across many pedagogical philosophies (Curren, 2007), but also in collective autonomy – from the Marxist and/or anarchist underpinnings of Democratic Schools, to the underlying assumption that alternative educational approaches value meaningful, non-hierarchical, creative human relations (Sliwka, 2008). In addition, though, I will attempt to question and extend the notion of autonomy – through a range of pragmatic and financial concerns to a sense that theorisations of autonomy could be still more 'collaborative' (as I put it in Chapter Eight) if they acknowledged the role of non-human materials and processes. For example, like many autonomous groups, some educators in the learning spaces I visited held anti-capitalist and or anti-neoliberal beliefs; but, at the same time, they had felt it necessary to engage with capitalist imperatives (such as charging for their services), leading to all kinds of personal and collective dilemmas about the morality of what they were doing. In effect, this will mean an understanding of autonomy as something that appears in diverse, even contradictory, ways in many alternative learning spaces – and that in some learning spaces may rarely appear at all. Thus, while retaining a sense of the diversity and almost contradictoriness of alternative learning spaces, the book develops towards a theory of *autonomous* learning spaces, an extended summary of which is presented in Chapter Nine.

In doing the above, this book does resonate with notions of individual autonomy, which, as I stated in the preceding paragraph, are quite familiar within theories of education, relating as they do to concepts of individual freedom, choice, independence and critical awareness (Biesta, 2006). However, while these individualised traits will appear in this book – especially in quotations from some practitioners – my key argument will be that individual autonomy should at best only be understood as a component of the kind of *collaborative* autonomy that I promote in Chapter Eight. It is here, then, that I accord in part with Biesta's (2006, p 4) critique of humanist education, which attempts to bring out 'rational, autonomous being'. For Biesta (2006, p 8), inspired by poststructural thought, the question is how to conceive of humanity, autonomy and education 'after the death of the subject'. In other words, Biesta argues that an individual-focused notion of autonomy is no longer viable, because humanist conceptions of the self have tended to be partial and exclusionary, and because notions of the inviolate self have been exploded by poststructural thought, which only ever sees beings in-relation to other beings (see Whatmore, 1997). Acknowledging that his approach looks a little like child-centred learning, he argues for a radically open conception of the subject that (following Levinas) questions how each individual can 'come into presence' in their communal environment (Biesta, 2006, p 9). But, for Biesta, one must look outside community as commonly understood – in terms of co-location and sameness of identity. Rather, community and therefore fulfilment comes from an engagement with the radical plurality of the world – with difference (whether religious, ethnic, gendered, sexualised, or whatever). Again, I agree with Biesta and try to show in this book how these ideas can be exemplified. Thus, in Chapter Seven, through the concept of 'love, spatialised', I show how alternative educators' attempts to foster individual autonomy often do *more* than this – how they are scaled-up into preparing children to acknowledge and act responsibly towards unknown others, often at a great geographical distance from themselves. However, as I indicated in the previous paragraph, in Chapter Eight of this book, I seek to do *more* still – to push notions of autonomy to a sense that is even more fully collaborative. In my reading, like the theorists of autonomy I have discussed in this section, Biesta (2006) also leaves little room in his expanded conception of the human subject for *post human* senses of self or subjectivity. That is, for those life processes (variously named 'non-human', 'natural' or 'material') that, I will argue in the next section of this chapter, are as equally constituent 'others' in the lives of human subjects as unknown or strange *human* others. It is, I argue, in acknowledging the politics and practices of 'life-itself' that it is possible to move beyond the problematic deployment of (human) nature that undergirds notions of individual autonomy – and about which Biesta, Barrow and others are rightly so critical – towards post human conceptions of learning in which *collaboratively autonomous* learning spaces might offer what I think are genuinely exciting versions and vision of life-itself (Chapter Eight).

Non-representational geographies and the politics of life-itself

A final, major source of inspiration for this book has been a range of broadly poststructuralist-inflected theorising that attempts to grapple with the vitality of life. While far more disparate than will appear to be the case in the following paragraphs, what holds all of these approaches together is an understanding that life is experienced, valued and governed in ways that exceed easy representation. By representation I mean not merely words, but the kinds of cognitive processes that are taken to characterise rational, logical and, by extension, 'scientific' ways of knowing the world. What I am about to suggest will seem obvious because these theories all bear witness to the kinds of tacit and experiential knowledges all of us hold about the world and which simply go without saying. But that is precisely the point; because they pertain to registers of the material, the bodily, the emotional and the affective, those knowledges appear ephemeral and ungovernable – making them, in the eyes of many commentators, all-the-more potent tools for those in power (Thrift, 2004; Connolly, 2008; Kraftl and Adey, 2008). If we accept that this is the case, then the task becomes a pressing one: to find ways of adequately understanding and conveying the vital and excessive forces of life-itself, and the ways in which those *may* be captured or controlled by powerful groups. This task has become variously impressed upon several disciplines in the past 20 years, with multiple perspectives on theorising materiality (Callon, 1986; Latour, 2005), emotion (Williams, 2001), affect (Sedgwick, 2003; Probyn, 2005) and the body (Butler, 1990; Turner, 2008). Amidst this bewildering variety, I want to write in this book from two, closely related variations on these themes: non-representational geographies and the politics of life-itself.

Non-representational geographies

Non-representational theorising in geography takes materiality, affect and embodiment together to forge more lively conceptions of *space* (for a particularly instructive example, see Thrift, 2000). As Doreen Massey (2005) argues so powerfully, for centuries space has been viewed as something static – a set of immovable points on a map; a container for the more interesting stuff of human–natural interaction; something that appears concrete, objectified, and, therein, easily represent-able. Yet, as I indicated at the very start of this book, space is so much more than this. When understood as 'spatiality', it is possible to see spaces as places that acquire meaning through human agency – that, for instance, may be commodified and put to work in capitalist systems of resource allocation, exploitation and exchange (Castree, 1995). Yet for Thrift, Massey and an ever-growing range of geographers, spaces may be livelier still. For, they argue, places do not simply acquire *meanings* that can be reduced to the logical dialectics of Marxist analyses of class. Rather, so much goes on before, around, and in excess of these cognitive processes of representation that spaces are so radically energised that they will always and already evade true representation. Herein lies what, for non-representational geographies (and related theorising in other disciplines), has been a virtually insurmountable problem: how to *account* adequately for the excessive liveliness of spaces.

The above caveat notwithstanding, non-representational theorising has spawned a remarkable range of work (for excellent overviews and collections of this work, see Lorimer, 2005, 2007, 2008; Anderson and Harrison, 2010; Thrift, 2007). Indeed, increasingly, children's geographers have taken inspiration from such approaches to theorise play (Harker, 2005), the seeming 'otherness' and inaccessibility of children's worlds (Jones, 2008) and the affective, embodied and material experiences that seem so central to what it is to be a child (Horton and Kraftl, 2006; Colls and Hörschelmann, 2009). However, I want to take just two examples that are particularly instructive for the subsequent chapters in this book and that I hope bring to life the implications of non-representational theory for those unfamiliar with geographical theories.

The first example refers to an impulse to move away from a view of architectural spaces (including schools) as pre-given, material containers for human action. Instead, geographers have sought to understand the complex relationships between humans (architects, residents) and non-humans (pipes, cables, bricks) that must hold together for buildings to hold onto their status as buildings (Jacobs, 2006). Indeed, if those relations fall apart or change too much, a building may fall down (Law and Mol, 2001). In this way, buildings are never finished but are ongoing achievements whose meanings exceed the (documented) intentions of their architects because they are used, performed (Lees, 2001), manipulated (Kraftl, 2006a, 2006b), felt (Rose et al, 2010) and played with in so many diverse, unanticipated ways (for an excellent example see Steven Saville's [2008] work on parkour).

Although, as previously mentioned, I want to distance myself from simplistic understandings of the determinate role of physical spaces in education, non-representational and vital materialist approaches offer important ways to re-theorise the role of material objects and 'natural' materials in learning. Childhood theorists have begun to take on the mantle of this work – Alan Prout's (2005) deployment of Actor-Network Theory being the most notable (see also Taylor, 2011). Yet, in my reading, educational scholars have been far slower to take up the insights of Actor-Network Theory (and related theories of materiality) than have geographers and sociologists. So, in this book, inspired in part by John Law's (2004) writings about mess in social science research, I seek to take account of the *messy* materialities that emerge in education spaces (Chapter Five). Moreover, I move beyond Actor-Network Theory to consider the value of theorising life-itself in terms of the natures and vital energies of learning (Chapter Eight).

The second example refers to emotion and affect. For several reasons, many scholars of emotion may be uncomfortable with being branded 'non-representational geographers' because their conceptual roots lie within earlier, feminist theories that sought to displace masculine, 'rational' ways of knowing the world (Rose, 1993). Thus, studies of emotion and affect have taken two divergent but nevertheless parallel paths (see Pile, 2010, for a rather polemical overview). To characterise a little grossly, emotional geographers have charted a range of what we might term 'expressed' emotions that are usually particular to how an *individual* feels – emotions like happiness, sadness, joy or fear (for guiding examples and reviews, see Anderson and Smith, 2001; Sharp, 2008; Bennett, 2009; Pain, 2009). Meanwhile, geographers of affect have sought to bear witness to modes of feeling, sometimes understood as atmospheres or temporary sparks of connectedness, that are *shared*. Thus, in the terms of non-representational geography (not, it should be noted, other disciplines like psychology), it is harder to name affects because they do not correspond to a single emotion, nor to a single agent. Rather, affects are multiple, extensive and distributed. Emotions may be directed outward, as, for instance, an individual projects fear onto a dark alley in a city; but emotions tend to be located within the cognitive processes of an individual agent. Affects, rather, begin in the interstitial space *between* agents – agents who may, incidentally, be human or non-human – and, therefore, are constitutive of the very lively but evasive forces that characterise non-representational notions of spatiality. In his important theorisation of hope as an affect, Ben Anderson (2006, p 741) puts it thus:

> first, flows of hope take place as trans individual affectivities which move between bodies; second, [...] hopefulness [is] a constellation of specific bodily background feeling, emergent from the expression of affect; third, actual hopes [...] emerge through processes of qualification and are distinguished by possessing a determinate object.

In other words, hope is an emergent property of a situation – an atmosphere, if you will – that may consequently be felt or expressed as an emotion (via qualifications that attach to a determinate object). I explore the production of *learning* atmospheres in several places in this book.

Whereas Actor-Network Theory has been arguably underused in education studies, the same cannot be said for the deployment of emotion and affect. For instance, Zemblayas (2007) traces the multiple emergence of emotion in education studies – from the emotion labour of teachers, to the undoubted importance of emotional investment (and passion) by students as part of their learning (see also earlier, seminal work by Valerie Walkerdine, 1988). I examine this work in more depth in Chapter Five, so here confine myself to noting that, in developing this work, this book focuses upon variegated kinds of emotions that characterise a greater range of learning spaces than most educational scholars have hitherto examined. In particular, in Chapter Seven I argue for attention to the emotions that characterise intergenerational (or, better, inter*personal*) relationships not merely as educational relationships but in terms of family and friendship (compare, for instance, Hopkins and Pain, 2007). Moreover, in Chapter Six I direct attention to the emotional and affective geographies of movement, wherein the cultivation of habit and spirituality are, I argue, a hugely significant part of the geographies of alternative education.

The politics of life-itself

Non-representational geographies overlap with theories of life-itself. Chiming with Actor-Network Theory, this work centres around two premises. First, that, as Jane Bennett (2010, p xvi) puts it so beautifully, seemingly everyday objects may have a 'thing-power' that affords them a certain agency – to surprise, to create, to connect, or to cause social relations to break down. This may, in effect, be because a particular piece of technology malfunctions or because a computer does something unexpected. However, it may also be because seemingly inert objects – even, in Bennett's (2010) analysis, base metals – have a kind of vibrancy if we look closely enough. At a microscopic level, every substance is made of atoms that are

> fields of distributed charge [...], flashes of charge that emerge from and dissipate in the empty space from which they are composed. Even when vast numbers of atoms are assembled in the macro structures of the perceptible world, their subatomic behaviour consists in the constant emergence, attraction, repulsion, fluctuation and shifting of nodes of charge: which is to say that they demonstrate none of the comforting stability or solidity we take for granted. (Coole and Frost, 2010, p 11)

The same is true at the universal scale: what we understand as 'life' is comprised of emergent constellations of matter/energy that flow, solidify and dissipate. Herein, Bennett (2010) shows how edible matter (foodstuff) flows through human bodies – from the take-up of minerals from the soil, as a carrot grows, to its gradual digestion in the human body (until some minerals become an indistinguishable part of that human body in the gut), to the flow of peelings into rubbish dumps, and excrement into sewage systems and eventually the sea. Thus, in a move popular with poststructural feminists in particular (Barad, 2003), the 'self' can no longer be viewed as contained within a body, for that body is always porous, leaky (Longhurst, 2001) and constituted by matter/energy that flows before, through and after it. Bennett (2010, p 48) captures this succinctly: '[a]ll organisms, not just humans, are animated by a life force, and thus all organisms have the power to bestow "form" on inorganic matter or on dead meat. It is this mysterious force called life' that transforms foodstuff into organic, animate existence.

The second premise of these efforts to theorise life-itself is that, increasingly, the contemporary world is a place characterised by efforts to manipulate, control and even create life. Nowhere is this more evident than in attempts to plan for and foreclose the future (see Anderson, 2010, for an instructive review), especially under neoliberal regimes of governance. Nikolas Rose (2007) argues that contemporary forms of neoliberal governance exhibit a heightening of attempts to regulate life-itself. He identifies a five-part schema under which these forms of governance are unfolding (Rose, 2007, pp 5-7), of which three are particularly significant here:

- 'molecuralisation', whereby contemporary biomedicine is attuned to the kinds of microscopic processes identified above, and especially to identifying vital entities (like genes) that can be manipulated in 'new practices of intervention [...] no longer constrained by the apparent normativity of a natural vital order;
- 'subjectification', whereby human beings are required not only to become responsible for their own bodies (Evans, 2006), but also may be governed by biotechnologies aimed to subdue and identify bodies of potential (terrorist) threat – at airport security gates, for instance (Adey, 2008; Braidotti, 2011);
- 'economies of vitality', whereby in contemporary biomedicine (for instance, in cures for cancer) '[l]ife itself has been made amenable to [...] new economic relations, as vitality is decomposed into [...] distinct objects – that can be isolated, delimited, stored, accumulated, mobilized, and exchanged [and] accorded a discrete value'.

The question then becomes whether and how it might be possible to escape this trajectory or 'velocity of change', as Braidotti (2011, p 11) puts it. This is where work on diverse economic practices and autonomous geographies (as previously discussed) may, in my view, be aligned with theorisations of life-itself. For, quite separately, Rosi Braidotti (2011) offers a way to further refine these projects not only in light of the social, political and economic premises of neoliberal capitalism, but in light of the increasing centrality of the governance of life-itself *to* those premises. Like Gibson-Graham – and with a striking, implicit spatiality – Braidotti argues for 'new figurations' that are 'not figurative ways of thinking, but rather more materialistic *mappings* of situated, embedded, embodied positions [... deriving] from the feminist method of the "politics of location"' (2011, p 13, my emphasis). Controversially, she eschews 'the lame quest for angles of resistance' or calls to 'overthrow the system' in favour of 'counter-actualised' praxes, experimentations 'brought about by collective effort' (Braidotti, 2011, pp 18-19). In my view, such experimentations could readily be exemplified by the diverse economic practices and autonomous spaces I have discussed in this chapter – and by at least some of the alternative learning spaces I examine in this book. She proposes 'to work critically from within in order to exceed the present frame', seeking to affirm 'the many [new] "centres" punctuating the global economy' that may contain the seeds of change (Braidotti, 2011, p 19). Specifically, she terms this a kind of 'dissonance' (Braidotti, 2011, p 20). Taking this as a musical allusion, one may see this as striking a new chord that includes at least some of the same notes as before; or, in Braidotti's own terms, as an affirmative refrain on life that seeks to open up the possibilities of the present – in the terms of what is presently available (see also Gibson-Graham, 2006, on starting with the 'here and now'). Thus, her point is neither to foreclose life via biotechnology or Margaret Thatcher's famous invocation that 'there is no alternative' to capitalism, nor to step outside or break from present life (for instance, via Marxist revolution). For the purposes of this book, Braidotti's work offers a powerful accompaniment to notions of 'diverse economic practices' and 'autonomy', because it again seeks to play with the possibilities that are opened up when avowed alternatives are viewed always already *in relation* to the status quo.

Conclusion

This chapter provides a theoretical toolkit for examining the spatialities of alternative education in ways that extend beyond previous studies of alternative learning spaces. Read together, the perspectives outlined in this chapter overlap and diverge in some fascinating ways, all of which could help build a theory of autonomous learning spaces. Beginning with geographies of education, I will combine attention to 'internal' processes taking place within schools and 'external' dis/connections outside the school walls. In order to understand these dis/connections fully, it will be important to explore the deployment of notions of autonomy, democracy, doing and feeling that are espoused by radical, informal and alternative educators (and scholars thereof). Each of these notions resonates in intriguing (but as yet unrealised) ways with non-representational geographies and theories of life-itself. For those approaches have much to add in terms of how feelings, materialities, habits and non-human natures figure in alternative learning spaces – something I will discuss in several chapters. Moreover, read against one another, the theoretical approaches outlined in this chapter offer overlapping but distinct ways to theorise 'alternatives' in ways that incorporate but exceed representation: from bubbles to prefigurative experiments, from counter-posed kinds of legitimacy to activism, from affirmative critique to dissonance. Notably, they are all somehow affirmative. It is striking that Gibson-Graham and a range of 'radical' pedagogical theorists critique the 'deficit' model of neoliberalism (both in terms of the economy and education), preferring one that explores existing capabilities (in terms of a community or a child). Thus, rather than choose one of these theorisations of alterity, I will combine them to show how alternative learning spaces operate across a series of registers and concerns – financial, political, habitual, affective, material and much more.

Thus, by combining the theoretical perspectives outlined in this chapter, it is possible in my mind to ask some hugely significant questions about the geographies of alternative education. The most pressing question revolves around using alternative learning spaces as case studies for 'outward-looking' kinds of critical work that Hanson Thiem rightly advocates. Notably, neither education nor learning, in even the broadest sense, are key concerns for theorists like Braidotti and Bennett; nor are they more than implicit concerns for Gibson-Graham or Pickerill and Chatterton. Yet, in a way inspired by those theorists, the geographies of *alternative* education are potentially so powerful because they enable us to reflect upon not only how education spaces are constitutive of neoliberal regimes, but also how they might operate beyond or in dissonance with them. In this way it is possible to ask about the extent to which alternative learning spaces resonate with but do something different from diverse *economic* practices (Gibson-Graham). It is also possible to ask whether and how alternative learning spaces mirror or exceed forms of *autonomy* in the ways understood especially by Pickerill and Chatterton, but also other autonomy theorists. In this way the rest of the book examines what might be gained from viewing alternative learning spaces as autonomous learning spaces.

THREE

Alternative learning spaces in the UK: background to the case studies used in this book

This chapter provides a systematic overview of the case studies discussed in this book. It is divided into rough 'types' for ease of reference, using the same typology found in Table 1.1. The chapter is intended as a touchstone for the later, thematic chapters, providing some historical, practical and theoretical background so that examples and quotations do not appear out of context. Each section includes an outline of the following with regard to each type: history, development and key proponents (where appropriate); main pedagogical principles and practices; academic research concerning that approach; significant 'moments' where that approach appears in this book. Each section ends with a note on the distribution of each type of alternative education in the UK (and elsewhere, where appropriate) and a note on the kinds of examples visited in the course of the research for this book. In terms of academic research, it will quickly become clear that there is relatively little research regarding some educational types, while there exist significant bodies of research on others. I conclude by summarising some significant areas for further development in academic research on alternative learning spaces, again making the case for more broad-based comparative, multi-site studies.

Care farms

Care farms exist throughout western Europe and North America (Sempik and Aldridge, 2006). In the main, care farms are working, productive farms that also provide some kinds of 'health, social and educational services' (Hassink et al, 2010). Such services are usually provided by farmers themselves, although in many of the examples I visited, extra staff with specialist skills (including education officers) are employed to engage with the public. As Hine et al (2008, p 1) put it: 'care farming is defined as the use of commercial farms and agricultural landscapes as a base for promoting mental and physical health, through normal farming activity.' Most farms are specifically engaged in 'caring' activities – 'health-promoting interventions that [...] use both biotic and abiotic elements of nature in treatments [that aim] to maintain or promote a person's social, physical, mental or even educational wellbeing (Haubenhofer et al, 2010 p 106). In practice, this definition combines two kinds of care: the therapeutic care that can be provided to a 'client' (the commonly used term), by a farmer, through the client's engagement with 'green' experiences; the act of caring for animals or plants, by clients, which, recursively, has some kind of therapeutic value. Evidence has begun to show that, quite commonly, the impact of working with animals, for instance, entails a range of positive emotional changes within a client that extends beyond the immediate human–animal relationship. As Berget and Braastad (2008) argue, a key outcome can be that clients are better able to enter into meaningful, trusting relationships with other people (see Chapter Eight).

A significant feature of care farms is that they cater for a wide range of clients. Visiting groups typically include disabled adults, children with special educational needs, pupils excluded from school for behavioural reasons, ex-offenders, drug addicts, the long-term unemployed and mainstream (usually primary) school groups. In terms of school-age children, the length and repetition of visits may vary dramatically – from occasional school trips by mainstream schools, to referrals for excluded pupils who visit for one or two days per week (or even more) over a period of weeks or months, with the ultimate aim of them returning to school, work or some other kind of training. The diversity of their clients often means that care farms are multi-use sites (Figure 3.1). At just the 10 farms I visited, some or even all of the following activities were incorporated:

- care for animals, including feeding, grooming, and mucking out;
- maintenance work, including building, repairing fences or pens, cleaning;
- 'nature' activities, including pond-dipping, preparing areas for wildlife, and forest school or similar activities;
- gardening/horticulture, including vegetable/fruit growing, tending, potting-on, cooking and eating edible plants;
- play and adventure playgrounds;
- interaction with public visitors, including tours and selling produce;
- educational visits by schools;

Figure 3.1: A typical urban care farm in the English Midlands, incorporating stabling, educational areas, open public space, allotments, animal enclosures, a shop and several other facilities on a small suburban site

- music therapy, including the use of natural materials to make instruments.

The roots of modern care farming extend back to the 19th century. For instance, Sempik et al (2010) argue that – despite their well-documented failings – Victorian asylums included elements of farming and market gardening that probably had several benefits for patients. More generally, the underlying principles of Green Care resonate with efforts in the early 21st century to 'reconnect' western societies with 'nature', somehow conceived (Hine et al, 2008) – something I discuss later in relation to forest schooling. There are, however, three more direct and recent influences upon care farming. The first influence is a political-economic one: an ostensibly neoliberal programme to transfer the responsibility for care from state institutions (like care homes) to community organisations and families. This has been termed the 'socialization of care' (Hassink et al, 2010, p 423). The intention is that those people who have previously been pathologised and institutionalised are able to live as 'ordinary' a life as possible – empowered through their ability to engage with and move between a variety of sites where they can take part in 'the reality of normal life' (Hassink et al, 2010, p 424). Care farms are but one of these sites. A second and related influence has been the retention of a link in some contexts between statutory care provision and care farms. In Germany, for instance, care farms are funded by and always linked to healthcare institutions (Haubenhofer et al, 2010). Indeed, in the UK, although care farms tend rarely to be directly funded by the state, they may receive referrals (and attendant funding) from education authorities, social services, prisons and other statutory service providers. The third influence upon care farming has been the growing difficulties faced by farmers in the UK and other countries (Hine et al, 2008). These pressures are diverse, including a series of health 'scares' (like BSE and foot-and-mouth), environmental difficulties and economic pressures. Therefore, while not all care farms in the UK have formerly been working farms, farm diversification has been a key driver in their rise.

In general, academic research has been relatively slow to keep up with developments in the care farming world, especially in the UK (Hine et al, 2008). For instance, Haubenhofer et al (2010) suggest that UK care farms have emphasised horticultural activities and green exercise: but even a glance at the previously mentioned list of activities that I have seen at just 10 care farms, or at the Care Farming UK website (www.carefarminguk.org), reveals a far more diverse range of activities. Another large gap in extant research is a glossing of the educational role of care farms. This is, to some extent, understandable, as the majority of studies have quite rightly attempted to evaluate the benefits to health and wellbeing of participation in the therapeutic activities offered at care farms. Yet, as I show throughout this book, many care farms explicitly dispel any notion that they are providing 'care'. Instead, they provide a structured series of activities and goals, over a period of weeks, that many of them characterise more as 'learning' than anything else. Indeed, the role of education within care farming is recognised, but only implicitly, in academic research. For instance, Burls (2008) reminds us that Bronfenbrenner's early development of the idea of eco-therapy was designed around the education of young children, and has since been developed in work with older, vulnerable adults (and hence the educational element has been lost somewhat). In the US, care farming is recognised as a kind of 'humane education' (Ormerod, 2008, p 288) that has parallels with 'human scale' education. And, most explicitly, Hine et al (2008, p 248) identify education as one of the four components of their care farming 'model'. Notably, they use the phrase 'alternative education' to describe the kind of learning taking place at care farms (Hine et al, 2008, p 248). Yet even in the latter example, neither education nor learning is afforded the kinds of more detailed, critical, empirical attention that is given to questions of 'care', 'wellbeing' or 'therapy'.

Care farms in Europe and the UK, and examples used in this book

As a result of the trends already discussed, the number of care farms in Europe has increased very rapidly. In the Netherlands – with arguably the earliest and best-developed network of farms – there were 75 farms in 1998 but over 1,000 by 2010 (Hassink et al, 2010; Haubenhofer et al, 2010). Other countries, including Belgium, Italy and Austria, each have around half that number, while in several other countries, such as Sweden and Finland, care farms were in their infancy by 2010 (Haubenhofer et al, 2010). A survey by Hine et al (2008) identified 76 care farms in the UK. However, my review of the Care Farming UK website (which as yet has no formal membership criteria and is not a mark of quality), revealed that, in early 2012, there were 183 care farms in the UK. The geographical spread of care farms is very uneven. In some regions there are dozens of farms (for instance, there are 30 in the West Midlands and 22 in the east of England). In other regions there are very few (just two in Northern Ireland and four in the north-east of England). Significantly, not every farm in the UK has been a working farm before becoming a care farm. Two of the farms I visited were city farms with an explicit community or educational mission; three had been allotments, large country houses, or were completely new projects designed and built as care farms; the remaining five had been or were working farms. As mentioned previously, all of the farms were diverse in terms of the activities available to young people – none of them just offered 'green care' but offered at least three additional services or activities (like a playground, shop or school visits). Apart from one farm, which was funded by the local authority's social services provider, none of the farms I visited were funded directly by the state. Several farms took individuals or groups on referrals from local authorities (see Chapter Six), while others relied on voluntary donations of money, material and labour, charging entrance fees to the public, selling farm produce and relying upon other sources of income. I visited care farms in Scotland, the north of England, the English Midlands, East Anglia and the south of England.

Forest schools

Like care farming, forest schools are a relatively recent introduction to the UK educational landscape. The story of UK forest schooling has been told several times but is worth repeating here. Forest schooling has its roots in the mainstream Danish early-years curriculum. That curriculum developed in the 1950s, with parallels in the Norwegian and Swedish contexts (Knight, 2009). It should be noted in passing that variants upon forest schools exist in countries like Germany (Grimm et al, 2011), Japan (Inoue and Oishi, 2010) and Switzerland (Lindemann-Matthies and Knecht, 2011), although the Scandinavian influence is always cited as the dominant one upon UK forest schooling. An integral part of the curriculum is time spent outdoors, usually in woodland, playing, lighting fires, and engaging in more formal learning activities, like playing 'nature detectives' (Figure 3.2). Often, following the kinds of 'autonomous' approaches to learning propounded by John Holt and others (Chapter Two), children are able to set their own agendas for play. In addition to the Scandinavian connection, there are three further, slightly less direct influences upon forest schools. The first is the large and diverse field of environmental education, which is also sometimes called education for sustainability. Environmental education has sought

Figure 3.2 Two six-year-old girls using magnifying glasses to play 'nature detectives' at a typical forest school in south-west England.

to improve children's (and society's) awareness of environmental processes, and especially of the impacts of humans upon the environment (Wooltorton, 2004). It has also sought to instil behaviour change by making the connection between knowledge and action (Amato and Krasny, 2011). While the emphasis in forest schools is on 'hands-on' engagement and play *with* nature, and the approach has a wide range of goals, children are also supposed to acquire knowledge about the local environment and sustainability issues (Ridgers et al, 2012). Given that the field of environmental education research is very well established, and given my focus on other themes in the subsequent chapters in this book, I will say little more about environmental education other than to acknowledge its influence upon forest schooling.

The second influence has been a range of writing – some of it polemical, even journalistic – on the decreased time that children in western societies are apparently spending outdoors, and especially in natural environments (for a balanced account, see O'Brien et al, 2000). A famous and provocative variation on this theme has been the theory that, as a result, today's children suffer from 'nature deficit disorder' (Louv, 2005). It is claimed, although difficult to prove directly, that lack of time spent in natural spaces, has led to increases in childhood obesity, and a range of psychological and emotional disorders (see O'Brien, 2009 and Knight, 2009, for brief summaries). I have to say at this point that some of these claims are based less on empirical research than upon the kinds of traditional social constructions of childhood that have further detracted from, rather than enhanced, children's freedoms (see James and James, 2004). However, it has been a little easier to prove a range of psychological, physiological and educational benefits from being outdoors, which I now outline.

The third influence on forest schools has been the longer-standing outdoor education movement. The influence of outdoor education is only recognised by some scholars (especially Sara Knight) but is arguably significant. The goals of outdoor education are manifold: to take children out of the classroom into an experiential learning environment that allows a 'personal connection with nature' (Harrison, 2010, p 3; Higgins and Nicol, 2002); to allow children to engage in risky play, for instance rock climbing, skiing, balancing or lighting fires (Sandseter, 2009); to facilitate a kind of physical 'journey' or exploration that may also allow a personal journey or period of reflection away from the routine environments of school or home (Allin and Humberstone, 2010). There are striking parallels with the goals and methods of forest schooling, including a shared commitment to the Swedish principle of *friluftsliv* – which, roughly translated, means 'living outside in nature'

(Backman, 2011, p 52, on outdoor learning; Knight, 2009 on forest schools). Again, while outdoor learning is not an explicit focus for this book, I will draw on this work to make arguments about movement/mobility (Chapter Six) and non-human natures (Chapter Eight).

The contemporary UK forest school is, then, a mixture of various approaches to environmental and outdoor learning. But it is the transformation of Scandinavian early-years curricula into UK forest schools that is most instructive, especially for what it tells us about forest schools as an 'alternative' learning space in the UK. Knight (2009) charts how in the mid-1990s, a group of early-years practitioners from Bridgwater College in Somerset visited Denmark to view outdoor early-years education in action. That group was inspired to set up forest schools in the UK, and from there the idea spread quickly. Today, one can become a formally accredited forest schools practitioner through three levels of OCN (Open College Network) training. The relatively speedy formalisation of forest schools is significant because, as Knight (2009, p 5) highlights, 'Forest Schools' (in name) do not exist in Scandinavia because 'the cultural norm is of regular access to the environment for the majority of the population', rooted in principles of free play, creativity and risk taking. 'Forest school' (as it appears in the UK) is simply integrated into Scandinavian mainstream early-years education in a way that is not possible in the UK – in part because outdoor experience plays a less fundamental, intrinsic role in UK schools and British culture, and in part because of increasing attentiveness to 'risk' and risk-mitigation in the UK (see Gill, 2007). It is therefore the case that educational alternatives – like forest schools – *become* 'alternatives' because of the way that they are constituted in relation to mainstream educational processes. This is something I pick up again in Chapter Four.

Out of the above contexts, a set of forest school principles has become increasingly solidified and formalised over time. The following list is a synthesis based on my own observations and what, for me, are some of the most significant academic texts about forest schools (Swarbrick et al, 2004; O'Brien and Murray, 2007; O'Brien, 2009; Knight, 2009, 2011; Ridgers et al, 2012):

- *Going beyond the familiar:* most forest schools take place in woodlands because they are places that children do not routinely visit. Forest schools are a break from the places, norms and, especially, rules of everyday life (and school). Woodlands are the ideal – but forest schools can take place in any environment where children can somehow engage with 'nature' in a space apart from everyday life. I know of forest schools taking place in a small corner of an adventure playground, on beaches, and in small, unloved patches of urban scrubland.

- *Repetition*: a central component of forest schools is that children should get to know a patch of woodland through visiting every week. Gradually, forest school practitioners build up children's confidence (and trust) so that they become increasingly able to explore and make decisions for themselves. Like care farms, most forest schools have a definite end-point (a song, a celebration, a shared meal) so that children have a definite sense of what they have achieved and where they are going next.

- *Managed risk*: children engage in activities that they would not at school or home. During this process, they build up trust with adults and one another so that they can gradually take and assess bigger risks. Initially, they may be allowed to explore an unknown area within the immediate vicinity of adults, but gradually they will be allowed to roam further, and engage in tasks like fire-lighting, den-building and the use of knives and saws.

- *Educating the 'whole child'*: there is an emphasis on children having time and space to make their own decisions, and to learn through play. Children can learn at their own pace. Learning is meant to be about forging relationships with others, engaging in conversation, improving self-esteem, happiness and wellbeing, and gaining practical skills. This can mean that learning processes and outcomes can be unplanned and contingent upon chance happenings; at the same time, for this to happen, there need to be strict temporal and spatial boundaries that are agreed by adults and children.

- *Forest schools are not just for young children*: while there is, as in Montessori education, an emphasis on early intervention, forest schools work with teenagers excluded from school and adults who are ex-offenders. Forest schools work from an ethos that the natural environment is an appropriate setting to change habits, emotions and relationships for the better.

- *Learning at forest schools can be linked back to National Curriculum objectives*. Forest schools share with all of the other alternative approaches cited in this book a conviction that what they are doing can support the kinds of learning that children do in school – including skills like literacy and numeracy. The point is that forest schools, again like other alternatives, allow children to acquire these skills in a different space, at a different rate, in a different way, from school.

I return to these forest school principles as part of my discussion in subsequent chapters of this book, but particularly in discussions of bodily movement, repetition, taking time, boundaries, interpersonal relationships and habit.

As is the case for care farms, research on forest schools has been described as 'emerging' (Ridgers et al, 2012, p 50), and many authors urge caution about the findings of early research (for example Knight, 2009). In a recursive sense, most research is practitioner focused, and has been geared towards producing, refining and evaluating the kinds of principles and practices I have just discussed (see Knight, 2011).Nevertheless, drawing on a larger and earlier body of research on outdoor education, extant research has taken three forms. First, several studies have evaluated the kinds of skills that children develop at forest schools – especially independence, teamwork, practical skills and imaginative play (see, for instance, O'Brien, 2009). Second, innovative research *with* younger children themselves has reinforced these findings, emphasising how children develop an interest in and awareness of nature, and how they have been inspired to share what they have learned with family and friends (Ridgers et al, 2012).Third, participation in forest schools has been proven to increase children's participation in outdoor activities, to improve behaviour, to foster greater senses of happiness and psychological wellbeing, and to bolster self-esteem (summarised in Knight, 2009; see also Swarbrick et al, 2004).Given the rapid increase in forest schools since the mid-1990s, academic research still remains patchy; apart from the study by Ridgers et al (2012), no studies explore the spatialities of forest schooling.The specific contribution of this book will be to place forest schools in the context of a comparative study of alternative learning spaces.

Distribution and types of forest schools in the UK, and the examples in this book

The number of forest schools in the UK has risen rapidly since the mid-1990s when there were none, at least by name, to at least 140 by 2009 (O'Brien, 2009). Given the continued rise and spread of forest schools outwards from west and south-west England, it can be safely assumed that, at the time of writing, there are over 200 forest schools in the UK. In contrast to other European contexts (especially Scandinavia), it is notable that forest schooling has had to become a nameable, discrete element of children's education – with its own qualifications and procedures – rather than an extension of (everyday) school life. However, this observation masks some diversity in forest school practice in the UK, especially in terms of its relationship with and positioning against mainstream education. For instance, in some contexts, children will be referred to forest schools by local authorities because they have been excluded from school, with the expectation that a dose of woodland for a day or two a week (sometimes for an extended period of months) will offer an alternative to school that will eventually allow them to re-integrate with a mainstream school. In other contexts, children from local primary schools will make special one-off visits or be transported to a patch of woodland weekly, for an afternoon, over a period of six weeks. Some forest schools run sessions for the public – for instance for parents and toddlers, who sign up through local children's centres or country parks.

All of the five forest schools I visited (although one termed itself a 'Nature Workshop') provided one or more of these services. They were located in Scotland, East Anglia and south-west England. The forest schools I visited were generally funded in the same way as care farms: they were either constituted as voluntary, social enterprise companies or as not-for-profit public limited companies and they tended also to rely on locally available grants, voluntary donations and, in some cases, personal investment by their founders. All of this simply reinforces the idea that although forest schooling is increasingly becoming a complementary element for mainstream education – especially in the early and primary years, it still feels very much like an '"alternative" or non-traditional educational project', as Swarbrick et al (2004, p 142) point out. I flesh out these arguments in Chapter Four.

Homeschooling

Homeschooling differs from care farming and forest schooling because, most commonly, children's attendance at school is completely replaced with education at home, on a full-time basis. As I discuss in Chapter Four, like Steiner and human scale schooling, homeschooling is figured as a more thorough-going *alternative to* mainstream education, rather than a temporary or partial replacement. In the majority of cases, the parents of a child take on the responsibility for homeschooling, although in 90% of cases it is mothers who generally stay at home to educate their children (Collom and Mitchell, 2005). There is considerable diversity in the routes taken by homeschoolers into home education: some see it as a natural extension of being a parent (or mother) and never send their children to school; others remove their children from school after a period of time, perhaps because their child has been bullied or because they do not agree with what their child is being taught. Less commonly, children may attend school 'flexibly' – for instance spending two days a week at school and three learning at home.

Unlike research on care farms and forest schools, there is a large body of research on homeschooling, although much of it is based in the US (although for UK-based examples, see Rothermel, 2003; Lees, 2011). A significant proportion of research has focused upon homeschoolers' motivations and, although I asked homeschoolers about their choices, I do not include my own data on this issue in the current book because it repeats the findings of an already saturated field of research (although see Kraftl, in press, 2013b). In setting the scene, for instance, Gaither (2009) depicts several contextual, macro-factors that have influenced the rise of homeschooling in contexts like the US. These include post-war mass suburbanisation, the rise of feminism, and disillusionment with the increased bureaucratisation and/or secularisation of mainstream schools. Given these various contexts, it is hardly surprising that the reasons given by homeschoolers for educating are diverse. (Indeed, thinking of the 35 parents I interviewed, all gave slightly different reasons for their choices.) While a little too quick to categorise, Collom and Mitchell's (2005, p 277) summary of homeschooling research is at least suggestive of this diversity. They state that 'the decision to homeschool is motivated by four broad categories of concern: (a) religious values, (b) dissatisfaction with the public schools, (c) academic and pedagogical concerns, and (d) family life'. In the US context, religion has been a key motivational factor, especially amongst politically conservative Christian families (Stevens, 2001) In the UK, religion appears to be a less significant factor (Rothermel, 2003). Indeed, in my (admittedly self-selecting) sample, the majority of parents emphasised their commitment to autonomous, child-led pedagogical principles ahead of religion or spirituality. Moreover, as Lois (2009) found in her rich study of homeschooling mothers, many homeschoolers emphasise that their decision to educate their children themselves is simply a natural extension of what any 'good mother' would do (see also Merry and Howell, 2009). As I have shown elsewhere (Kraftl, in press, 2013a), this justification can also be influenced by what Holloway (1998) calls 'local parenting cultures' – the kinds of parenting practices popular amongst the peer groups in which mothers take part.

While much research has attempted to focus on documenting the demographic profiles and motivations of those who homeschool, there have also been many excellent studies about the experiences of homeschooling itself. For instance, some authors show how homeschoolers became highly politically mobilised, in the first instance in lobbying for the legalisation of homeschooling in the US (Stevens,

2001) and, later, as a social movement campaigning for freedom from state intervention (Collom and Mitchell, 2005). I touch briefly on questions of activism in Chapter Four. More importantly, I observe that the majority of work on the social organisation of homeschoolers (especially Stevens, 2001) tends to assume some kind of higher political or religious motivation for families to come together. Instead, in several instances in this book, I turn the lens back onto some of the social groups that UK homeschoolers organise, where it is apparent that these are often informal, loose, amorphous gatherings, characterised by considerable diversity, and where it is the kinds and qualities of the *interpersonal relationships* fostered within those social spaces that holds most meaning (Chapter Seven).

In a different vein, several authors show how homeschooling is equally characterised by diversity when it comes to learning styles. Some parents strictly follow national curricula or one of an increasing range of learning programmes that can be purchased online, while others follow child-led principles of learning from the beginning (Stevens, 2001). Interestingly – as I found in my interviews – a large number of parents begin trying to 'do school at home' but soon realise that, for a variety of factors, they go through a gradual process where they allow their children increased freedom to follow their interests, wherever they may lead (compare Holt, 2004; see also Neuman and Aviram, 2003). While my findings about the *biographies* of homeschooling families reveal little of much novelty, in this book I take advantage of my research at other alternative learning spaces to put homeschoolers' experiences of learning into context. In doing so, I proffer a range of new ways to understand homeschooling that have not been developed in previous research: for instance, how autonomous homeschoolers articulate a particular way of negotiating tensions between 'mess' and 'order' (Chapter Five), and how these resonate with the approaches taken by care farm and forest school practitioners; and how homeschoolers emphasise movement and mobility in learning in ways that cross-cut those ideas in other learning spaces (Chapter Six).

Homeschooling around the world, and the examples in this book

Homeschooling takes place in many contexts around the world, but is distributed very unevenly. In the US, around 2 million children are home educated (about 1.7% of the total student population) and this figure is steadily rising (Gaither, 2009). In the UK, 50,000-150,000 children are homeschooled, although this is an estimated figure and the total is likely to be towards the upper end of this range (Conroy,

2010). By contrast, in countries where homeschooling is illegal (like Germany), there may be only a few hundred families practising home education (Kunzman, 2009). Demographically, it is estimated that between 75% and 90% (Bielick et al, 2001) of US homeschooled children are white. In terms of familial and educational status, an early study (Mayberry et al, 1995) found that 97% of homeschooled children lived with married parents, and that 76% of homeschooling parents had post-secondary qualifications. The picture appears to me more diverse in the UK, where Rothermel (2003) found that roughly one in eight homeschooling parents were working class and, in contrast to the US, only 49% held post-secondary qualifications. From my own qualitative study, I encountered substantial diversity, including four single mothers and several minority ethnic and religious families. Several families (especially the four with single mothers) described themselves as working class or less well-off, although the majority of families had sufficient finances for one parent not to work at all. When it came to learning styles, the majority of families in my study (31 of 35 families) neither did 'school at home' nor followed a pure 'child-led', autonomous approach. Rather, they erred towards the latter but included some elements of more 'school-like' learning – whether in organised groups or through curriculum materials they had bought or acquired. The remaining four families followed a curriculum (two followed the UK National Curriculum) as closely as they could. Most of the families (27) lived in London or south-east England; the remainder lived in the English Midlands and south-west England.

Democratic and human scale schooling

Homeschoolers are a prime example of an alternative educational approach that foregrounds the importance of interpersonal relationships to children's learning. In fact, as I show in Chapter Seven, this is something that characterises many alternative approaches to learning. This is equally evident in democratic and human scale approaches to learning. While these two approaches can be understood separately (Carnie, 2003), there is so much that ties them together that it makes more sense to discuss them in the same section. Indeed, I have visited schools that primarily call themselves 'Democratic' or 'Human scale' but which in their educational philosophies and teaching practices actually combine both. Another important thing to bear in mind about these approaches is that the philosophical bases of democratic and human scale schooling have important connections with other alternative educational approaches – such as forest schooling (Knight,

2009) and Montessori schooling, as well as explicit philosophical and political connections with the ideas underpinning autonomous social movements (for example Pickerill and Chatterton, 2006). Moreover, there are some fascinating cross-overs with mainstream education, which I outline later. It is for this reason that, although relatively few such schools exist in the UK, they form an important part of several chapters in this book, but especially Chapters Five and Seven.

If one were to distil out a key difference between democratic and human scale schools, it would be that the former foreground children's voice in decisions about their education, whereas the latter emphasise the importance of the scale of the environment in which learning happens. It is therefore still instructive to say a little about the varied roots of these two approaches. Democratic schools are arguably better known, because they are couched in at least a century of critical thinking about pedagogy (see also Chapter Two). Democratic schools are so 'alternative' because they do not merely promote children's voice in their learning, but in most aspects of a school's organisation (Carnie, 2003). In many schools, this approach is formalised in a whole-school council where every member – teacher or pupil – has one vote and, depending on the school, those votes have equal weighting, no matter the age or status of the individual. It is thus conceivable that some uncomfortable decisions can be taken, although it is usually the case that because those decisions are debated in detail within the entire school community beforehand a kind of situated common-sense prevails. Thus, as Mabovula (2009, p 219) summarises, democratic school governance is centred around particular principles, including 'inclusion, motivational communication, consensus, deliberation/dialogue, collaboration, and conflict resolution.'

It is important to recognise that the values underpinning democratic schooling are not – as may be popularly believed – simply designed to prop up an artificial island of democratic alterity somehow divorced from the rest of society. Rather, democratic educators suggest that a reconfiguration of the interpersonal power relations within a school will actually *better* prepare children for everyday life outside the school. On the one hand, they aim to prepare children to leave the school with self-confidence and creativity, which would ideally mean that they engage in somehow more meaningful, democratic kinds of connection with others in the course of their everyday lives (Carnie, 2003). It is almost as if those children are being equipped to take with them a 'liberal democratic notion of justice on a global scale by 'expanding' [...] their sense of responsibility and obligation to others' (Pashby, 2011, p 427). On the other hand, democratic schools might be viewed as prefigurative or experimental spaces where the advantages *and* disadvantages of alternative modes of democratic ordering can be *worked out* in practice. Clearly, it is the *process* of trying to do democracy differently that matters: it is perfectly acceptable to make mistakes. Indeed, in all of the democratic schools I visited, staff members were as equally keen to point out their failings as their successes!

John Dewey is a key influence here. Dewey initiated one of what can be viewed as a series of global antecedents to the democratic schools that exist worldwide today. His temporary 'Laboratory School', founded in Chicago in the 1900s, has endured as a key influence upon educators seeking to build a more 'democratic society' from schools located both within and outside mainstream education systems (Schutz, 2001, p 267). A similarly early and famous example that does continue to exist today is Summerhill Free School, started by A.S. Neill in the 1920s – a school famous for providing children the choice whether to attend lessons (in practice, most do) (Carnie, 2003).

Other than the work mentioned previously, academic research on democratic schools themselves has been very patchy in comparison to the range of theoretical work critiquing and developing the philosophical foundations of democratic forms of education (on the latter, see for example Friedrich et al, 2010). Nevertheless, there have been some important in-depth studies of democratic schools. For instance, Davina Cooper's (2007, p 625) study of Summerhill demonstrates beautifully the shifting conceptions of property ownership that constitute the 'variegated social life' of the school. In another study of four democratic schools, Dobozy (2007, p 115) identifies three principal features of those schools: a sense among teachers that their schools were 'out of the ordinary'; a series of negotiated school rules rather than punitive lists of what children can and can't do; child-focused approaches to teaching and disciplining rather than a uniform approach.

Upon reading about such features, it becomes evident that the principles underpinning human scale schools overlap considerably with democratic schools. Indeed, human scale schools emphasise student participation and the kinds of democratic values and especially governance/decision-making processes mentioned above. However, the main difference is that they conceive of 'the primacy of human relationships' (Harland and Mason, 2010) in a slightly different sense that is not only underpinned by democracy but by *scale*. Thus, as Carnie (2003, p 17) puts it so well, 'Human Scale Education believes that smallness of scale helps to create the interpersonal relationships that enable children and young people to become confident and resourceful individuals, capable or respecting and caring for each other and for the environment.' The term 'small' usually refers to the physical size of the school in terms of the number of pupils (usually less than one hundred), the class sizes (usually smaller than in mainstream schools) and, very often, the size and intimacy of the school buildings (Carnie, 2003). In the case of the buildings, some examples of human scale schools are explicitly 'home-like' in quality, aiming not to replicate the large, impersonal, institutional spaces of mainstream schools (Figure 3.3). However, a key consideration for this book (examined in Chapter Seven) is that the notion of scale propounded here is not determined principally by the physical structure or size of the school but by a commitment to smallness: to a human scale and process of 'rehumanizing' most broadly conceived (Cook–Sather, 2006, p 329). This is why interpersonal relationships and community decision making are accentuated. Like several alternative approaches (forest schools, Steiner schools), human scale schools aim for a holistic education, wherein the learning of curriculum subjects does happen, but the connections between and beyond those subjects are also emphasised. Other than a highly instructive evaluation by Harland and Mason (2010), and a brief chapter by Carnie (2003), I know of no studies of

Figure 3.3 The interior of a typical human scale school in London. Originally a semi-detached house, the building has been extended. Downstairs there is a school-like classroom with old-fashioned desks, but in this upstairs room efforts have been made to include home-like furniture and a colour palette not reminiscent of mainstream schools.

human scale schools in the UK, nor of studies of schools elsewhere that have an approach underpinned explicitly by *smallness of scale*. There is thus considerable scope for extended academic research on this growing movement of schools, and within the confines of this book I can only offer some starting points (I visited four specifically 'human scale' schools, as discussed later). However, given the emphasis upon scale (understood in various ways), this is one obvious example of an alternative educational approach that lends itself to geographical analysis. Human scale schools therefore figure in my discussion of the material spatialities and mess/order (Chapter Five), habit (Chapter Six) and interpersonal relations (Chapter Seven).

I have already indicated that both democratic and human scale schools present some important connections with other forms of education, both alternative and mainstream. But the connections go beyond education. For instance, several human scale schools in the UK form part of wider spiritual communities of practice (see Chapter Seven for an extended example). Moreover, while human scale *education* may not be familiar to many readers, other parallel deployments of the term 'human scale' may be. For the term is aligned with grassroots or 'alternative' approaches to economic development that concentrate on the provision of basic human needs, upon holistic understandings of development, and upon an understanding that human environments (especially cities) should be inclusive, hospitable, beautiful, safe, vital and humane (Cruz et al, 2009; Francesco, 2009; Guillen-Royo, 2010). In this book I begin to trace some possible points of connection between human scale education and these other, arguably more extensive understandings of the human scale. In so doing, I directly broach two issues of central conceptual importance to my argument. First, given the connections with alternative economic practices (which are central to Gibson-Graham's work), I question to what extent it is possible to observe fruitful connections with alternative *educational* practices – not only with regard to human scale schools but also in relation to other examples used in this book. Second, given the reference both to 'basic needs' and 'vitality' in non-educational deployments of human scalar thinking, I observe possible points of connection – that in some cases are more than merely conceptual – with the notions of vitality apparent across several examples of alternative education in the UK (Chapter Eight).

Global and UK distribution of democratic and human scale schools, and the examples in this book

It is important to recognise that the values underpinning democratic schooling have had important influences upon mainstream schools, to varying extents. For instance, famously, the Italian city of Reggio Emilia has run a network of schools (now 34 of them) underpinned by a communitarian notion of democracy since the early 1960s (Fielding and Moss, 2011). In the UK, schools such as St George-in-the-East, begun in a disadvantaged area of London in 1945, became one of the 'most radical examples of a democratic secondary school within the state system of secondary schooling' (Fielding and Moss, 2011, p 9). Moreover, democratic schooling has formed part of mainstream educational policies in several countries, for instance in social-democratic educational reform in post-war Norway (Volckmar, 2008). Elsewhere, in South Africa, for instance, attempts have been made to democratise the governance structures of mainstream schools and to empower learners to have a voice about their schooling (Mabovula, 2009).

Outside of the mainstream sector, there exist approximately 200 democratic schools in over 30 countries worldwide (www. idenetwork.org). As well as six known schools in the UK, there are further contemporary examples in Brazil (unsurprising, given Freire's influence), the US, Japan, and Palestine, among other places (Le Tendre, 1999; Brent Edwards, 2010; Levy and Massalha, 2010). Since there are so few examples of democratic schools outside the mainstream sector in the UK, I was only able to visit one school; however, it is worth noting that democratic principles underpinned each of the four human scale schools I visited (as mentioned later) and several of the other educational alternatives included in this book. The school I visited was Kilquhanity School (real name), in south-west Scotland. The school was begun by John Aitkenhead in 1940, and was heavily inspired by A.S. Neill's Summerhill (for further details, see Chapter Four). The school closed in 1997 but was re-opened in 2002 following investment by a Japanese university professor. It now has links with a free school in Japan that sends pupils and teachers on lengthy exchanges every year (the resident teaching staff are both British and qualified teachers). Given that my interviews were with these two teachers (who were also former pupils), most of my discussion of Kilquhanity relates to the pre-1997 closure of the school, although I do draw upon relevant observations from my visit as part of my analysis.

Since it is scale that is the starting point for human scale schools, there is likewise considerable diversity among those schools in terms of the pedagogies and curricula they adopt. Many teachers are, admittedly, influenced by the writings of E.F. Schumacher (2011 [1973]) in his text *Small is Beautiful* – although readers familiar with that text will know that it is a far-ranging critique of modern institutions and political systems that touches on environment, economy and other aspects of everyday life as much as education. Therefore, although affiliating themselves with the Human Scale Education Movement (HSEM) (www.hse.org.uk), all four of the schools I visited (in London, East Anglia and south-east England) drew on a range of educational approaches. Most included elements of Montessori education and democratic schooling; some had developed their own curricula based around long-term project work negotiated by teachers and pupils; some drew on non-western spiritual principles and practices (including Buddhism and meditation); while one school (actually a network of schools) provided a space where badly bullied children could go to recover and continue their education. At the time of writing, it is unclear how many independent human scale schools there are in the UK, although I would estimate that there are between 10 and 20 schools. A slight complication is that the HSEM has had a growing impact within mainstream schools as well as alternative schools, especially in the UK, where the Movement was founded. The same is true of an earlier, related movement – the US Coalition of Essential Schools – by which the HSEM was in part inspired (Harland and Mason, 2010). Thus, in 2006, the Calouste Gulbenkian Foundation funded 39 English secondary schools to 'design and implement human scale education innovations', which in many cases involved trying to break down a larger school into a system of schools within schools (Harland and Mason, 2010, p 9). However, my focus in this book will be upon examples of human scale schools that are positioned outside the mainstream sector.

A final case study included in this 'type' is Findhorn (real name). A charitable trust formed in 1972 by its members, Findhorn is best known as a spiritual community, although it describes itself as a 'spiritual community, learning centre and ecovillage' (www.findhorn. org). Findhorn is located on the north-east coast of Scotland, not far from Inverness. Several hundred people live at Findhorn, and it could be termed an 'intentional community' (Sargisson, 2000), although most residents resist this term. The community contains dozens of homes, mainly of ecological design, as well as several community centres and resources (Figure 3.4).

Figure 3.4 Eco-houses and communal area at Findhorn, north-east Scotland. Along with the community members, the physical spaces of the community are viewed as part of a resource for learning. In this way, Findhorn typifies the combined social and spatial elements that I understand as the *spatialities* of alternative education.

Although Findorn is not a school (and is not a 'human scale' or 'democratic' school by name), I have included it in my study and in this section for three reasons. First, it constitutes a unique but important example of an alternative learning space. It is important because it is not a school but offers many of the kinds of educational experiences that other alternative schools do offer, and which quite frequently replace or complement mainstream schooling. Second, it aims to be 'an international centre for holistic education, helping to unfold a new human consciousness and create a positive and sustainable future' (www.findhorn.org). Findhorn's approach, with its emphasis upon love in learning, the quality of interpersonal relationships and upon spirituality, resonates with that of other human scale educators (see Chapter Seven for a detailed analysis). Third, Findhorn is unique in relation to many human scale *schools* because, both pragmatically and philosophically, it is more intimately connected with 'outside' public communities, both near and far. For instance, since 2010, Findhorn has run a 'building bridges' outreach project with local schools (and I interviewed the project coordinator), while also providing a resource for international visitors, many of whom stay at the community and take courses. Through this project, it was also beginning to take referrals of 'at-risk' young people from local schools (as do care farms and forest schools). For these reasons, Findhorn appears at several important junctures in this book.

Steiner schooling

Unlike human scale schooling, Steiner schooling is one of the best-known examples of alternative education. While in several countries, like Germany, Steiner schools are often state funded, there are (at the time of writing) only two state-funded Steiner schools in the UK (in Hereford and Frome), although both are funded through the *Free Schools* programme and not conventional funding mechanisms (see Chapter Nine). Steiner schools also follow an alternative curriculum and thus Steiner schools can properly be described as alternative – they seem to 'provide something which other forms of schooling do not' (Woods et al, 1997, p 26). The principles and practices of Steiner schooling are well documented (Calgren, 2008) and have been explored in some excellent studies over the past 15 years (especially Woods and Woods, 2006; Oberski, 2011). I have also published several articles about a Steiner school in Wales, and draw in part on this work for the present book (Kraftl, 2006a, 2006b). However, for readers not familiar with that work, this section offers a brief introduction to Rudolf Steiner's rich and complex philosophies, before drawing a picture of contemporary Steiner schooling and noting some significant themes in academic research.

In his philosophical work, Rudolf Steiner (1909, 1919) combined an interest in several fields, including Christian teachings, Goethe's writings, paganism, farming, and newly emergent studies of child psychology. Steiner developed a theory of human being, spirituality and the world that was anthroposophical: a version of phenomenology where the experience of a human subject was not merely submitted to introspective, subjective reflection but also to a kind of 'higher' objectivity (Oberski, 2011). Steiner's approach sought to submit the whole realm of human experience *to* thought – including thinking itself. In common with other alternative approaches to education (as discussed previously), Steiner's work has been influential in many other fields, including architecture and, most notably, in biodynamic farming practices and the Camp Hill movement of therapeutic, mutual communities for people with 'learning difficulties, mental health problems and other special needs' (quoted from www.camphill.org. uk). But it is in respect of Steiner's unique theorisations of the growing child, which form much of the basis for the Steiner curriculum, that his work is perhaps best known (Kraftl, 2006a). As Rawson and Richter (2000) argue, Steiner's view of child development is one of a gradual process of awakening that progresses through a series of stages (see also Carnie, 2003). Over time, balanced growth – comprising physiological, embodied, emotional, reflective and spiritual components – is a process of 'bringing forth', or more clearly expressing, whatever it is that makes a person unique (Oberski, 2011, p 9). Thus, the aim of Steiner education is not to form followers of anthroposophy but to see an anthroposophical understanding of human development as a cipher for 'awaken[ing] young people to the spiritual and ethical dimensions of human life and to enable them to be free and independent thinkers and to make decisions for themselves' (Woods and Woods, 2006, p 317). Importantly, that independence is a form of autonomy (see Chapter Two): not egotistical self-centredness but, rather, a self-consciousness that enables an individual to critically reflect upon their place in and responsibilities to the world (Oberski, 2011).

In principle, then, the ultimate 'vision' of Steiner education is little different from that of other approaches to education – including homeschooling and democratic/human scale approaches. Like those approaches, Steiner education is underpinned by the kinds of child-centred, democratic and autonomous pedagogies discussed in Chapter Two. Indeed, Knight (2009) recognises the influence of Steiner in, first, Scandinavian approaches to early-years education and then in the forest schools movement in the UK. However, there are also crucial differences – both in terms of what Steiner schooling looks like and in terms of how that schooling is intended to produce a well-rounded, self-aware adult subject. First, in terms of the curriculum, a child progresses through three (more or less developmental) stages at a Steiner school. The first stage (ages nought to six, but spent in the kindergarten from three to six) is geared around playing and doing; children do not learn to read or write (Carnie, 2003). Children listen to stories, engage in 'homely' activities like baking, sing songs, and are encouraged to imitate their teachers (who, in a model of informal education, 'facilitate' rather than teach) (Kraftl, 2006a). At stage two – the 'heart of childhood' (ages seven to 13) – children move on to more formal education. They learn to read and write and engage with subjects that look like curriculum subjects taught at mainstream schools. However, much of what they learn is taught through movement (for instance, learning letters through literally walking their shapes), and artistic experiences are integrated into science teaching and vice versa (Woods et al, 1997). As I have argued elsewhere, in this way the holism of the educational experience in a Steiner school takes on a flavour of 'performance art'

(Kraftl, 2006b; Chapter Six). A child's teacher will follow their class into the third stage (ages 14–18), 'where there is an increased emphasis on developing the young person's capacity for abstract thought' (Carnie, 2003, p 47). In those schools that take students to age 18 (there are relatively few in the UK), pupils learn subjects in three- or four-week blocks with a specialist teacher. Many of those schools will enter their pupils for standard national examinations (GCSEs and A-Levels in the UK). Another feature of Steiner schools is the attention to the design, layout and decoration of material spaces, which I examine in Chapter Five (see also Kraftl, 2006a; Kraftl and Adey, 2008).

Critically, all of this is orientated – implicitly, until the third stage – to the fostering of critical *and* spiritual reflection among young people about their individual place in the world. Children are never taught directly *that* they are undertaking any special exercises to intuit these kinds of reflection. Rather, the three different stages allow a building towards 'free' reflection that mirrors Steiner's intuitive knowledge about children's development: stage one aims at the development of the will, stage two at the development of feeling, and stage three at the development of thinking itself. Thus, art, movement, rhythm and games are not meant simply to foster creativity or innovation (as in some other alternative educational approaches). Rather, as Oberski (2011, p 14) puts it: 'the actual purpose of [creative] activities lies much more in the development of pupils of willing, feeling and eventually intuitive thinking through the imagination faculty, which may later foster moral imagination'. Steiner education, then, aims somewhat intangibly but nevertheless pointedly towards a performative, emotional and embodied rendering of a caring, empathetic and responsible disposition to the world. The spiritual dimension (both Christian and non-western) is critical here. This is because it is through critical reflection around 'the spiritual aspect of a person [that] a world reveals itself which is exalted above the outer world perceived by the physical senses and the inner world of the soul' (Woods et al, 1997, p 27). Given the existence of some excellent previous studies of Steiner schooling and spirituality, I do not say much more about the 'moral imagination' in this book (see Woods et al, 1997; Oberski, 2011). Rather, with this work in mind, I explore some related examples taken from other alternative learning spaces, which resonate in some significant ways with Steiner's writings (something I show in Chapter Seven).

Academic research on Steiner schools is much better developed than that on other kinds of alternative education. That research is also located in some quite disparate publications and academic disciplines, so it is difficult to talk of a coherent body of research on Steiner schooling per se. Nevertheless, there are at least four notable features of this work. First, there are broadly education-focused studies that evaluate the learning outcomes of Steiner-educated children (which often compare favourably with those in mainstream education, especially on artistic and creative faculties) and the organisation of teaching in Steiner schools (for example Cox and Rowlands, 2000; Woods and Woods, 2006; Stehlik, 2008). Second, there are studies that explore the social and material construction of childhood in Steiner schools (Kraftl, 2006a, 2006b) and that focus on the experiences of children themselves (for example Rivers and Soutter, 1996). On the latter, a fascinating longitudinal study by psychologists showed that students of Steiner schools (as well as Montessori and New Schools) adjusted better to the transition to higher education from school, exhibiting less stress and greater life satisfaction and academic performance(Shankland et al, 2010). I return to look at the materialities of Steiner schools – and especially the design and decoration of their buildings – in Chapter Five. Third, in light of the previous discussion of intuitive and critical self-consciousness, some studies have focused on the kinds of citizenship and sociability afforded by Steiner education (for example Stehlik, 2009). A particularly notable Swedish study found that, compared with pupils of the same age group in mainstream schools, 18- to 19-year-old Steiner school pupils 'more frequently expressed interest and engagement in social and moral questions' (Dahlin, 2010, p 165). Fourth, there are those articles (discussed earlier) that explore spirituality in Steiner schooling in light of a larger body of work on spirituality in education (Woods and Woods, 2008; Ahern, 2009; Oberski, 2011). Notably, although not as broad in scope as this book, several of the above studies either assess the role of Steiner schooling in respect of mainstream curricula (for example Woods et al, 2005; Dahlin, 2010) or compare Steiner schooling with other alternative educational approaches (Shankland et al, 2010).

Global and UK distribution of Steiner Schooling, and the examples in this book

It is estimated that there are around 1,000 Steiner schools around the world, on every habitable continent (Oberski, 2011). Given previous estimates (800 in 2006), the network of global Steiner schools appears to be growing steadily but slowly (Woods and Woods, 2006). At the time of writing (April 2012), my review of the UK Steiner Waldorf Schools Fellowship website (www.steinerwaldorf.org) shows that, in the UK, there are 30 Steiner schools, 11 specialist kindergartens, and 12 'interest groups' probably intending to register as Steiner schools with the Fellowship in the future. The majority (around three quarters) of these schools are located in south and central England. For this book I undertook research at four registered Steiner schools and one 'interest group': one school was in Wales (the basis for my earlier and subsequent published research), the others were in the south of England, East Anglia and the English Midlands. All of the schools were fee-paying (although some varied their fees depending on family income), and all of them exclusively followed a Steiner curriculum.

Montessori schooling

Montessori education shares some similarities with Steiner schooling and some of the other approaches discussed in this book. It is, like Steiner schooling, widely understood as an explicit (usually private, fee-paying) 'alternative' to mainstream education (Cossentino, 2006; Shankland et al, 2010). Moreover, like many forms of alternative education, it is concerned with educating the 'whole child' – especially the Rousseauian belief in drawing upon all of the child's senses during education (Hainstock, 1997). Indeed, the philosophical roots of Montessori education (in Rousseau, Pestalozzi and Froebel) are shared with several other approaches (on forest schooling, see Knight, 2009).

Maria Montessori (1870–1952) was the founder of the Montessori approach. Initially working with children in an Italian psychiatric clinic, she was surrounded by peers who viewed mental disabilities less as a physical impairment and more as a result of deficient education (Hainstock, 1997). Like Rousseau, she believed in children's natural ability to learn. She theorised that contemporary institutions of care and learning in Italy were simply not appropriate for many children's needs. As a result, initially at the psychiatric clinic where she worked, she was involved with her colleagues in developing a series of repetitive, graded exercises designed to improve children's motor skills (Hainstock, 1997). Taking her approach outside the psychiatric clinic, she then formalised those exercises in her first proper 'school', set up in the slums of Rome in 1907 (Carnie, 2003). Frequently referring to her approach as a 'scientific' one, she continued to revise and develop her views on children's learning based upon ongoing observations of children in the classroom. A little like Steiner, she argued that children under the age of six followed an innate path of human development that – given an environment in which children could freely choose from a series of exercises and activities – it was nevertheless possible to nurture in an optimal way. Again, like Steiner, she identified stages or 'planes' to children's development, although these differ somewhat from Steiner's (Grazzini, 1988). The first plane (birth to six) was the time in which children's minds were 'absorbent', as they acquired language and sensitivities to others. The second plane (six to 12) involved the lengthening of the child's body and a period during which they engaged in more socialised rather than individual learning. The third plane (12 to 18) was the period of adolescence, during which Montessori observed turbulent emotional and physical changes in young people, and when adolescents were involved in a search for external validation of their own self-worth. The fourth phase was the period of independence gained during young adulthood (18 to 24).

Although attending to the full range of childhood and youth experiences, Montessori is principally known for her work with younger children (the first plane). As discussed later, her approach has spawned thousands of Montessori nurseries and pre-schools all over the world. Perhaps the clearest expression of Montessori's method is in the book written by her son (and collaborator): *The Human Tendencies and Montessori Education* (Montessori, 1966). Together they developed a series of principles that underpinned their understanding of human nature and, therefore, of the values underpinning education. Those principles included: orientation to the environment gleaned through meaningful interaction with the world; manipulation of the environment; task-based or vocational work (also Cossentino, 2006); order, exactness and repetition, both for real-world applicability and the development of the mathematical mind (Montessori, 1966).

In the context of the first plane (from which all the examples in this book are taken), the principles mentioned above are translated into a series of methods with which many early-years educators will be familiar. For instance, the learning environment in Montessori classrooms appears highly ordered, with neat shelves on which are laid out materials and tasks (Chapter Five). Since order is so important, the materials are always laid out in exactly the same places each day, so that the child 'knows their place' in the world and can gain confidence from the environment. There is a keen attention to detail, where the colour, texture and shape of learning materials are central to children's ability to benefit from their involvement with an activity. So, if a child is counting wooden blocks, those blocks should all be the same colour and shape so that children are not distracted from the task at hand – counting. Montessori called this the 'isolation of principle' (Carnie, 2003, p 76). Indeed, for this reason, copies of many of the original materials designed by Maria Montessori for use in her schools are still used in many Montessori schools today (Carnie, 2003). Using these materials, children engage in activities that are somehow purposeful or geared to the real-world, and which usually involve some measure of physical movement. Following Montessori's beliefs about education, children are free to choose any activity they wish. But while children may be free to choose any task, that choice is underpinned by a careful manipulation and ordering of the classroom environment by the teachers (see Chapter Five and Figure 3.5). Each classroom contains a series of age-appropriate tasks that would generally not be available to older or younger children (Hainstock, 1997). Meanwhile, Montessori teachers observe each child, in depth, every day, recording the tasks in which they have been engaged as an individual, and helping them to make choices when necessary. This is something I explore in more detail, and compare with other alternative learning spaces, when I discuss 'taking time' in Chapter Five.

The explicit attention to the material environment makes Montessori education – like Steiner education – an exciting topic for geographical study (Chapter Five). However, as I indicated at the very beginning of this book, I am not simply interested in the significance (or otherwise) of the *material* settings in which alternative education occurs. Rather, I aim to explore the diverse spatialities that characterise different forms of alternative education. Thus, it is striking that despite an attention to seemingly minutely scaled, material details, Montessori education also shares with Steiner schooling a sense of connection between the small and large scale. Specifically, in *Education and Peace,*

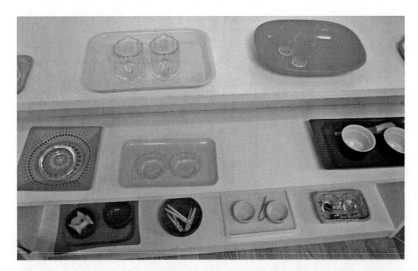

Figure 3.5 A shelf in a typical Montessori classroom. Note the carefully arranged objects, always placed in the same place on the same shelves, and designed so that children can fulfil tasks without adult direction. The objects are designed to help children acquire skills relevant to everyday life.

Montessori (1992) argued that education had a central role to play in the promotion of world peace. Her view was that the development of children according to their natural developmental path, with repetitive physical activities at the core of their learning, could produce freer, more empathetic individuals predisposed to peace, democracy and the resolution of conflict (Hedeen, 2005). There is much in common here with other pedagogies developed early in the 20th century – such as the inner-city playground movement in the US, where it was believed that physical exercise and discipline could train the inner character of children and ultimately make them better citizens (for example Gagen, 2004). Importantly, the jump in scale is not just from small to large. In other words, a Montessori education does not just begin with the material details that surround each individual child. In my own visits to Montessori schools, it is clear that teachers also 'start big' in some of their work. For instance, in direct contrast to mainstream primary education in the UK, children learn about the solar system, the sun and the earth *before* they learn about their more immediate, local environment, so that they have a sense of where they 'fit in'. Indeed, there are several published examples of children learning about geography in ways that seem incongruous with early-years education. For instance, Herbst et al (2008) describe a one-year programme where three- to six-year-old children in a Montessori school were introduced to basic principles of earth sciences and glaciology. At the end of the programme, children could successfully describe, in basic terms, these basic principles. The crux here is not only the factual element of learning but also the political facets stimulated by this process of 'starting big'. As Herbst et al (2008, p 220) point out, this introduction to basic earth science was *also* anticipated to 'contribute to a more careful and respectful attitude towards their environment'. Thus Montessori education involves a two-way process of 'scale-jumping' that combines the intimacies of classroom learning with a global or 'Cosmic Education' (Herbst et al, 2008, p 220) towards the ultimate goal of world peace. Like Steiner education, this approach is redolent of the interplay between 'self-cultivation' and 'world-making' found in Gibson-Graham's (2006) approach to diverse economic practices. Similarly, therefore, Montessori's notions of a 'Cosmic Education' figure in my discussions of the 'up-scaling' of habit in Chapter Seven.

Like Steiner education, Montessori education has received relatively significant attention from academics, although never, as far as I know, from geographers. An important facet of studies in other disciplines has been critical discussion about the capacities of Montessori education to educate for citizenship and democracy (with sometimes indirect reference to Maria Montessori's writings on peace). For instance, Brunold-Conesa (2010, p 259) argues that while Montessori schools claim to 'promote values associated with global citizenship [...] to prepare students [for...] an increasingly globalized world', the relative lack of secondary-level Montessori schools in most countries means that those goals cannot be seen to fruition. Elsewhere, other studies point to the positive effects of Montessori education in the development of children's problem-solving and coping strategies, the development of school communities, and conflict resolution (Shankland et al, 2009; Rule and Kyle, 2009; Hedeen, 2005). Since this book is not concerned with the 'effects' of alternative education on children, I do not seek to contribute to these debates. Rather, with a focus on the spatialities of learning, I will build on the discussions of scale, materiality and habit mentioned above.

Global and UK distribution of Montessori education, and the examples in this book

Montessori education is globally widespread. In the US, there are over 3,000 registered Montessori schools, most of which are pre-schools for three- to six-year-old children (Hainstock, 1997). The vast majority are fee-paying, private schools. In the UK, there were over 700 Montessori schools registered in 2003, mostly nurseries (Carnie, 2003) and, like all of the approaches discussed in this book, it is safe to assume that that number has increased since then. Given Montessori's own travels (for instance to Asia) and the global interest in her methods, the influence of Montessori education can be found in India (Hainstock, 1997), Japan (Kai, 2009), Germany (Koinzer and Leschinsky, 2009) and many other countries. There are various institutions and training courses geared to the advancement of Montessori education. The main international organisation is the Association Montessori Internationale (AMI), founded by Maria Montessori herself in 1929 and still responsible for training teachers around the world (www.montessori-ami.org). The AMI has several national branches, including one in the UK (www. montessorisociety.org.uk). However, it is not the case that Montessori's methods have been received evenly around the world. In the US, for instance, several critics found her focus on specific material tasks too didactic and contended that it concentrated too much upon cognitive rather than social development (Hainstock, 1997). Moreover, Montessori's methods have been interpreted in different ways: different schools may follow Montessori's methods to varying degrees, and of the relatively few schools catering for older children (above six) many combine Montessori approaches with the National Curriculum. Thus, as Carnie (2003, p 71) argues, 'only a handful are considered to be pure Montessori schools'. In the research for this book I visited three Montessori schools, all of which were nurseries (for children aged three to six). I chose these schools because all three attempted to put Montessori's principles into practice as accurately as they could, and all of their teachers were Montessori-trained. I also include some additional materials when discussing Montessori schools: a lengthy interview and two-day period of observation carried out on my behalf by a colleague – Sophie Hadfield-Hill – at a Montessori school in the US; reflection from several homeschooling parents who had sent their children to Montessori nurseries; and material from three of the four human scale schools I visited, where Montessori's methods were an explicit component of their educational approach.

Conclusion

Taken as a whole, the different sections of this chapter point to some of the rich diversity of educational alternatives that currently exist in the UK. While in many cases the figures concerning the number of practitioners or schools are unreliable, it does seem to be the case that most of the educational 'types' covered by this book are expanding. In some cases (like care farming and forest schooling) that expansion is very rapid. This is, then, for many reasons, an important point at which to publish a book about alternative education, and especially one that compares a range of increasingly popular approaches. At this stage it is worth offering three words of qualification about this approach, of which I am all too aware. First, while the coverage of this book is relatively considerable in terms of the range of the case studies it includes, it is still only partial. As I mentioned in Chapter One, I have excluded various forms of what could be deemed 'alternative' and – certainly following Falk et al's (2009) definition – 'informal' education. At the same time, and second, it is also the case that there is far more diversity within each educational type than I have had space to acknowledge in this chapter. It should not be inferred that even Steiner schools, with a well-developed curriculum, are somehow all the same, let alone that each educational type is 'alternative' in the same way. A third issue that I have not been able to broach fully here is that there are many points of connection *between* each approach. Sometimes these are deliberate, sometimes coincidental, but in some instances they are profound: I discuss some of these connections in Chapters Four and Eight, although again I cannot provide more than a few indicative examples. All of this means that the book is necessarily selective. There is simply not space to introduce or discuss each of my 59 case studies in detail. Rather, my intention from now on will be to tease out a range of common and divergent themes from my extensive study visits, in order to build an argument about autonomous learning spaces.

The above caveats notwithstanding, I have included material from an extensive range of case studies because I am convinced by the merits of a comparative approach, grounded in experience of a large range of alternative learning spaces. This will mean glossing over some details that might be apparent in more classically 'ethnographic' study of fewer spaces (Cook, 2004), but, given that I rely heavily on quoted materials and some relatively 'thick descriptions' (Geertz, 1973, p 3), I hope that the empirical details will afford the reader at least some sense of the context of each individual learning space. In some chapters I also include some longer 'case studies' that should bring some particular examples to life. Ultimately, this should mean that the book still has much to say about the educational alternatives *not* included as case studies, even if in a conceptual rather than more empirical sense. While theory building is important, it should also mean that some of the more practical implications of my conceptualisation of autonomy will appear all the more robust (Chapter Nine). This is in no small measure because, as I have also repeatedly mentioned, there is a relative dearth of comparative studies of alternative education, and especially those that we could say are 'social-scientific' rather than focused upon educational outcomes, acquired skills or attainment. This is also because, looking across the summaries presented earlier in this chapter, there are variegated resonances with the notions of autonomy highlighted in Chapter Two: from the decision-making processes apparent in Steiner and democratic schools, to the ethics of love, care and cooperative responsibility sought by Montessori and human scale schools, to the support offered by care farms and forest schools for local communities to become more self-sustaining and less reliant upon neoliberal political regimes or global commodity chains (see also Chapter Eight). Specifically, this book is influenced by contemporary social-scientific approaches in human geography, and I will show that much of theoretical and practical relevance can be gleaned from looking at the *spatialities* of alternative education. In this chapter, I have begun to highlight from the perspective of individual approaches to alternative education what some of these spatialities might be. Already, certain common themes are apparent – from the scale-jumping between intimate bodily movements and global senses of citizenship exhibited within Steiner, Montessori and informal education (Chapter Seven), to the centrality of movement/mobility to Montessori, home and forest education (Chapter Six). These and other spatialities are examined in the chapters that follow.

FOUR

Connection/disconnection: positioning alternative learning spaces

One of the central aims of this book is to consider what makes alternative learning spaces 'alternative'. I began this task in Chapter Three, where I outlined some of the principal pedagogical and organisational features of the educational types included in this book. In many cases, it is those kinds of features – from conceptions of child development to the role of the teacher – that explicitly mark out those spaces *as* alternative (Sliwka, 2008). At the same time, many of the case studies (and the organisations representing them) promote themselves as somehow alternative to, or different from, mainstream education in the UK. Two brief examples should illustrate this. In the first example, Steiner schools compare their approach to the 'early specialization and academic hot-housing' they observe in mainstream settings (http:// www.steinerwaldorf.org/). Thus, the official Steiner Waldorf Schools Fellowship UK website presents 10 key points regarding the 'distinctive education' provided by Steiner schools (http://www.steinerwaldorf. org), including creativity, (lack of) assessment and individuality. In the second example, home educators express similar sentiments about mainstream schooling in a very different, and sometimes more overtly politicised way. Even by its name, one of the main UK home education support groups – Education Otherwise – implies alterity from the mainstream. That organisation's description of home education begins 'Home education (HE) is an alternative to school; it is parents' right in law to keep primary responsibility for the education of their children instead of delegating it to a school' (www.education-otherwise.net).

Clearly, there are some distinct pedagogical, organisational and definitional features that mark out learning spaces as 'alternative' (Woods and Woods, 2009). However, the aim of this chapter is to begin to present a more complicated and nuanced picture. I do so by drawing directly upon the views of educators and learners involved in several of the alternative learning spaces that served as case studies for this book. I introduce the first of my spatial frames of reference – connection/disconnection – as a way to understand the ways in which organisations and individuals position themselves in respect of the mainstream. I consider diverse issues, which include but are arguably far more diverse than those covered by previous theorisations of alternative education (Chapter Two). I reflect on issues such as how alternative educators 'distance' themselves from the mainstream, how they try to relate to and provide a resource for local communities, and how children feel when they talk to adults and other children who have attended mainstream schools. It will become apparent that the positioning of 'alternative' learning spaces is often multiple and shifting, incorporating many kinds of connection and disconnection, sometimes simultaneously, with several 'mainstreams' – including local authorities, local communities, members of the public, and mainstream schools. To complicate matters, I also chart points of connection and disconnection with other 'alternative' practices – some explicitly educational, some not.

I conclude the chapter by arguing that it is sensible to understand the positioning of alternative learning spaces as a negotiated process, often simultaneously incorporating multiple forms of connection and of disconnection. I term these multiple forms of connection and disconnection *dis/connection* – a *combination* of modes of engagement and separation that must be carefully managed and that is rooted as often in pragmatism as it is in pedagogy. Doing so may appear to be an exercise in dualistic thinking, but the forward slash is meant to symbolise complexity: it points to the simultaneity of connection and disconnection at many alternative learning spaces, with multiple mainstreams (and alternatives). This leads me to argue that such forms of dis/connection represent the first of several versions of *autonomy* that, as I suggested in Chapter Two, should be an important way to theorise the geographies of alternative education.

Conceptual dis/connections: critiquing and empathising with mainstream education

It will come as no surprise that the vast majority of educators and parents in my research were engaged in alternative education because they harboured deep-seated reservations about mainstream schools. Many of these critiques were levelled at neoliberal policies on education, which have pervaded in the UK for some years, and which I have already discussed in Chapters One and Two. Most respondents were not necessarily *anti*-school, but critical of the kinds of *spaces* that contemporary mainstream schools had become.

"I had a vision that [bullied children] had to be educated in a house, in an alternative space from a mainstream school. They weren't going to go to a school. It's a fear of the institution that smells, looks, feels, sounds like a school. Schools are vast places with long wide corridors that go on forever, stairs where kids kick you, you go across the campus. It had to be the antithesis of whatever that was. Small, intimate, home-like, cosy. Kids had to feel 100% safe here." (Anne, director of small schools network, East Anglia)

"I've tried to get rid of the artifice at school. So they might take a few years to complete a piece of writing, or have three pieces of writing on the go at one time. And so on." (Judy, headteacher of a small school, England)

Both Anne and Judy had attempted to abolish the 'artifices' (as Judy had it) of school – both environmental and social. They had created knowingly *alternative* environments for children's learning, which were distinct from mainstream schools. Like many alternative educators, they used their critiques of contemporary schools as part of the process of legitimising their own approaches. This is a different process of distinction than the focus upon (lack of) professional accreditation and interpersonal relations outlined by Quirke (2009). I encountered this discursive strategy many times, especially among homeschooling mothers, who were frequently challenged about their decisions to home educate (see also Lois, 2009). Some homeschoolers referred to horrendous incidents at school, such as bullying by staff or pupils, while others found that schools restricted their children's creativity or individuality. Immediately, space mattered: I have argued elsewhere that homeschoolers observed a kind of discursive spatial dualism between school (an institutional, depersonalised space where children were separated from their parents) and home (an intimate, family space where parents and children could be together) (see also Merry and Howell, 2009; Kraftl, in press, 2013b).

In the above ways, almost all advocates of alternative education promoted *some kind* of 'separation' between mainstream schooling and their own approaches (mirroring Woods and Woods, 2009). However, a large proportion of the same respondents also used their disconnection from mainstream schooling as the opportunity for a more connected reflection on *any* space in which education occurred.

"Well I think we have to redefine what we mean by schools. Not getting rid of them. Use the word, but radically change it. What's also obvious is that square rooms and walls don't fit a lot of children's learning styles [...]. Even a fantastic teacher, with endless resources, in a school room, is never going to help the child learn. Not compared with a natural environment or any outdoors environment. That's the bottom line, we aren't here to teach, we're here to encourage the child to learn, to give everything we can to facilitate that." (Joanne, forest school practitioner, south-west England)

"It's all about scale. If you have a big school, the headteacher can't have as big an influence. You might never meet the headmaster as a pupil. Here, you would. Masses to do with space and numbers. But there can be disadvantages. At times the school was too small. There wasn't a big enough variety of friendships, of ideas, of vibrancy. It can get too close, because teachers need to step back too. Instinctively I would say 15 to 20 [pupils per class] is the best size." (Harry, teacher and ex-pupil at Kilquhanity democratic school, Scotland)

Thus, neither Joanne nor Harry was anti-school; nor were many of the other teachers and parents I spoke to, including many homeschoolers (who traditionally are viewed as being anti-school). In fact, their critiques (and especially Harry's) are equally valid for any kinds of mainstream *or* alternative education. Thus, as several scholars have it (for example Fielding and Moss, 2011), these are examples of how alternative education practice may prompt critical reflection on education in its broadest sense, in these cases on the quality and scale of school environments. They both exhibit an openness to "radically" changing or informing mainstream school environments, rather than circumventing them. Indeed, Harry is as critical of Kilquhanity – where at times the classes were *too* small – as he is of mainstream education.

Joanne and Harry imply that in some alternative education practices there is a kind of implicit connectedness with mainstream schooling that at least operates at the conceptual level. It is almost as if, although engaged in radically different pedagogies, there is an underlying sense of commonality effected by the impulse to educate children. Thus, even homeschoolers – some of the most ardent critics of neoliberal education – retain a kind of residual or potential connection to certain facets of mainstream schooling.

"I have no contact at all with our LEA [local education authority]. I did send them a letter saying that my daughter wasn't going to school. I then never heard from them again. We do keep a folder, take photos of what they do. We pick up resources. I suppose just in case someone asks us, really." (Charlotte, homeschooler, south of England)

"I was always the mommy. I never thought of myself as a teacher. Because there's this social construction of school, and that constantly makes you reflect, there's something different sometimes between learning and whatever else. It's a kind of dialogue: is this the right thing? Like a moral guide on your shoulder." (Mary, homeschooler, London)

"The more I then read into research into HE [home education], I wondered, why do we send them to school at all, why do we have the school system, it seems completely nuts. On the other hand, it is part of the culture, there is a school system, and to say no, you'll never do that, seems to really cut off completely. So I go in regularly [to a local primary school] with them because I teach maths club in the school." (Katie, homeschooler, London)

Mary illustrates the kind of discursive spatial dualism between home and school that, as I argued earlier, is common among many homeschoolers. But the most significant thing about all three of the above quotations is that each parent retains a kind of connection with mainstream schooling and the National Curriculum in particular. For Charlotte, this was implicit and tokenistic – "just in case". Very differently, like Joanne and Harry, Mary saw herself as engaged in an ongoing "dialogue" with school that offered a kind of moral compass for her teaching and parenting approach. And, differently again, Katie occasionally visited a local primary school with her children in order not to "cut off completely" – even though she believed school was "completely nuts".

If Mary was involved in an ongoing dialogue between home and school, it was also the case that several educators gave a far more direct sense of how their status as 'alternative' was far from clear cut. A Steiner school teacher from the English Midlands put it best:

"When we started the school, we fought the whole notion of being alternative – then [in the 1980s] it maybe had stronger connotations – hippy. Our view is that we are complementary. Our timing may be different, and our approach, but we are an alternative to the National Curriculum, in that sense, but in terms of education, it's complementary." (Michael, Steiner school teacher, English Midlands)

Thus, even though Steiner-schooled children usually attend full time, Michael was keen to argue that what they offered was "complementary". This was perhaps because his school, like many UK Steiner schools, only educates children until the early teenage years, and therefore most Steiner-educated children will go to a school following the National Curriculum for their GCSEs and A-Levels (qualifications usually taken between the ages of 15 and 18 in the UK). However, Michael also provided a sense of the dynamism of the relationship between alternative education spaces and the mainstream, wherein to be branded 'alternative' during the 1980s might have had "stronger [negative] connotations" than it does today. In this sense – as I will demonstrate repeatedly in this chapter – notions of alterity are constantly negotiated.

Upon talking with young people – especially homeschooled children – I was struck by how they too attempted to negotiate their way between the alternative and the mainstream.

> "I think it has become part of my identity. I'm sometimes like, oh no, there's a school group. These children that go to school, they've got no imagination. Say we go to a museum, they're just there to behave badly, not to learn, they don't care about anyone else. Some of them are OK, don't get me wrong, but, like, I kind of feel sorry for them. So, like, I know, we are home educated for a reason." (Marie, homeschooled young person, aged 12, south of England)

> "The other school kids are too young to go to school. They can't even speak properly because they're in a uniform. Six or seven is fine, I think, to go to school. But four is too young. [I ask how she came to this conclusion.] I don't know – it's just too young" (Pippa, homeschooled young person, aged 13, London)

I discuss public interactions between homeschooled children and other children and adults in Chapter Six, so here I simply want to highlight how critiques of mainstream schooling are internalised by homeschooled children. Like Woods and Woods (2009) I do not want to spectacularise this as a form of 'brainwashing' about mainstream education but, rather, to observe a kind of empathy – albeit a little patronising – apparent in what both Marie and Pippa said to me. That is, they each hold a passion – rather than resentment – about being homeschooled and consider that as young people they would not want to be subject to some of the restrictions and behavioural traits they have seen displayed by *some* mainstream-educated children. However, both Marie and Pippa have internalised some dangerous assumptions about mainstream-educated children that are shared by exponents of the 'crisis in childhood' thesis, which rather over-determines the 'state' of contemporary British childhoods from an adultist perspective (see Scraton, 1996).

Whatever one's interpretation of these quotations – and I suspect these will vary by reader – my point is that Marie and Pippa were engaged in processes of critical reflection about education that was not simply about dismissing or disconnecting from mainstream education. According to my analysis thus far, it would appear that it is actually quite rare for alternative educators to isolate themselves from other educational systems, even if at this stage such an inclination resides at the level of a *potential* willingness to engage in conceptual dialogue rather than anything more (active). Indeed, it is notable that even some of the strongest critics of mainstream schooling, and those labelled as 'alternative' tended to prefer a combination of 'separation' and 'engagement' (in Woods and Woods' [2009] terms). Alternative education was, and is, therefore not defined against mainstream education but through critical, often empathetic, engagement. I explore in the book's conclusion what the more practical implications of this conceptual 'willingness to engage' might be, but in the next section I move from conceptual to more pragmatic, active forms of dis/connection.

Pragmatic dis/connections

The previous section emphasised the conceptual dis/connections between alternative educators and learners and mainstream schools. In this section, I explore dis/connections that are altogether more pragmatic, considering matters of educational policy, financing, the referral of learners from mainstream schools and teacher training. Once again, it will become clear that there are far more connections than disconnections with the mainstream, but that those connections may endure for shorter or longer periods of time. Hence, I am arguing that temporality matters as much as spatiality here. I therefore begin this section by looking back in time: I reflect upon some of the historical interactions between mainstream, state-sanctioned education policies and the very existence of alternative education spaces. For more established educators, who reflected on their own experiences of mainstream teaching and teacher training prior to the 1990s, there were clear historical antecedents for their current work.

> "I taught at a comprehensive [mainstream secondary] school. There was also a city farm on the same site. So I taught science as well as the city farm unit, on the school site. At the time, the upper band did exams, the lower band didn't. The lower band went away with a vocational profile – horticulture, mechanics, home economics, things like that. Then it became politically unacceptable not to offer formal exams. But my experiences there have stayed with me [goes on to give examples]." (Tony, care farm, Scotland)

> "I think the training I got in mainstream teaching gave me a terrific grounding. Before I went, having been a pupil here [Kilquhanity] I thought I knew a lot about education because I came from a different background. I realised that there were other people that were saying no, this is the way to go about it. Because you *can* evaluate this and that. You can actually become too personalised. So I actually use my training here." (Harry, teacher and ex-pupil at Kilquhanity democratic school, Scotland, emphasis added)

Tony and Harry highlight two separate but related points. The first is that, historically, certain elements of mainstream schooling apparent in England before the introduction of the National Curriculum (in 1988) resonate with some alternative approaches. For instance, as Tony suggests, vocational training was a key facet of comprehensive schooling (albeit tiered) when he was teaching in the early 1980s. Elsewhere, in primary education, there was a move in some local authorities to promote pupil-centred learning (redolent of democratic and human scale pedagogies) during the 1970s (Burke and Grosvenor, 2008). The second point is that, in a Scottish context, Harry argued that his teacher training in the mainstream system made him reflect critically upon the approaches taken at Kilquhanity. Specifically, this led him to critique two foundational beliefs for many alternative educators – their aversion to testing and their promotion of personalised learning (Sliwka, 2008). In both cases, it is important to highlight the influence of (admittedly historical) mainstream education policies and practices *upon* alternative education spaces. Thus, as I began to argue in the previous section, alternative and mainstream education spaces are mutually constituted in multiple ways and we should not simply view alternative education spaces as loci for critical reflection upon the mainstream.

Kilquhanity is, in fact, an interesting case study because its relatively long history straddles successive periods of policy making (this time in Scotland, where the curriculum differs from England and Wales). Its founder – John Aitkenhead – was told by A.S. Neill (the founder of Summerhill School) that Scotland could not support a democratic school like Summerhill. But Aitkenhead did set up a school, and during its early years the educational policy environment in Scotland was very permissive. As a former pupil and another current teacher put it, "John could do whatever he liked, with whomever he liked." The situation then became more complex, as Christopher went on to explain:

> "It was then established that there was a Scottish Education Department; they decided that all independent schools should be registered as a school. Most of the independent schools registered within six months [...] it took John 14 years to become fully registered. The education inspectors were actually very warmed by what John was doing and were very supportive. They had other reservations but not about the education itself. [...] Today, the state should consider the range of opportunities that exists. There's a continuum of alternatives from Gordonstoun to Summerhill to here. So we wouldn't criticise state education as a bad thing. Many alternative forms of education – Montessori, Steiner, here – have had their influences on the state system and vice versa. And the reality is, fascinatingly enough, that the *awareness* of what the state system could be about, is far more opened for debate today." (Christopher, ex-pupil and current teacher, Kilquhanity democratic school, Scotland, emphasis added)

I include this long quotation because it illuminates several broader, important issues; it is also worth noting that Christopher had worked for many years as a respected mainstream secondary teacher and school inspector in England. This brief vignette about Kilquhanity's history illustrates something of the dynamic negotiations between the mainstream (in this case, mainstream policymakers) and individual educational spaces. Understood in this way, in the 1940s and 1950s alternative educational spaces (at least in Scotland) were ostensibly 'separate', in Woods and Woods' (2009) terms. Interestingly, however, the more recent formalisation of inspections was actually a supportive one and, while the consensus among some commentators might be that educational alternatives are being foreclosed today (Conroy, 2010; Fielding and Moss, 2011), Christopher's feeling was the reverse – that there was in fact currently more openness to debate.

Remaining in Scotland, other practitioners were positive about the prospects for greater pragmatic inter-connection between their learning spaces and mainstream schools. They focused specifically upon the mobility of disadvantaged pupils, at risk of exclusion from school. Under the (then) new Scottish Curriculum for Excellence, it was anticipated that those young people would be able to benefit from a *range* of alternative learning spaces. This led to discussion of several pragmatic as well as pedagogical issues.

> "Should we become SQA [Scottish Qualifications Authority] accredited? What we're finding is that the schools we're working with are happy for us to do it through various agreements – whether it's because X [pupil] has never attended, or whatever they need, they're happy to take them on." (June, forest school practitioner, Scotland)

> "A new part of the curriculum in Scotland, is the 16-plus [years old] learning agreement; kids who are on negative destinations, not into employment or college, have the right to create their own curriculum. The kids and the person working with them have it. It's one hour a week to a whole week. They have a whole big pool of stuff to choose from. So here at Findhorn we've started a new department – Building Bridges, which will be going for four years, to connect more locally between us and the community. So in that sense I think we need to be alternative and complementary. We need both – classrooms and people like us. There is a space for both. Both need to change too. They need to come together to get rid of the old and create the new. The new Scottish government, and these new Activity Agreements, it recognises you need some alternative schools, and a range, at that." (Sarah, education officer, Findhorn, Scotland)

Clearly, both June and Sarah were optimistic about the new Scottish curriculum. As Christopher had stated from his viewpoint at

Kilquhanity, it appeared that the Scottish government was aware of the role of alternative education providers, especially for young people at risk of school exclusion. It was therefore particularly interesting to see that Findhorn – which is foremost a spiritual community, with a secondary educational mission – had in 2010 set up a new department specifically aimed at forging *connections* with the local community and its schools. At the same time, Sarah recognises that the process of connection required some distinction – it was important for Findhorn to remain "alternative" in some way because it was in having a *range* of alternative choices for young people that the Activity Agreements would work best. This is a hugely important point, to which I return in the chapter's conclusion.

In England, too, several organisations had entered into referral and funding arrangements with local authorities. These had been long term in some isolated cases, while in many cases these arrangements could be short term and uncertain. Moreover, some practitioners listed just one referral and/or funding arrangement whereas others relied on several.

> "We are [county council] owned and employed. Originally we were a site for the rehabilitation of ex-servicemen. We changed into a learning disability centre in the late 1970s and now serve the county and [nearby large town]." (Christine, care farm practitioner, south of England)

> "Different ways that they get referred to us. School referrals if they are having difficulties with the academic side, so they try to do an alternative vocational curriculum with them. We've always worked closely with SEN [Special Educational Needs] schools in the area. It's a real wide range of kids. Providing a facility that they're happy with and comfortable to come back to. We also work with RNIB [Royal National Institute for the Blind], for long-term placements. We take some through [local voluntary agency]. We used to get them through the day centres, but most of those have closed down now. Referrals from care workers that have used us as a facility before. The list goes on!" (Ursula, care farm practitioner, English Midlands)

These examples notwithstanding, the vast majority of alternative learning spaces in my study could not rely solely on state funding for their survival. This is, in effect, one of the simpler criteria by which these spaces may be judged as 'alternative'. Almost all alternative schools charge fees for attendance; many care farms and forest schools charge the public for courses, entrance to their sites and guided tours; and many providers of alternative education rely on donations in the form of time or money. This means that, in effect, many learning spaces have had to register as businesses (usually social enterprise or public limited companies). However, this has caused significant debate and controversy in many instances. For instance, I know of several schools of different types that have not charged low-income parents and have asked them to volunteer their work instead to pay fees in kind. This has led to two contradictions. On the one hand, it has fulfilled the social function of these schools, allowing low-income families to attend, but has increased a burden on those families' time, since they have to commit to working at the school in addition to their other obligations. On the other hand, some schools have experienced significant financial difficulties because so few families in their catchment area can afford full fees (see Kraftl, 2006a). In practice, this has meant that at least one small school, in a disadvantaged area of London, has seriously considered moving premises (but had not done so at the time of writing). A further issue has been that many alternative educators hold left-leaning, sometimes anarchist, and in some cases anti-capitalist political convictions. They have struggled to reconcile charging fees – especially to disadvantaged families – with their beliefs, even when those fees come indirectly from the state.

> "So this mum said, 'My son has direct payments [from the local authority to support his education], we'll pay.' I said, 'I don't want to make profit.' But she said, 'No, from our point of view, this is a good experience for our son. Don't feel guilty. There's nothing incompatible about paying for it.' He still comes in now incidentally. He started at 18, he's now 25. So suddenly we had more and more paying fees. I felt awful, it took me years to get over the charging fees. I'd spent years in public service, and it's a different mindset – it's a business model now. But there are a lot of advantages to it. We're not now chasing funding for things. I can concentrate on doing a good job and still provide the service I set out to in the first place." (Tony, care farm, Scotland)

> "I have my own public limited company. If we were state-funded, we'd be part of the local authority. You would lose your local autonomy so you would not be able to control the quality of your product. I'm not averse to being blockfunded

by the state, but at the moment we're now able to ensure that everybody who receives a service from us finds it at the very least valuable, and gets an individual experience. It's important for us to be socially accountable. That's why I'm not a private, self-employed individual." (Joanne, forest school practitioner, south-west England)

These quotations illustrate how pragmatic concerns – especially financial – are tied up in the kinds of conceptual negotiations of alterity that I discussed earlier. Moreover, these pragmatic considerations are central to the very constitution of alternative learning spaces. For it is in their ongoing interaction with local authorities, in their dealings with government policies and inspectors, and with their practices steeped in historical trends in mainstream teaching, that practitioners forge all kinds of connections *and* disconnections with the mainstream. Importantly, it is through careful negotiation of these dis/connections that practitioners like Joanne are able explicitly to claim 'autonomy' (rather than that they are 'mainstream' or 'alternative'). However, these dis/connections do not only matter in and of themselves: as both Tony and Joanne recognise, they are also intimately entangled with the material, interpersonal 'experiences' that learners acquire. I attend to some of these experiences in later chapters.

Community dis/connections

In this section, I explore how alternative learning spaces position themselves with regard to their local community. In other words, rather than emphasising their relationship with policy makers and other educational providers, I focus upon how educators relate to members of the general public who do not form a routine part of their learning community. I attend to the issue of scale in this section, since most respondents considered their publics to exist within the *local* community. My analysis should be read in light of two issues I raised previously in this chapter. First, Michael's sense that staff at his Steiner school had to resist the notion of being 'alternative' in order to gain acceptance among the local community. This is an impulse that pervades several of the examples in this section. Second, the ways in which alternative learning providers have adopted fee structures that aim to encourage socioeconomically disadvantaged members of the local community to engage with them. As will become clear, financial considerations underpin many of the connections that alternative learning providers make with their local communities. This was particularly evident at an urban care farm in the English Midlands, where being "cost-effective" intersected with their vision that they should be open to anyone who wanted to visit, especially from the local community.

> "It's for the local community, initially. Aiming at two lower income housing estates [names two urban estates that both experience socioeconomic disadvantage]. As the years have gone by, it's spread further and further afield, particularly on the educational side. And that's because several of the other facilities around here have got more expensive. So we've tried to be as cost-effective as we possibly can. For lower income groups. And that means we're literally open as a farm. There's no one on the gate. It's a visitor problem more than anything else. On a sunny day, we have visitors with alcohol or they've been down the pub. We can set the standard with the user group, not the general public. You deal with it once it's here. Like any open venue. You have to start from being welcoming – you can't have an entry policy." (Ursula, care farm practitioner, East Midlands care farm)

While Ursula's care farm took referrals from an increasingly large catchment (particularly for education), her vision was still one of service to the local community. In fact, she wanted their connection to be a deep and "welcoming" one: since they had "no one on the gate", no "entry policy" and, in fact, did not charge for entry (asking for donations). Their working assumption was an empathetic one: an immediate predisposition to being "literally open", dealing with any problem – and they had experienced many tensions – "once it's here". Through an inclination to welcome people first, and deal with problems later, they had attempted to dismantle *any* sense of separation or disconnection with the local community. Instead, they relied upon the attributes and skills of individual staff to work with the different and unexpected demands that could be made upon them – which is for many democratic educators an important trait.

More generally, it is the case that forest school and care farm practitioners seek more than other alternative educators to emphasise their relationship with local communities. This was particularly the case for sites that were located in or adjacent to urban places (see also Knight, 2009). Admittedly, many forest schools and care farms are situated at some distance from large settlements, in rural areas of the UK, and may not have such an obvious or immediate 'local' community. It might, then, be assumed that a slight spatial separation – often requiring a car or taxi journey for visitors to their sites – might mitigate their relationship with the local community. However, several practitioners pointed out that their ideal was to be *both* separated from and easily accessible to their client groups. In many cases they saw great pedagogical and therapeutic value in having to travel, for a short distance, to a place that removed them from their everyday lives.

> "Actually, it's not just forest school – the thing about the sessions is that you *are* remote from the community, physically and, you know, mentally. That you *have* walked a bit, come by car, you have travelled to be here. There's a little bit of a journey to get to where you're going. It doesn't have to be *far*, in fact ideally not. So it's not a dream, but it might as well be dream-like, because it's so distant from that environment where you're somebody's son, somebody's husband, giving you an opportunity to explore stuff. All I *know* for sure is that it is transformative, but we have to find a way to measure and capture that, if we're going to convince budget-holders that children need it. [But] the first thing that we do is always make sure that we're as close to the people who want it as possible. That's important from a bigger perspective, because one of the things we're trying to do is save our woodland and give our woodlands another use. And it's also saying, look, this is just down the road from you. This is *yours*, for you personally, if you want it." (Joanne, forest school practitioner, south-west England, original emphasis)

Joanne worked in a small and relatively poorly maintained patch of woodland a few hundred metres from a disadvantaged housing estate in a large town in south-west England. When I visited the site for a nature workshop with toddlers, it transpired that many of the families had never before visited the woodland – some not even knowing it existed – despite living just five minutes' walk away. In Joanne's view, this unassuming and slightly forgotten patch of greenery was a perfect location because it provided enough of a journey (physical and metaphorical) to engender some 'distance' from everyday life. It constituted a very different kind of space but at the same time was local enough for people to feel a sense of connection, of belonging – that the place was "yours", as Joanne put it. The physical act she describes is a banal one – a short walk: but bound up in that act is a journey that, she argues, may be "transformative". Once again, we see interplay between separation and engagement – a particularly local, *spatial* form of dis/connection – that is constitutive of the *kind* of alternative educational space that places like forest schools try to create. It is also important to note that Joanne at once emphasised her financial separation from the local authority (in a quotation mentioned previously) *and*, at this later juncture, pressed for greater evidence to convince "budget-holders" of the transformative power of these kinds of dis/connection.

It became evident that the notion of the 'journey' was also important in breaking down barriers and misconceptions that, many educators felt, were held about their being 'alternative' learning spaces. Since many care farms train and employ both young people and adults with learning difficulties, they can in certain circumstances be stigmatised. This is why several of the care farms I visited were open to the public, and why that openness was specifically articulated – by practitioners during interviews with them, in their public signage, and in making certain areas accessible to the public with no entrance fee. For instance, at one care farm in the south of England, the public were able to wander freely around the garden centre component of the farm (Figure 4.1). Every effort had been made to make the garden centre look as 'normal' as possible – both to encourage public visitors and to provide employees

Figure 4.1 An 'open' part of a care farm in the south of England.

(all of whom experienced learning difficulties) the opportunity to interact with the public in as 'realistic' a setting as possible. As one of the managers of the farm pointed out:

> "At the shop, we actually employ an adult with learning difficulties. He's come through the employment side, and he's paid. It has to be as realistic as possible, as much as we can achieve that whilst still providing the service we provide and safeguarding our clients. And it's where they pay an entrance fee to go round the farm park. And it's important to have that interaction, the customer interaction – it could be formal in the shop, or informal in the car park. The community come to us, not us going out and about. It helps reduce stigma, and gets different groups of people together who never would have met. Everyone learns something who comes here, even though we never set out for that to happen deliberately." (Yvonne, care farm practitioner, south of England)

Thus, while the official 'client' group at the farm must travel to work and learn there, Yvonne also considered that it was vital to have "the community come to us" to help "reduce stigma". It is important, still, that the farm can be a safe and therapeutic space for vulnerable adults, and the staff at the farm work hard to set boundaries and routines so that their referred clients are safeguarded appropriately. It cannot therefore be *entirely* open because the core aim of the farm is to provide care and learning for those clients, not to educate visitors or make money from the garden centre. It is, then, "as realistic as possible" – with the added, informal benefit that "everyone learns something who comes here" – even if that is not the immediate intention. Again, this is a form of dis/connection – boundary-setting that is at once contingent upon particular kinds of engagement – predicated upon journeys to and from the local community.

It is significant that in Yvonne's experience these spatial dis/connections have led to unanticipated, informal kinds of learning. These could be conceptualised as 'knock-on' forms of education stimulated by meaningful but everyday engagements with social spaces that are somehow *provocative* of learning. In the case of Yvonne's farm, learning was provoked by the public's engagement with their clients, getting "different groups of people together", and making the *space* as realistic as possible. In a different context, homeschoolers also found that they provoked unanticipated forms of learning by simply being visible with their children, in public spaces, when the majority of children would be in school.

> "It's [homeschooling is] a very public statement. And for some reason, an awful lot of people find it incredibly challenging. You know, you can go to the supermarket and someone will say, 'Oh, not at school today?' And I'll say, 'No, they're homeschooled.' And that's the cue for any kind of reaction from 'Good on you' to 'How can you do that?' to 'Isn't that illegal?' I get a bit fed up with it, to be honest. It's tiring, in public, having to explain my own private family decisions to just about every stranger. But on the other hand [...] I feel I've got a role to educate other people about it so I do feel that I should take the time to give a proper response." (Rowena, homeschooler, London)

As Lois (2009) argues, homeschoolers are frequently called upon to justify their decisions to home educate their children, and tend to have a variety of discursive and performative strategies that they employ when they are challenged in public spaces. As I explain in Chapter Seven, homeschooling children also employ a range of strategies in their dealings with others who have not been home educated. For both parents and children, as Rowena indicates, this can be 'tiring'. Indeed, as mentioned several times previously, it is the case that educators across various settings must work hard to foster engagement with different publics and think very carefully about how they present themselves. By being out in public with their children during school-time, homeschoolers are immediately marked out as 'alternative', even if they follow the National Curriculum at home. Thus, when they are challenged by a member of the public they have a choice about whether and how to supplement their disconnection with a certain aspect of the mainstream – school – with a momentary connection. As Rowena felt (mirroring the majority of my interviewees), her immediate response was to look beyond her aggravation and fulfil what she saw as her "role to educate other people".

In several ways, then, I have shown in this section how alternative educators tend to be *outward looking* in their disposition to the local communities and publics with whom they may engage. Some consider that they have a crucial social role to play in providing a learning resource for disadvantaged local residents, and that they should be "open" to welcoming anyone who wants to visit. Others emphasise the (short) journey that learners should make to a space that is close enough to be accessible and meaningful, but *different* enough in feel to make it "transformative". And some educators attempt to engage the very publics that might stigmatise what they do, provoking unanticipated kinds of informal learning in the process. It is equally the case that many alternative schools, in particular, find it hard to engage with their most local communities. In part, this is because they are misunderstood or simply not known about by local families whose children do not attend, as has been the case for at least one Steiner school I visited. In part, this is because, realistically, the demand in some parts of the UK for Steiner, Montessori or democratic schools is so limited that they tend to have regional, rather than local, catchment areas. As Ball et al (1995) showed in their seminal exploration of 'circuits of schooling,' it is not unusual for parental choice around independent, fee-paying schools to occur at the regional scale in the UK. Indeed, that alternative independent schools attract relatively few pupils per year is an indication that their circuits of schooling are probably even larger than all but the most elite independent schools. It is, therefore, hardly surprising that there is a considerable difference between such schools and forest schools or care farms. By their very nature and financing, the latter kinds of learning space are able to position themselves more readily with regard to local publics and forge richer and more diverse local community connections.

Alternative dis/connections: "little people can do big things"

I have argued thus far that alternative learning spaces are involved in a variety of dynamic and multi-faceted relationships with what – for ease – I have called 'mainstream' organisations and practices. These relationships are characterised by many kinds of connection and disconnection, which can be deep, local and enduring but can equally be ephemeral. However, as I pick up in my discussion of autonomy in the chapter's conclusion, alternative educators and learners are also involved in relationships with other, 'alternative' organisations. I will trace just a few of these relationships in this section, starting with relationships *between* different alternative learning spaces. I then explore some of the relationships between alternative learning spaces and other alternative spaces that cannot immediately be classed as 'learning spaces'. Significantly, some of these overlap with the kinds of diverse economic practices that have stimulated much recent interest amongst geographers and others (Gibson-Graham, 2006).

It seems relatively obvious to say that learning providers are involved in networks, organisations, support groups and communities of practice that are pertinent to their approach. Some of these are national or international organisations, often with a strong presence on the internet in the form of websites, blogs and discussion groups. I included mention of some of these in my introduction to different approaches to alternative education in Chapter Three. It also goes without saying that different educators draw in different ways from these networks. For instance, many UK-based Steiner schools tend to meet annually for a sports event (mimicking the Olympics) that takes place at a Steiner school in the south of England. Quite differently, the majority of care farm practitioners belong to a national body – Care Farming UK – but, among those I interviewed, very few of them drew upon the organisation, or its website, for either information or support. Indeed, many practitioners viewed themselves as quite independent and disconnected from other care farms, each with a unique approach and history couched more in interaction with the mainstream than with other alternative learning providers. Indeed, several experienced care farm practitioners were concerned that a farm's inclusion in the Care Farming UK database (http://www.carefarminguk.org/allcarefarms. aspx) could be interpreted as a mark of quality or accreditation (at the time of writing, it is not).

Elsewhere again, it has been repeatedly been recognised that homeschoolers in the UK and other countries (notably the US) have been remarkably successful at setting up pressure groups, social gatherings and collective learning opportunities for their children (Stevens, 2001). While their use of the internet for teaching resources is well documented (Bauman, 2001), I found that homeschoolers were particularly notable for their use of the internet in mobilising connections between families, and for their very varied usage of online forums and discussion groups.

> "I heard about homeschooling and then I actively researched it. I joined a national organisation, and got information, I read books, I started contacting people locally, who were on the contact lists and the mailing lists [online], and started getting ideas of how it worked in reality. The HE community is very active online – forums, lists, resources online. It probably makes online spaces another learning space – a virtual space." (Rowena, homeschooler, south of England)

"It's a way of passing on information. As a single parent I belong to a Google group that's specifically for single parents home educating. And also for exchanging ideas – it's a way of people sharing information, letting us know what's happening with the law. In a sense those spaces are important, knowing there are lots of other people out there. It's invaluable as a support for me." (Charlotte, homeschooler, south of England)

"To be honest we're not that involved [in online communities]. They don't support us so much as they inform. [... I] don't see that I need support as such, I don't feel vulnerable. But others do. They can draw support from the sense that others have done it before them." (Olivia, homeschooler, English Midlands)

In the above ways, homeschoolers presented differing kinds and intensities of dis/connection with online networks and organisations. All homeschoolers are, on the one hand, very clear that what they do is a *family* endeavour. They have, after all, chosen to educate their children at home. However, at the same time, parents chose to be involved to very different extents in a variety of networks that required interaction with other families. Very often, this meant 'face-to-face' gatherings and community learning events; however, this also meant engagement with more formalised groups with an online presence (such as Education Otherwise). For mothers like Rowena and Charlotte, these were crucial resources, offering emotional support, information and a sense of affirmation – "knowing there are lots of other people out there", as Charlotte put it. Conversely, Olivia represented one of a series of mothers – admittedly with more experience of homeschooling – who tended to connect with online communities in a much patchier way. For, precisely because of the *child-led* approach they took (see Chapter Three), they were directed as much by cues internal or unique to their family as they were by external support.

Homeschooling parents were also interesting because several recalled how they had experimented with various non-mainstream alternative schools before they began homeschooling. Most commonly, they had trialled Montessori and Steiner schools. Significantly, in many cases, they had found such schools equally as problematic as mainstream schools, in part because they held quite particular parenting philosophies that, it transpired, were not particularly compatible with the strictly determined tasks set out in Montessori schools, for instance. This had caused several parents to be very critical of and to distance themselves from other alternative kinds of education. However, I encountered just as many connections as disconnections. For instance, some homeschooling families attended forest schools or visited care farms as part of their weekly routines. At one small school in North London, I met a mother and her two children whom I had met the previous summer at a homeschooling group, and who had just begun trialling the school for two days a week. It transpired that, at that school, several homeschooled children had attended for often extended periods over the previous few years; a similar experience was replicated at a couple of the Steiner schools I visited. In Scotland, I found that one care farm in Scotland was well known to young people who also attended a forest school some 20 miles away, and that that same care farm would potentially be linking up with the 'Building Bridges' programme at Findhorn (see Chapter Three).

I could go on listing some of these connections, which were practical as much as pedagogical, incidental as much as deliberate. However, I want to end this chapter by exploring notions of autonomy, which are couched in politics as well as pragmatics. In the remainder of this section, I want therefore to attend specifically to the political motivations that characterised *some* forms of connection between alternative learning spaces, and between learning spaces and other kinds of alternative practices. One could, loosely, term these the 'activist' elements of Woods and Woods' (2009) three-fold schematisation of alternative education, although it will become clear that less spectacular forms of political engagement were at play, too (see Horton and Kraftl, 2009). Nevertheless, some of my respondents specifically indicated that they had been involved in particular forms of activism that they suggested were either directly or indirectly related to their educational approach, and which tied them into particular social networks or social movements (see also Collom and Mitchell, 2005).

> "They [homeschooling networks] bring people together. We went and lobbied parliament last year [in protest at the Badman Review]. We had a big picnic outside – that was organised through the internet. There is a big activist element. I will go along to stuff. There were several hundred of us that went with our kids." (Charlotte, homeschooler, south of England)

> "We went to lobby our MPs. Which was quite interesting. It was a really nice atmosphere, us kids got together

spontaneously. We started making up rhymes, it was really funny. It was like, this is parliament, this is where all the laws are made. We kind of hung around in there. It was interesting to be part of that. Little people can do big things!" (Rebecca, homeschooled young person, aged 18, London)

It is important at this stage to highlight that there are equal numbers of homeschoolers who are not as politically active (although they may be engaged); in fact, it was repeatedly made clear to me that it was often homeschoolers who had never sent their children to school who were the most involved in activism and political lobbying. But it is nevertheless important to acknowledge the different kinds and intensities of connection between political activism and some alternative educational practices. As Rebecca highlighted from her point of view as a young person, taking part in political action may be an affirmative experience. Her use of the phrase "little people can do big things" seemed more than anything to sum up the purpose behind homeschoolers' demonstrations at Parliament Square. I interpreted this phrase as having a double meaning. On the one hand, Rebecca encapsulated a sense that these experiences of activism consolidated the sense of efficacy that a minority group, comprised of diverse political and religious convictions, could gain from *coming together* in this way. On the other hand, she was emphasising the political agency that young people could have – not only in the context that they are physically smaller, but in terms of their (lowly) social status in UK society. Note also that this political statement mirrors the pedagogical belief in children's agency that underpins many of the (child-led) approaches that home educators take.

The connections between alternative education space and 'alternative' and/or activist political convictions were not confined to homeschooling – but in many cases these beliefs 'bubbled under' everything that happened within those spaces.

"I've also got a background in protest and civil disobedience, especially environmental non-violent direct action, as well as a deep rooting in feminism and Marxism. [But] at the moment we're working with children to try and give them tools to survive their families really. And by just being in a natural environment to intrinsically develop respect, and love, of nature. But that background of mine bubbles under all of that." (Joanne, forest school practitioner, south-west England)

"John [Aitkenhead] placed adverts into publications like the *New Statesman*, a journal called *New Era* – they said things like 'Kilquhanity for Freedom and Democracy'. He was inundated with pacifists and conscientious objectors, not just from the UK but the US too. A lot had formed communes – they were like-minded people who were ostracised from society. The other perspective is the anarchist movement. I don't think John or [A.S.] Neill would directly associate themselves. But I think we could. John always quoted this thing that education was the generation of happiness. That was William Godwin, the father of the anarchist movement. A lot of [...] anarchist ideas about children's education are the same as what we are doing here. Philosophies of anarchism in terms of communities. And it links into what was fashionable in the 1960s and 1970s – small is beautiful – Schumacher, and we jumped on the bandwagon a bit. That was the experimental, sometimes activist element." (Christopher, ex-pupil and current teacher, Kilquhanity democratic school, Scotland)

"I feel it's more alternative for our beliefs but there is the nod to people like Schumacher, of course. The philosophy, neo-humanism, there is a series around the world through Ananda Marga, and even others, that is the ethos that makes us alternative, because I know teachers in the state system, they hear about it, if you visit you get more of a sense, because it's small, it's very family-like. I'm sure there are lots of schools like that. It's not so much that we're not mainstream, just that it's an alternative approach. We do use the National Curriculum occasionally – neo-humanism is more about taking methods, more eclectic, picking things that work with the qualities of children – story and games, that the children learn through love, and joy, playing games and listening to stories." (Helen, small school practitioner)

These three quotations are illustrative not only because they tie alternative education into a whole range of political movements, publications and beliefs. Rather, they also demonstrate the important point that the "alternative" (Helen) or "experimental"(Christopher) status of such spaces is not only a matter of external dis/connections with other people, places and politics (Fielding and Moss, 2011). Like many educators, all three of them connect their accounts of politics with some of the spatialities *internal* to their approaches – what it is about learning spaces *themselves* that makes them somehow different. They therefore anticipate three themes that I explore in later chapters where I look at those spatialities. Joanne and Helen both note the implicit relationship between their 'deep rooting' in political and spiritual philosophies and their impulse to simply help children 'survive' life itself, or work with their inherent 'qualities' (Chapter Eight). All three – but especially Christopher – acknowledge the implicit influence of anarchist thinking upon the smallness of scale and interpersonal relations that are key to many alternative learning spaces (Chapter Seven). And Joanne and Helen accounted for how their political affiliations very often intersected with spiritual understandings of the natural environment, childhood and love (intersections I explore fully in Chapter Eight).

Conclusion: dis/connection and autonomy

This chapter has provided a detailed account of some of the many kinds of connections and disconnections that constitute alternative learning spaces. Inspired by Gibson-Graham's (2006) call to map diverse economic spaces, this chapter has begun the parallel and by no means separate task of mapping alternative learning spaces. I have incorporated but also sought to add considerable complexity and dynamism to three previous theorisations of alterity: Fielding and Moss's (2011) slightly disconnected view of common schools as prefigurative, experimental microcosms; Quirke's (2009) particular focus on training, accreditation and legitimacy; and Woods and Woods' (2009) instructive – but knowingly reductive – three-fold schema of 'separation/engagement/ activism'. My purpose has not been to dismiss these theorisations but to attempt to add further nuance. Specifically, this chapter has argued that, without exception, alternative learning spaces must negotiate and combine many forms of connection and disconnection, which often shift over time. Thus, their relationships with 'external' systems – whether mainstream schools, government inspectors or political activist networks – may, I have suggested, be viewed as forms of *dis/ connection*. It is in this way that I argue alternative learning spaces aim less to be fully 'alternative' but rather *autonomous*. I take my definition of autonomous social spaces from Pickerill and Chatterton (2006; see also Chapter Two). Given that their work focuses on *social* spaces, I want in this conclusion to emphasise both the considerable overlaps with their work but also some points of departure that are particular to alternative *learning* spaces. I do so by summarising the features of the four kinds of dis/connection discussed in this chapter. These I take as the beginnings of a theory of autonomous learning spaces, which I hope will complement and extend Pickerill and Chatterton's work, and which I will develop throughout the rest of this book.

Conceptual dis/connections

Superficially at least, many alternative educators view what they do *as* alternative, and attempt to distinguish themselves from mainstream education. Specifically, they critique and attempt to abolish the *spatial* 'artifices' of school − long corridors, institutional smells, and so on. Simultaneously, few are completely 'anti-school': they empathise with school pupils, and argue for the redefinition of schools − including their own schools, in some cases − as part of a process of reflection in which alternative and mainstream educators should engage. Moreover, many educators retain connections with schools that are both literal and metaphoric − from viewing the National Curriculum as a 'moral guide' to occasionally visiting local primary schools. These connections are therefore *spatialised* because they combine social and spatial processes. In doing so, most acknowledge that they present some *kind* of alternative but attempt to resist the idea that they *are* alternative in a simplistic, static sense that would imply separation. Conceptually, then, the vast majority of alternative learning spaces are in fact autonomous because they are rarely inward looking (Pickerill and Chatterton, 2006). However, rather than (or in addition to) offering dis/connection as a form of anti-capitalist critique, alternative educators present a conceptual version of autonomy premised on pedagogical reflection: on what schools are for and what education could look like.

Pragmatic dis/connections

Whereas Pickerill and Chatterton focus upon the political and performative elements of autonomous social spaces (what they term 'praxis'), I have argued that pragmatic dis/connections are of vital importance to understanding alternative learning spaces (see also Woods and Woods, 2009). These connections worked in both directions between alternative and mainstream educational systems. Sometimes, such dis/connections could be historical − embedded in decades-old teaching practices that were, more often than not, acquired in the mainstream educational sector. In other cases, dis/connections with government policies and inspectors shifted over time − from complete ignorance by the state, to support, to suspicion, to a sense that the UK educational mainstream is now more open than ever to alternative approaches. Contemporary dis/connections were characterised by changing funding and referral arrangements. There was a sense that – in Scotland at least – the new mainstream Curriculum for Excellence actually *required* a kind of landscape of alternative choices in each region so that 16-plus year-olds could choose between a range of complementary but out-of-school activities. Recursively, though, funding caused complex pragmatic *and* philosophical difficulties for many alternative providers – in charging admission fees they could be too expensive for more disadvantaged learners, but at the same time many could not survive without, in part, being businesses. Pickerill and Chatterton (2006, p 3) argue that autonomous social spaces are concerned with the 'revolution of the everyday'. In a utopian sense, the impulse to live differently is easiest to carry out *within* autonomous spaces. I have turned that argument around, though, to acknowledge the fundamental role that everyday, pragmatic considerations – that have not undergone revolution, but look very much like those in mainstream capitalist societies – are a formative part of the vision that alternative educators have. I insisted several times that in order to fulfil their social role, several practitioners have had to bite the bullet – especially when it comes to operating as businesses.

Community dis/connections

I argued that financial considerations were also embroiled in the ways in which alternative learning spaces engaged their local communities. Most educators held some kind of a vision of their broader publics, which were often positioned at the local scale. Geography really mattered here: dis/connections with the community were rooted in some particular spatialities. Some learning spaces had thought carefully about the kinds of boundaries they set for public admission – negotiating a need to be 'open' (and hence not charge at all for admission) while safeguarding the vulnerable clients who were referred to them. In some cases, they relied on the skills of staff not so much to prove their legitimacy as educators or child-friendly practitioners (Quirke, 2009), but to manage whatever unexpected mix of people or situations came through the door next. In other cases, certain boundaries were retained in order to create as 'realistic' a space as possible, *so that* members of the public could engage with diverse (often stigmatised) social groups – to 'break down barriers'. Furthermore, forest school practitioners espoused almost a kind of optimum distance between their sites and the local community – far enough to require a walk, close enough to have meaning and foster place attachment (Relph, 1976), but different enough in feel to engender some kind of literal and conceptual escape from everyday life. Finally, I emphasised the importance of unexpected (informal) kinds of learning that were the product of encounter – when a homeschooling family were challenged in the street, or when vulnerable adults mixed with families visiting a care farm. In these ways, I added some empirical flesh to Holloway et al's (2010) call for geographers of education to expand the range of sites they study (farms being one of their suggestions). Moreover, Pickerill and Chatterton (2006) acknowledge *that* autonomous social spaces must engage 'other' communities (both local and further afield), but attend overwhelmingly to connections with other alternative/autonomous practices (discussed later). Rather, I have indicated just some of the many ways in which autonomous learning spaces *do* connect (and disconnect) with 'mainstream' publics that are more diverse still and which in many cases would not consider themselves alternative/autonomous.

Alternative dis/connection

Notwithstanding my observation about local communities, many alternative learning spaces *were* involved in the kinds of local, national and international networks, both online and face-to-face, that Pickerill and Chatterton argue characterise autonomous spaces. Indeed, both conceptually and pragmatically, there are significant cross-overs between the kinds of networks in which alternative educators and autonomous social groups are involved (for instance with shared roots in activism, anarchy and the 'small-scale'). Importantly, if some groups (like homeschoolers) may sometimes appear separate from the educational mainstream, many families were part of intricate support and information networks, often online. There were also significant cross-overs between different kinds of alternative learning – from some passionate critiques of Steiner and Montessori schooling by homeschoolers, to co-working between care farms and forest schools.

This chapter has, then, showcased multiple and dynamic forms of external dis/connection that might enable us to begin to conceive alternative education as autonomous. As I have argued in this concluding section, the concept of autonomy that I have begun to sketch out in the chapter is one that stretches and even questions other uses of the term (Sitrin, 2006; Pickerill and Chatterton, 2006). In particular, I have paid greater attention to pragmatic concerns and connections with local, ostensibly 'non-autonomous' communities, than has previous work. This has allowed me to argue that *multiple* forms of dis/connection are constitutive of a sense of autonomy – of doing something different, but doing something that requires and benefits from many kinds of connection with 'outside' organisations, financial systems, policies, training guidance, and much else besides. This is not always the case: as Woods and Woods (2009) observe, there are some examples of 'separatist' educators and communities who are perhaps neither able nor willing to connect what they do with either mainstream or other alternative practices.

However, this chapter has found that such 'separatist' groups are in the minority. More commonly – from the seemingly privatised realm of the homeschooling family, to the relative remoteness of forest schools in far-flung rural areas of the UK – the majority of educators saw what they did internally as at least a small part of something *bigger*. Beyond the examples cited in this chapter I have, for instance, come across homeschoolers involved in local food-growing cooperatives and the UK Transition movement, and forest school practitioners seeking to foster diverse 'communities of inquiry' that will support families with tough lives. I therefore pick up this issue of being part of something bigger, and these specific examples, in Chapter Eight. I am not arguing that the forms of autonomy exemplified in this chapter are necessarily or always reflective of those more familiar understandings of the term (discussed in Chapter Two). As I have argued, it is important to remember that there is considerable diversity across different types of alternative learning spaces, and it would be dangerous for me to suggest that they are *all* autonomous, in the same ways. Thus, in some learning spaces, I am asking whether autonomy means something different from how it has been understood in experimental social centres or Argentine social movements. In those learning spaces, autonomy may be something more temporary, less spectacular, more pragmatic, less politically radical, perhaps even privatised (in a financial sense), and in some of those spaces it may not always be appropriate to talk about autonomy at all. But, given the democratic and loving relations that undergird the vast majority of alternative approaches (which I discuss in Chapters Two and Seven, respectively), some resonance with previous theorisations of autonomy is retained. Nevertheless, in several other learning spaces, the resonances with other notions of autonomy are more obvious, because they propound versions and visions of life-itself that seek to extend beyond neoliberal maxims, and to collaborate with others in doing so. In those instances, however, the lesson of this chapter has been that we can understand autonomy to be something even more multi-faceted, complex and dynamic than has hitherto been the case. I pick up this particular argument again in Chapter Eight.

FIVE

Mess/order: materials, timings, feelings

Historically, it has been assumed that the term 'space' delineates something that is static, bounded and restrictive. In contrast, philosophers have tended to concentrate on the creative possibilities evoked by concepts of time (Massey, 2005). More recently, however, geographers have stressed that it is impossible and undesirable to divorce our understandings of time and space (Dodgshon, 2008). This is another reason that I began this book by arguing for the study of *spatialities*, not simply the physical spaces in which learning happens. In the production of spatialities, society and space are constantly being remade together, in dynamic ways. Thus, the term spatiality has always implied a certain liveliness: a demand that we study space and time together, even if ways of doing so have varied enormously.

This chapter is about some of the selected spatialities – the co-implicated spaces-and-times – that characterise alternative learning spaces. I therefore explore temporal and (physical) spatial process together. Whereas Chapter Four focused (crudely) upon 'external' connections with other educational systems and networks, this chapter is principally concerned with spatialities 'internal' to alternative learning spaces. While in reality there are many overlaps, my overriding interest in this chapter is in how alternative educators *combine* spatial and temporal techniques to make learning happen *within* their respective settings. This may seem a rather convoluted and complex endeavour: but if we are to take the spatialities of alternative learning seriously, it is, as I will show, completely necessary. Thus, I continue to ask what makes these spaces different or 'alternative': but I now am turning the lens on the ongoing processes of *making* those spaces themselves.

Since this chapter broaches a potentially enormous topic, my 'take' on the spatialities of learning will be more particular, and will proceed as follows. Empirically, I will attend to three aspects of the learning environment, which combine temporality and spatiality: the creation of order, the absence of uniformity and material objects, and the presence of mess. But, as already indicated, I do not want to see these three concepts as completely separate. Thus, my overall argument will be that, in managing these two elements *together*, alternative learning spaces are characterised by an interplay between mess and order (or *dis/order*). I will argue that many alternative educators view the former (mess) as a more evident and desirable part of their approaches than mainstream educators. As I discuss throughout the chapter, I do not therefore view mess in a pejorative sense. In any case, my purpose in this chapter is not simply to document different kinds of messy or ordered spatialities. In addition, I ask what alternative educators hope to achieve by negotiating dis/order, particularly in terms of what children (should) learn, and how. I will argue that dis/orderly spatialities are often geared to the production of particular modes of *feeling* – not only emotions, but affects and atmospheres. It is in creating those modes of feeling that capacities for children to learn are constituted. My discussions of feeling and materiality will be particularly significant, not only for geographers of education, but education studies more generally. I therefore begin the chapter with two brief conceptual contexts, inspired by some of the work outlined in Chapter Two. First, I contextualise my discussion of feeling within what Zembylas (2007) argues is a rather unbalanced engagement with issues around emotion (and especially affect) in education studies. Second, I argue that while few studies of education have yet engaged with theories of materiality (like Actor-Network Theory), some particular gains could be made from doing so. In the rest of the chapter I then exemplify some of these gains through several different versions of mess/order that I encountered during my research.

Emotion, affect and education studies

Michalinos Zembylas (2007) argues that emotion is not a new topic for education researchers. He documents how, as part of a more general turn to emotion in the social sciences, attention to emotion has grown since the late 1990s. However, he also notes how that work has been quite patchy in its conceptual and methodological coverage. Usefully, he suggests a three-fold categorisation of educational research on emotion. First, he argues that there has been a relative wealth of studies on the psychological, internal or individual emotions that emerge in educational settings, where '[i]nformation is gathered about the causes of emotion, the way a teacher or student felt', and so on (Zembylas, 2007, p 60). Second, he documents how many scholars have pursued social constructivist studies of emotion in education that are attuned, unlike individual approaches, to sociocultural contexts. The assumption at play here is that emotions are less individual responses than acquired forms of interpretation about how one should feel in a given situation. This had led to an array of studies about emotional relationships and emotion management, which in part influence this chapter. Third, Zembylas (2007) argues that some studies have attempted to overcome the individual/society divide implied by the first two approaches. To overcome this divide would be to emphasise the relationality of emotion (see also Bondi, 2005) and the role of the human body in feeling, mediating and managing emotions. As in non-representational theory (Chapter Two), emotions are not merely created by language but by gestures, expressions, movements and habits that tend to be hard to represent (Thrift, 2000). Here, the focus is commonly on *affect*, rather than emotion. Affect is understood as a collective and inter-subjective feeling productive of a situation and, unlike in the first two approaches, neither the sole property of society nor the individual (but both) (see also Anderson, 2006).

Despite work by selected scholars (Probyn, 2005; Hickey-Moody and Crowley, 2010), Zembylas (2007, p 67) argues that poststructuralist approaches to affect are 'theoretical tools that have not been used as much in education'. This is a hugely significant point for geographers because, as Kenway and Youdell (2011) rather bluntly put it, 'to our knowledge no emotional geographies of education exist' (see also Holloway et al, 2011). Their excellent special issue represents one attempt to address this lacuna. Yet, the papers in *Emotion, Space and Society* – like those that Zembylas reviews – are curiously silent on issues of *materiality*. This speaks of the absence of materiality in studies of education, and in particular the role that material objects may play in constituting particular learning atmospheres – something I began to address in some earlier work on Steiner schooling (Kraftl, 2006a). This absence is problematic for two reasons. First, as I highlighted in Chapter Two, poststructural theorists such as Jane Bennett (2010) and Bruno Latour (2005) have pressed for a recognition of the agency of non-human materials in constituting society and, specifically, in constituting affects. I am, then, in part influenced by livelier conceptions of materiality allowed by Actor-Network Theory, for instance – of how walls, desks, carpets, toys can play an active role in shaping social experience. But regardless of how much 'agency' one affords all that stuff, I am more generally convinced by a reassertion of materiality in helping us to explain how the world takes place (Anderson and Tolia-Kelly, 2004). Second, as I highlighted in Chapter Three, a call to 'rematerialise' our understandings of the world would not be particularly contentious for many alternative educators. Many approaches – Montessori, Steiner, care farm, forest school – pay close attention to the materials and physical environments in which learning takes place. At the same time, their conceptions of materiality are irrevocably entwined in the ways in which they adopt certain rhythms and routines in order to foster specific learning atmospheres (that is, particular kinds of affects).

In this chapter, then, I offer one particular way to address the lacunae in academic research on education identified by scholars like Zembylas, Kenway and Youdell. But I start from the (initially daunting) proposition that it is, both conceptually and empirically, simply not productive to consider the different registers outlined thus far (rhythm, materiality, affect) apart from one another. Thus, I focus upon dis/orderly spatialities, in which conjoined deployments of time and material space are entangled with the production of learning atmospheres. As I proceed through the chapter, the reasons for grappling with this complexity should become clear.

Taking time, creating order, fostering affects

Despite my observations at the very beginning of this book, almost all alternative educators would see *some* kind of a role for the physical, material environment in children's learning. But my argument in this section is that, looking across a range of alternative learning spaces, we see how the materialities of the learning environment maybe deployed and managed in very different ways. For instance, in some care farms and forest schools, outdoor environments are viewed as a 'toolkit' that can be mobilised according to the day's activities. In Steiner schools and Montessori schools, the physical environment is supposed to mirror, or resonate with, the developmental 'stage' of children. Some educators (including homeschoolers, Steiner and Montessori teachers) are keen that children use the 'right' materials, which may be 'natural', 'authentic', or both. Thus, while the latter parts of this chapter focus on less orderly materialities and temporalities, I want to begin by discussing the role of material *order* and the importance of 'taking time' to create that order. Specifically, I explore how material, *spatial* order and notions of taking *time* are entwined in several ways to produce certain kinds of affects or learning 'atmospheres' (see also Kraftl, 2006a).

In several settings, educators play close attention to the materials they provide for children's learning. These materials include toys, craft equipment, tools, counting beads, shapes, and all manner of other things. Nowhere is material order more evident than in Steiner and Montessori classrooms. In those cases, learning materials conform to particular criteria of texture, colour and form. For instance, Montessori schools operate Maria Montessori's 'isolation of principle' (see also Chapter Two). Here, children would learn to put objects in size order with simple wooden blocks that are all the same colour and shape, so as not to distract from the task at hand (Figure 5.1). Therefore, all of the Montessori schools I visited sourced their learning materials from approved suppliers, often at some expense. As one teacher put it:

> "The most important thing is that you have all of the materials that are useful and very Montessori. And at child height that children can access, not the adults. It comes from their learning, and the space reflects that." (Yvette, Montessori teacher, south of England)

While a Steiner classroom looks very different, similarly close attention is paid to the kinds of materials that are included. In a Steiner kindergarten, for instance, there is an emphasis upon softness: upon natural, untreated, but smooth wooden toys and soft, light-pink cloth (Figure 5.2). Again, those materials can be sourced from specialist suppliers. In both cases, the quite particular qualities of learning materials have been carefully chosen to reflect the developmental stages through which children pass. So, for instance, the wooden shapes used in a contemporary Montessori classroom for children in the first plane (ages three to six) are a relatively accurate version of the shapes first developed by Maria Montessori, following her in-depth observations of children during the early 20th century.

Figure 5.1 An illustration of learning materials in a Montessori classroom.

Figure 5.2 An illustration of learning materials in a Steiner classroom.

It is the case, then, that the carefully ordered materials that populate Montessori and Steiner classrooms are the result of detailed engagements with and reflection upon how children learn: of *taking time* to observe the learning process. Recursively, those materials are meant to allow children to take their own time to learn and to develop as individuals – an underlying principle of many alternative educational approaches (Sliwka, 2008). Hence, we already see one way in which temporality and materiality are entwined. This recursive relationship between taking time and the material order of the learning environment was not confined to Montessori and Steiner schools. For instance, home educators emphasised that their intimate relationship with their children meant that they had a keen sense of how their children interacted with different materials.

> "I look at colour and I look at content, and I think, can we work with this? Texture and content are important. I wouldn't have known this if I haven't spent so much time with them over the years. So with my older daughter, what the paper feels like. It's a very sensory thing. I think it's a girl thing. Stationery lights their world. The look and the feel. But she loves thin, tissue, crisp paper. And she loves a new book. The smell." (Dana, homeschooler, London)

I am not suggesting that teachers in mainstream schools do not reflect in similarly careful ways upon the learning materials that populate the classroom. Indeed, a plethora of specialist catalogues and websites exists from which teachers can choose those materials. Yet alternative learning spaces do frequently look and feel different from most mainstream schools. In some cases, this can be because the learning materials themselves are different – take the preponderance of wood in the Steiner kindergarten, or the equipment used in the Montessori classroom for measuring, pouring, balancing, cleaning and other 'normalisation' activities (see Chapter Six and Figure 6.1). But, more generally, this is because each individual toy or piece of equipment does not simply fulfil a function in and of itself. Rather, objects are enrolled into something larger – both in terms of physical scale and pedagogy. What I mean is that educators attempted to create overall effects – and *affects* – in their learning spaces. Those effects and affects were meant to flow from a careful combining of different learning materials, framed within the larger physical structure of the classroom itself (the colour of the walls, for instance). As I have already suggested, it is this production of affects that interests me, rather than what any individual material object looks or feels like.

I am suggesting, then, that the diverse material constituents of a learning space are frequently designed and *ordered* to produce particular learning effects and affects. These processes of material ordering work recursively with the idea of taking time to observe children, and allowing children to take their time with their learning. Let me provide three examples of what I mean. First, in the Montessori method, the aim is to produce certain 'effects' in the child, which are both 'biological' (their 'natural development') and 'social' (preparing them 'for the environment') (Maria Montessori, cited in Hainstock, 1997, p 77). To do so requires 'special circumstances' that are a combination of 'a suitable environment, a humble teacher, and material objects adapted to their needs [...] a pedagogical experiment with a didactic object [...] awaiting the spontaneous reaction of the child' (Maria Montessori, cited in Hainstock, 1997, p 77). In this way, the Montessori classroom provides a carefully structured set of didactic learning activities – shelves full of different exercises for counting, pouring, moving, sewing and so on. Children are afforded choice but the classroom, taken as a whole, directs them towards particular kinds of physical activity. However, for Montessori, it was only in limiting choice and activity, through didactic learning materials, that the spontaneity within every child could be awakened. Thus, while more didactic than any other alternative learning space, the Montessori classroom is, in the grander scheme of things, meant to afford an *atmosphere* in which individuality and creativity may be fostered.

The second example is taken from Steiner schooling. As I noted earlier, the Steiner kindergarten is meant to be a very simplistic, uncluttered space with a carefully chosen set of materials and toys. But, as I have argued elsewhere, the kindergarten is a material manifestation of a particular construction of childhood (Kraftl, 2006a; Kraftl and Adey, 2008). It is supposed to be *homely* – furnished simply but in a welcoming style, filled with the smell of baking, with a teacher whose disposition is (regardless of gender) supposed in part to be 'motherly' (Figure 5.3). It is supposed to be protective and 'womb-like' – with pink, wavy walls and small cubby-holes into which

Figure 5.3 The 'homely' interior of the kindergarten at Nant-y-Cwm Steiner school, Wales.

children can withdraw. And, it is meant to reflect the psychological needs of a young child – colour (and the *right* colour) being paramount in the Steiner approach. Temporality and materiality are combined again – this time in the sense of introducing the *right* colours and *right* kinds of material order, at the *right* time in children's lives, so that children are not rushed into having their 'critical faculties' awakened too early (at least as far as Steiner was concerned):

> "Colour is significant for the younger children. We can argue about what colour it should be. Steiner talked about a peach blossom. I think it gets pinkified at various kindergartens, some I couldn't be in because it was too intense, some too soft. There's a judgment to be made. I went to one and felt ill – there was too much muslin, too much pink, I felt I was sitting in a marshmallow. We're not trying to awaken children's critical faculties in the kindergarten, but we need some clarity. That colour is mirrored within

the child as Steiner puts it." (Michael, Steiner school teacher, English Midlands)

A third example comes from Findhorn in Scotland. Findhorn has a series of sanctuaries for prayer, reflection and meditation, one of which – the 'nature sanctuary' – looks strikingly similar to the kindergarten at Nant-y-Cwm Steiner school (compare Figure 5.4 and Figure 5.5)). As Sarah put it:

> "One of the wee gems is the nature sanctuary. It looks like a hobbit house. It's designed for singing and a sanctuary to support nature connection. It doesn't matter how you think your voice sounds, doing even an 'ommm', you can feel the vibrations of the voices around you, coming through the building, the curved walls, the floor, the earth, and you feel it. We ask the school kids who visit to do it. And it's fascinating, just to do a rolling 'ommm'. And also just to sit in silence, to breathe. It just totally drops all people out of our ego. And it's like wow – that's why we brought them here, to plant that seed of change in them." (Sarah, education officer, Findhorn, Scotland)

Figure 5.4 The exterior of the kindergarten at Nant-y-Cwm Steiner school, Wales.

Figure 5.5 The exterior of the nature sanctuary at Findhorn, Scotland.

As part of a so-called 'critical geography of architecture' (Lees, 2001), I have called, with Peter Adey, for greater attention to the kinds of affects that can be created and manipulated through material, architectural spaces (Kraftl and Adey, 2008). In my view, the same goes for studies of education where a livelier conception of the role of architectural spaces should be possible. This is what we mean when we say that affects can be created and manipulated *through* architectural spaces. We are neither suggesting that a classroom or meditation room can determine those affects, nor that it is a simple background or container in which learning can take place. Rather, as Montessori so astutely observed, the affects afforded by a space are a dynamic mixture(or an assemblage, in the words of poststructuralists) that, in the examples I have provided so far, may be highly ordered by human agents. Like Montessori, I want to account for a greater range of agents – both human and non-human – in the production of educational affects. Thus, I agree with her that those affects are a combination of three things, which are present in all three of the above examples: first, the qualities of the space itself – from the colour of the walls in the Steiner kindergarten to the sonorous qualities of the earthy, echoing walls in the Findhorn nature sanctuary; second, the non-human materials that populate a learning space – the haptic qualities (tactility) of carved wood or soft cotton sheets (Steiner), or the 'didactic' qualities of jugs and containers that are meant to afford a very narrow series of activities (Montessori); and, third, the agency of humans who interact with, manipulate and, especially, *order* those materials in order to create particular affects.

As I have argued, the ordering of material spaces is quite often achieved through 'taking time'. This may mean taking time to observe children, so that learning materials can be fashioned to precise proportions, colours or textures. Or it may mean ensuring that the volume and feel of a space encourages learners to "just sit in silence", as Sarah put it. As I have argued, temporality and materiality operate recursively in the ordering of educational affects. In the next section, I pick up on Sarah's inclination that sometimes children should just be afforded the time and space to sit in silence, in order to add nuance to this recursive relationship.

Taking time and making space: the *absence* of 'uniform' materialities/temporalities

Thus far, I have argued that the imperative to 'take time' was, in some alternative learning spaces, recursively connected with the careful management of material learning environments. But the imperative to 'take time' goes beyond the examples cited above, and beyond the careful management of the *presence* of material objects. For, on the one hand, the notion of 'taking time' is reflected in one of the most common criticisms of contemporary mainstream education across virtually all alternative, informal and radical pedagogies. That is, in the sense that children are constantly pressurised and therefore lack the time and conceptual space to develop at their own pace (for example Illich, 2002 [1970]; Holt, 2004; Gatto, 2009; Fielding and Moss, 2011). On the other hand, in this section, I want to show how some alternative educators try to relax (but not dispense with) order somewhat so as to escape what they term the 'uniformity' of mainstream school environments. In part, as I will show, this move is predicated on the *absence*, rather than the presence, of material objects.

> "I struggled with autonomous learning because I love it so much. My husband [...] comes home and we, say, went to a steam fair yesterday – 'What did you learn?' 'I don't know – nothing!' And he's like [...] well, you can imagine. Then four weeks down the line, they'll come out with an absolute gem. It takes time to foment. Thank you! It happens on every level." (Dana, homeschooler, London)

"Taking time is a really key issue. Projects really roll over very fast in the early years – that's natural to those kids. The older [children] are capable of extending in more depth. No rigid cut-offs. We have to look out and listen. Sometimes they can go on too long and they flag. So actually getting the time *right* is more important." (Judy, headteacher of small school, original emphasis)

In the above quotations, taking time is understood less as affording *more* time, in the ways I highlighted earlier. Rather, as Judy points out, it implies "taking time" to avoid "rigid cut-offs", in a way that is somehow more relaxed about when, how and where learning happens. This was a matter of *attuning* to the temporalities of children's learning, however quick or slow. This process of attuning is something that has become overtly formalised within some alternative learning spaces, and especially the Steiner and Montessori curricula (Chapter Two). A second issue here is a kind of relaxed stance to the *outcomes* of learning experiences. Dana indicates that it can take time for experiences to "foment" – in a sense that children knew or articulated something that they did not previously. The implication is not to escape formal 'learning outcomes' but to re-negotiate the level of control over when those outcomes maybe expressed and how they can be acknowledged. It is a re-balancing of temporal order and disorder in favour of a slightly less rigid (but not necessarily less robust) learning process.

As I have repeatedly argued, the concept of 'taking time' was intimately linked to the materialities of learning. Thus, the relaxation of rigidity observed by Dana and Judy related in other cases to the relaxation of the material and temporal "artefacts of school", as one educator put it (Chapter Four). In some learning spaces, this meant a certain *absence* of particular objects, practices, routines and spatial configurations.

"There isn't the pressure that the school environment brings. There's the conforming, uniform structure of schools. Uniform [clothes], books, pens, desks, facing the front, all the rest. Here there's the feeling, oh, we're going there, for a reason [...]. And there's the idea of we have an hour of science, English, then we go and do something else. They would also have more control over the space as well, than they would at school. Generally the parents expect them to be in the lessons. Sometimes they have to drag them in.

But generally over time they want to be in lessons." (James, teacher at organised homeschooling group, London)

"It's just not having it contrived – oh we'll go to the park and play now. It's having that space just to sit and get bored, and then start reflecting on things. Just sitting for hours in a tree and just staring. I think that's important emotionally. To be happy, on your own, in an open space. Where you don't always have to be surrounded by people, or technology, or stuff, or noise, or things to do. She then learns things, and then makes her own discoveries, and then comes back and tells me and I learn. So we use the libraries a lot. We sit there, spend time, get books out. Just sitting there. The Barbican is great, it looks like it was designed with children in mind. The choice of books, she really likes the atmosphere in there, the design. It's a place you can just spend time." (Charlotte, homeschooler, south of England)

James indicates that the "uniform structure of schools" is productive of a pressurised *atmosphere*, achieved through the materials (clothes, books, pens) and social practices ("facing the front'") that promulgate uniformity. While the quotation is from a homeschooler (who had been a mainstream teacher), this sense of temporal-and-material uniformity is something that many alternative educators have tried to escape. For him, then, the concept of taking time is as much a process of dismantling some (but not all) sense of uniformity: retaining some structured lessons but allowing children time to choose their play and to organise the classroom. Material and temporal *order* is reduced, but not foregone completely. It is a mixing or reconfiguration of order *and* disorder. For James, this reconfiguration was productive of an alternative kind of atmosphere that seems to draw children into learning.

Charlotte's discussion of emotion and affect is rather different. She values the opportunity for her daughter "just to sit and get bored". Anderson (2004, p 739) argues that boredom is not simply a negative state of alienation or disenchantment but, in a phenomenological sense, 'takes place as a suspension of a body's capacities to affect and be affected forged through an incapacity in habit'. Like Harrison (2009), he argues that inaction and vulnerability are not simply meaningless forms of withdrawal from the world. Rather, as Charlotte suggests, boredom may be emotionally and therefore pedagogically productive. For her, it was important to find spaces that afforded the capacity to be bored. Crucially, these could be spaces that were relatively *free* of human interaction, noise, "technology, stuff", like the park; sometimes these were spaces that were carefully designed to allow people to just spend time (the library). The significance was that these were both places that afforded the ability for *children* to introspect, make discoveries, and develop emotionally. Again, the implication was that in mainstream schools, the balance between order and disorder had swung too far in favour of the former – that schools were overflowing with highly contrived material stuff, rules, regulations and routines (see also Kraftl, 2012). Thus, she felt that children do not have the time or space to get bored in the kinds of ways that Charlotte deemed so productive. I return to the question of habit (mentioned in the Anderson quote), in the next chapter.

I asked children themselves about the effects that they thought flowed from 'taking time'. Leah's response was particularly enlightening.

> "I don't think I'd go to school if it wasn't for the farm. I feel really relaxed. Because I'm not under pressure, in a class of 30 kids [... I] wasn't expected to read and write, to pass exams. I was a snotty girl, I got bullied constantly [but] at the farming club, I was just me, I could do things successfully, I was allowed to be myself, it was a safe space." (Leah, young person, aged 17, care farm, East Midlands)

Leah had been struggling to attend mainstream school before being referred to a care farm. However, the atmosphere fostered at the farm (a "safe space") had afforded her time, space and control and an absence of material and social pressure. It had also been instrumental in her eventually returning to her local secondary school, and thus, in her case at least, had been a productive experience.

In this section, I have suggested that taking time can be better characterised as a style of attunement or orientation – to the affective capacities of a space to allow one to 'just sit', and to the different temporalities through which children may express what they have learned. While in previous sections I have discussed the *presence* of particular material objects, in this section I have almost argued the reverse. That is, materiality still matters: but it was in many cases the *absence* and/or relaxation of the 'uniform' symbols and artefacts of mainstream schools that, educators argued, afforded a more relaxed time and space for children to develop. Certainly, some children themselves agreed with these sentiments, although I shall return to some rather different experiences later.

Dis/orderly materialities: "it's making mess manageable"

The previous section highlighted the relaxation of material and temporal order in some alternative learning spaces. This section explores the idea that some learning spaces are not merely more relaxed but explicitly seek to make time and space for *dis*-order and notions of *mess*. I should point out that the notion of 'mess' was only *expressly* articulated at around a third of the learning spaces I visited. Nevertheless, I came across the idea in some guise when visiting at least one example of every 'type' of learning space, although it was more prevalent in homeschool, care farm and human scale settings. My discussion in this section is therefore prompted foremost by these empirical considerations. But before I turn to these analyses, I briefly contextualise them within the work of one theorist of materiality – John Law – whose brand of Actor-Network Theory explicitly makes space for mess.

It is widely agreed that many elements of the world are so complex that our attempts to represent or control them simply reinforce the ambivalence of our knowledge about the world (Bauman, 1990). This is, indeed, the premise for non-representational thinking in geography. It is also the flip-side to contemporary forms of neoliberal governance, scientific intervention and, arguably, education policy, all of which attempt to carefully survey and manage life-itself (Chapter Two). In this context, John Law's (2004) book *After Method: Mess in Social Science Research* is hugely significant. For, on the one hand, Law argues for a recalibration of social-scientific research methods in a way that might enable social scientists to recognise some of the mess of the world. Some experiences, feelings and occurrences – like hunger, train crashes, laboratory experiments – cannot be reduced to singular terms or simple theoretical explanations.

Thus, we *could* see laboratory experiments (as an example) as linear processes that lead from a defined goal to a clear finding – this is how they appear in the pages of scientific journals. But we could also view experiments *as* experimental – as a series of ongoing, contingent decisions from a series of possible outcomes. Experiments *play* with and are a process of negotiation through the mess and chaos of an excessive world. Ultimately, the majority of the things that happen in any experiment – the dead-ends, the test-runs, the explosions, the animals or plants that do not behave as expected – do not make it to the pages of an academic journal. There are multiple realities, of which the one encapsulated by one's 'findings' is but one. But, Law asks, 'if there are different realities, then lots of new questions arise. How do they relate? How do we choose between them? How should we choose between them?' (Law, 2004, p 13).

Law argues (2004, p 7) that these are *political* questions about how the world ends up as it does, and how we engage with the world. I pick up these political questions again in the chapter's conclusion. My point in this section is to ask, empirically, how ideas of mess and disorder relate to alternative learning spaces. This section is an attempt to grapple with mess from the perspective of education and, specifically, those involved in *doing* education. Thus, my questions look like Law's (see quote), but are slightly different: how do alternative educators deal with mess in their learning spaces?; how do they valorise, play with or negotiate mess, in the context of the kinds of order outlined in the previous section?; and, ultimately, what are the implications of mess for how teachers and learners engage with the world? I begin to answer these questions – for they are immense – by looking at some versions of mess that I encountered in my research.

First, as much as the careful ordering of a learning space may provoke particular *emotions* or *affects*, material mess may do the same. As Maura highlights, simply having "stuff around" can provoke all kinds of learning experiences.

> "The messy play, especially for those children who've not had it before, you watch their reactions. They're like, 'Oh wow, goo!' Which is cornflour and water together. Watching it go from runny to solid, just picking it up. It's just amazing for them. Sand, wet, dry, you can create anything with that. Pouring, filling, running, sandcastles. For some children, sensory connects with them. Some children don't want to be doing what you can see – what you can smell, feel, taste, hear instead. That makes them develop in whatever they're doing." (Maura, care farm practitioner/play worker, East Anglia)

> "It's not vital to have all the stuff around, but it really helps. It's just that opportunity, bubbling away in the background there, to just pick something up and run with it. It leads to all kinds of learning. And that reminds me, he used to be into bows and arrows, and he broke one of the windows in the house, caused a right mess, so we used that as an exercise of going to the glaziers. He was only seven. He measured it all up. Got the right size frame. Went and got the putty.

And he fitted the window. There's education everywhere!"
(Annette, homeschooler, London)

Thus, while highly ordered material objects may afford some learning affects, messy materialities may afford other experiences. Specifically, Maura and Annette identify with an impulse to *play* with mess. For them, that can have several learning outcomes – for instance, allowing children the opportunity to "develop in whatever they're doing" when other activities may not support that development. Interestingly, in the UK context, "messy play" has become part of mainstream education (for instance in many children's centres), so mess is not in this sense unique to alternative learning spaces. However, there is resonance here with Fielding and Moss's (2011, p 6) support for the 'hundred languages' model of learning for democracy – of finding diverse materials and activities appropriate to the many registers in which children learn. Certainly, alternative learning spaces emphasise a *range* of messy activities that, building on the previous section, take a somehow more relaxed stance to mess. Thus, some activities (like breaking a window) are far less directed than timetabled 'messy play' sessions, or bounded playwork activities (Russell, 2012), which usually happen in children's centres or playgrounds and are therefore bounded in time and space. Thus, in Annette's case, learning is non-teleological, non-linear, disordered – in the sense of being spontaneous to and 'running with' whatever happens. I return to the question of teleology later in the chapter. But the point here is that mess is vital to a contingent, spontaneous approach to learning: "all the stuff around" presents an "opportunity, bubbling away in the background" (Annette). Again, we see how temporality and materiality are entwined, this time through mess.

The second version of mess relates to its symbolic or visual import. Frequently, the presence of mess was invoked as a material reminder that some good-quality learning had taken place. This was particularly the case for homeschoolers:

> "In a family space it's shared. You have to constantly try to *create* a space for learning. For a long time, we didn't *eat* at our table, because it was piled with fodder. I, for a while, I used to like that. Because it was covered with stuff, with books, with sticky, with glitter, leaves, a skull, this and that, it was really disorganised [...]. And I loved it when my husband came home and said, 'It looks like you had a great day.' And I would say 'Yes, we did. We did this and this and this and this and it was really cool.' They [children] couldn't like

tell him [what they'd learned]. And so the mess, it showed him what we'd been doing. It's all so ad hoc. [But] we did create a flow and structure from it. But then it also feels like there's loads of holes in what we could have done." (Mary, homeschooler, London, original emphasis)

"It can be stressful when thinking about the home. More when people come to visit, actually, and they don't know what I do with my home. Mess is important to other home educators too. It's just part of what their home becomes. [...] At the end of the day, you look at it and you think yikes, what happened today? But then you think, well, a lot!"(Hannah, homeschooler, south of England)

For Mary, the kitchen table was a material prompt to discuss with her husband what her children had learned. In both temporal and spatial terms, the material remnants of mess provided a kind of a historical trace that *child-led*, spontaneous learning had happened. In much the same way as does Law (2004), Mary recognises that *all* forms of learning are partial, with "loads of holes". Thus, many homeschoolers struggled with the physical and pedagogical "mess" of what they do – that they do not take the structured approach adopted at mainstream schools. But, at the same time they realised that"mess is important" (Hannah).

This struggle to reconcile mess with the "flow and structure" of learning (as Mary put it) leads to a more general and third observation about the status of mess in alternative learning spaces. For, rarely was it the case that material mess – glue, bits of glitter, the odd skull – was sufficient in itself for good learning. Therefore, it is more appropriate to speak in terms of the interaction of mess and order (of 'dis/order'). I implied the importance of dis/order in my earlier discussion about the relaxation of uniform temporalities/materialities. However, this term is crucial for understanding how mess is accommodated, sometimes in quite extreme ways, but is very often also *managed*.

"One of the problems is linking animals with people, in an open farm setting. You have to think about the everyday public, it gives some limitations. You go to some places [other care farms], it can be absolute chaos, because no one is going be upset by manure everywhere, or trip over something, or someone going off on one in the corner – all kinds of mess! Here you have to think about the public at the same time. We try and keep the groups that are working behind fences almost. That's why we have so many paddocks. We need to have the chaos, but it's making mess manageable." (Ursula, care farm practitioner, East Midlands)

"We try to create certain atmospheres. You go to any home educating house and it will be a complete tip! Because, you'll tend to have posters on the wall, children's work up, great piles of writing and drawing, and glue and glitter and books everywhere, half-finished crafts, junk, pine cones everywhere. At the same time you try and keep things fairly clear to give a feeling of space and opportunity and inevitably they get stuff out. I try to open the back door to give us an illusion of space." (Rowena, homeschooler, London)

In both of the above examples, mess is made "manageable" (Ursula): there is an attempt to create some kind of a balance between order and disorder – some kind of overall dis/order. At Ursula's farm, the pedagogical value of mess is weighed up against the practical and legal considerations of being an open farm, and their broader mission to serve the local community (Chapter Four). Therefore, their solution has been an overtly spatial one – to partition the farm into a series of "paddocks" wherein mess can be contained but can still be entertained. In Rowena's case (without the health and safety constraints), she balances her "complete tip" with the need to still "keep things fairly clear" – to give "an illusion of space" wherein "certain atmospheres" can be promulgated. In her case, Rowena wanted to achieve a feeling of material excess that would stimulate her children's creativity.

Dis/order, unlearning and the non/teleological: "setting out a slightly rickety framework"

It is at this point that John Law's (2004) work is once again instructive. For – albeit with attention to social-scientific methodology – he makes two crucial points. First, he argues that attentiveness to mess should not be read as a call to dispense with methods that are tethered to a sense of order. Rather, he views these as complementary. This is one thing that I have argued for above – a sense of mess/order encapsulated by the term 'dis/order'. Like the term 'dis/connection' (Chapter Four), I mean for this term to be understood non-dualistically, in order to symbolise multiple and dynamic interactions between order and disorder. Second, Law also displays an interest in temporality. On the one hand, he emphasises the insensitive *speed* of much social-scientific method, which seeks to 'short-circuit' the world by rendering it explainable through a series of methodological and narrative short-cuts (like models and isms) (Law, 2004, p 10). Rather, he calls for engagements with the world that are 'slow and uncertain' (Law, 2004, p 10). On the other hand, he emphasises that such efforts – to 'take time', as I have put it already – presage new forms of spontaneity and sensitisation to the world. Most tellingly, he calls this a process of 'unlearning' (Law 2004, p 10). The parallel with radical pedagogic theories – especially Illich's (2002 [1970]) notion of 'de-schooling' – is evident.

Law's work can help us understand notions of 'unlearning' (or at least doing something different from mainstream education) across many alternative learning spaces. For, there is an assumption (for instance about child-led learning) that alternative educators think that there should be no prescribed outcome to learning– that learning is almost wholly a non-teleological, non-linear and spontaneous exercise. Rather, the picture is considerably more complex than this, as my examples taken from Steiner and Montessori schooling showed. Most frequently, though, as I have argued (as does Law), the impulse is to combine order and disorder, teleology and non-teleology. Most alternative approaches to children's learning valorise some kind of *increased* openness to contingent happenings and spontaneity (see also, for instance, Stevens, 2001; Neuman and Aviram, 2003). Significantly, as much as this would be expected in homeschooling settings, this is also the case for Steiner and Montessori schools, despite the careful attention to material/temporal order I highlighted above. Indeed, in the Montessori classroom, material/temporal order is meant to afford an atmosphere of freedom that will enliven children's creativity (Carnie, 2003). Thus, for instance:

> "they [children] don't have a set seat. They can go backwards and forwards. Teachers start off [each day] by talking with them, they choose what they want to do, but with a conversation – if we find a child knows all his colours, we encourage them to move on." (Jeanette, Montessori teacher, English Midlands)

Indeed, I rarely encountered any individual or group engaged in learning that was wholly non-teleological. For many practitioners, it was this that made what they did *learning* and not something else (like care). Most educators sought some kind of progression, even if this was more relaxed or seemingly "full of holes". So, following the approach that I take throughout this book, it is better to think of differing combinations of teleology and spontaneity – of learning as *non/teleological*. This would, of course, be something that could be said for mainstream schooling too, and therefore the difference most respondents observed with mainstream schooling was one of degree. That is, they thought that they made space for non-teleological, spontaneous forms of learning to a greater degree than did their mainstream counterparts.

It would be possible at this juncture to trace endless specific versions of non/teleological learning. However, I will confine myself to some indicative examples, with some particular regard to children's experiences. First, most homeschoolers characterised their approach as a kind of toned-down or 'semi-formal' version of child-led learning. They attended several weekly classes and social events, but at the same time valued the flexibility to be able to take their children travelling (sometimes for months), or off to museums, at a moment's notice. But, ironically, an effect of this flexibility was that some of the children I interviewed found that their days were filled with organised activities:

> "I'll explain my whole week. Monday morning I have sewing lessons. [...] That's really fun. Then I have a break. I suppose from learning. [...] Then I go to pottery that starts at 1. Usually for an hour but I do an extra half hour, often it's on my own the last half hour. It's all homeschooled children 'cos it's during school time. Then one of my friends comes round. She comes around for a play. After Guides I come home. And that's one day. And phew!" (Jena, homeschooled young person, aged 10, London)

Evidently, we had only got as far as Monday at this point and we spent a further 10 minutes talking about the rest of the week. While I interviewed homeschoolers from a range of socioeconomic backgrounds, it is quite appropriate to observe the classed nature of some of these routines. Jena's experiences resonate strongly with middle-class parenting strategies that require considerable levels of financial investment, and which take place in the educational mainstream as much as outside (Katz, 2008) – even if, in some cases, "it's all homeschooled children".

A second important point of discussion revolves around the status of rules. Contrary to popular (but not academic) opinion, even the most politically permissive learning spaces have rules. In fact, one of the teachers at Kilquhanity democratic school informed me that at any one time there could be hundreds of rules, some decided by the children and some by the teachers. At a care farm in East Anglia, which incorporated an adventure playground open to any children from the surrounding community, the importance of rules was made very clear, despite the prevalence of material and temporal disorder:

> "There's got to be rules. The children have to collect kindling, learning what's dry, what's wet. Then making the fire. Then how they sit around the fire. It's all part of that progression. I also think, places like this, you need to experience challenging behaviour. We're here to oversee. We're facilitators. We'll intervene. We wouldn't let them bash hell out of each other. But they have to experience, you shouldn't do that, it feels bad to make someone feel bad. It's a space to just be, kind of between the school and the street. It's more supervised, not controlled, but it's not so regimented, it's not so organised – you see that in the physical space – look at the play equipment, it's slightly ramshackle, paint peeling off, a bit rough, not like the commercial playgrounds, and that's the point. And the children are drawn to it and it's a space where they can work some of these things out on their own. It's a mix of us just being here, setting out a slightly rickety framework."
> (Maura, care farm practitioner/play worker, East Anglia)

Maura's care farm was located in a socioeconomically disadvantaged area of a large town. As with other similarly located care farms (Chapter Four), the manner in which they engaged with the local community was key. In this case, there had been careful consideration of the kinds of rules that were and were *not* required in order that this could be as much "a space to just be" as some of the other spaces I have discussed in this section. Maura highlighted how their rules facilitated *both* spontaneous kinds of informal learning and more formal learning (or "that progression"). In a similar way, several forest school practitioners (who also work with fires) indicated how they clearly delineated *spatial* boundaries around and within their sites in order to provide the room for children to light fires, use sharp knives and engage in 'risky' play. Maura was also very clear that their farm was a kind of complementary space, situated between school and the street, where children could encounter "challenging behaviour" within a safe but not restrictive setting. Of equal significance was the resonance between these rules and the material environment. The farm and its playground provided a space that was messy, "a bit rough" (Figure 5.6), but still afforded some

Figure 5.6 A typical example of an adventure playground that is intended not to over-determine children's play and socialisation.

sense of order – a "rickety framework", as Maura put it. It was this framework that meant "children are drawn" to the farm in an affective sense. Thus, Maura's experience neatly encapsulated the interplays between teleology and spontaneity, and between timing, materiality and affect that I am trying to foreground in this chapter.

Children themselves reflected on the relative merits of rules, boundaries and set routines – and the absence thereof – in some important ways. The views of homeschooled children as regards rules were particularly instructive because they varied so much (bearing in mind that the two young people quoted next were brother and sister). Both of them had experienced mainstream schools and homeschooling at different periods during their lives.

> "It [mainstream school] was kind of weird, the way you have the different classes, then packed lunch, and then you had another few classes and you had a big break, then there's this bell and you line up and you walk back in. You had a teacher for the whole time you were there. Oh that must be a nightmare. The lining up was a competition of who could get to the front of the line. There were toys and go-karts and things. There was one class everyday who had priority over the toys. If someone else asked, they'd ask and they'd

have to give it to you. It was funny. It was very controlled. And that was my experience of going to school." (Jena, homeschooled young person, aged 10, London)

"Most of my [homeschooled] friends were kind of going weird. About half keep trying to break rules and stuff. A lot smoked, which I didn't really agree with. It's partly them being teenagers. But I also know a girl's a bit older than me. She smokes, she drinks, she bunks off learning, she's throwing it away. She's not even 16 yet. I just didn't want to be with that really. It is just some of them, but maybe you actually need more structure, when, like, you're about my age." (James, homeschooled young person, aged 15, London)

Given the earlier discussion of school as a 'uniform' space, Jena's perspective – and her bemusement at the institutions of school – indicates something of the appreciation that homeschooled children have for the relative freedoms afforded by homeschooling. James reflected in a similar way about his own experiences of attending school. The obvious difference between the two quotations, though, was that James acknowledged the importance of rules. Astutely, James pointed out that this was probably related to age. Indeed, several homeschoolers pointed out how, when their children entered the teenage years, they had gradually had to adopt more and more 'formal' teaching styles, registering their children for classes, and setting out greater ground rules and learning outcomes. The resonances with other alternative pedagogies are evident. Steiner's third developmental stage (ages 14–18) emphasises the need for greater structure as young people develop the capacity for abstract thought (Chapter Three). Indeed, at one Steiner school, this was described to me as "*discipline*, which is [...] a horrible word, but, take the word disciple out of that, and you've got [...] the relationship, it's one based on a great warmth between the teacher and the child" (Paul, Steiner teacher, cited in Kraftl, 2006a, p 493, emphasis added).

The third version of non/teleological learning I want to highlight relates to the issue of *progression*, which has surfaced in several of the previous quotations. Alternative educators in my study were in virtual unanimity about the inappropriateness of constantly setting targets for children's learning. But, at the same time, as Knight (2009, p 21) points out in the context of forest schools, 'blocks' of learning need 'beginnings and ends'. There is, then, always an interplay between what Tony (quoted next) calls "nebulous" activities and the need for targets – between the representational and affective aspects of learning.

> "We talked to the person from [local authority]. And fundamentally I couldn't make her understand what we wanted to do. If I'd said someone comes in and does a six-month course, they do six weeks on chickens, six weeks on baking, and then they come out with an SVQ, they'd have said, yes, we understand that. But because I say we have this toolbox, we bring individuals in, we look at what their identified needs and targets are, it was all a bit too nebulous really, for them to get to grips with it. The idea of individualised approaches wasn't there at that time. You have to have an end point, yes, or a destination, where are you going next? [But] targets are not always objective. Sometimes it's about trying to find how someone's *moved* in a direction. Can we say he is more confident? [...] And we introduced this question – how do you feel today? So this girl had an OK day here, but here's it's fantastic. And you can see that change over time." (Tony, care farm practitioner, Scotland, original emphasis)

> "Historically, people were placed here and stayed here. We have people who have been here for 34 years. The aim is now, things have changed, they get what they need from us, and they use it as a pathway, then they move on, if they're able to. We do kind of look at their progress. There's nothing formal at the moment, it's informal. But that's the way we want it to be in future. Have an aim, come in, support them, and an exit point." (Yvonne, care farm practitioner, south of England)

For various reasons (funding being one), both Tony and Yvonne have felt the need to introduce monitoring and evaluation tools at their care farms. As Yvonne states, this represents a historical shift from informal learning to the kinds of outcomes-led engagement that haven driven recent UK government policies around youth work (Cartwright, 2012; Davies, 2012). Since care farms must negotiate two imperatives – learning and care – they cannot dismiss targets wholesale. Currently, they offer various combinations of two kinds of learning – learning for the experience itself (intrinsic learning), and learning for progression (like return to school, college or employment – extrinsic learning). Both

Tony and Yvonne saw the need for an "exit point" but at the same time were cynical about the ways in which the kinds of learning that took place at their farms could be measured. They had both grappled with ways of accounting for the non-representational, affective elements of their work. For instance, Tony struggled to reconcile the experience of 'being moved' – which was as key to his work as 'moving on' – with attempts to document the emotions proper to 'being moved'. In other words, Tony had toyed with the 'self reports and survey instruments' that Zembylas (2007, p 60) characterises as the methods of the 'individual' approach to emotion in education. He had found these satisfactory in part, but, evidently, both he and Yvonne were still working on ways to find adequate methodologies for representing that work.

Bringing it together: a case study of a human scale school

In this chapter, I have tried to distil out the component times and spaces that constitute the dis/ordered spatialities of alternative education. I have moved through different intensities of order and disorder: from the carefully organised material environments of the Montessori classroom, to the (managed) mess evident in care farms, homeschool settings and human scale schools. The chapter should be read as a whole, then, as a theorisation of the diverse forms of order and disorder that are at play across different learning spaces. Before I conclude, however, I want to offer one longer 'case study' that will, I hope, give readers one sense of how *multiple* dis/ordered spatialities emerge in practice. The case study is from a human scale school in England; all of the quotations are from the headteacher, Judy, whom I have already briefly quoted in this chapter. I have given the school the pseudonym 'Wheatfields'.

Wheatfields caters for children aged four to 11, and represents an alternative to mainstream primary schooling in a medium-sized town in England. The older class caters for children aged seven to 11 (a greater age range than in mainstream schools). The teaching and learning follows a problem-based approach that leads to in-depth, long-term project work rather than a series of set subject-based lessons. At the beginning of a project, the children will be engaged in conversation, usually initiated by a question asked by a child. The conversation will usually be about a 'real-world' topic of interest – like climate change or sustainable housing. The teacher acts as a facilitator, by introducing activities – like more structured reflection, research, or play. The teacher is supposed to be 'non-knowing': "we collect questions, facilitate this buzzy reflective discussion, keep observing and collecting possibilities".

Judy pointed out very strongly that what they did was "very open-ended, but not child-centred". It flowed from children's own interests but was still structured. Thus, once the class had agreed on a project, each child would agree to undertake certain activities as part of a particular group – for instance, research, building, painting, or writing. The teacher would ensure that each child stayed part of the group and that the group completed their activities. Thus, "it's very boundaried. There is more freedom than you would usually find. But there are clear parameters. Once you stay with your group, that's who you stay with until it's finished. You hang on with the boring bits."

Judy was clear that what they did was "freer than in most settings" but at the same time involved very careful setting up. She indicated that teachers did not have formal lesson plans (as at most schools) but had to be attuned to the needs of each group during the day (spontaneous). In the longer term, teachers had to be aware of what the natural course of the project would be, with projects often lasting a whole term (taking time). At Wheatfields, teachers negotiated both material and temporal mess in a particular way. As Judy stated:

> "The space needs to be messy, you need to allow for it and cope with what might look like chaos to be expressive and free. The messier work stuff happens here [see Figure 5.7]. But they make mess. It's counter-intuitive to make mess. But you really need to. So we create different spaces for different stuff – some with carpets, for more controlled activities, some without, where they can make mess."

Interestingly, like other human scale schools, Wheatfields drew on a range of pedagogical influences, including elements of the Montessori curriculum. Thus, as Judy highlighted in the above quotation, the school included a range of spaces – some ordered, some messy, some a mixture of both. The dis/ordered spatialities of Wheatfields school led to a conceptualisation of learning that both resonated with and differed from mainstream schools. (Like James, who figured in an earlier quotation, Judy had also worked as a mainstream teacher.) As Judy described, it involved an attentiveness to the non-representational ways in which children "have been moved", as Tony put it in an earlier quotation. At the same time, the teachers and children were still encouraged to assess those embodied, emotional changes through a particular language: the language of habits.

Figure 5.7 The messy learning space at 'Wheatfields' school.

"We don't assess subject skills but which learning habits children learn and hang on to. They have portfolios, and they [children] use the language of learning habits, from Guy Claxton and others. What they do is children write about and document in work or photographs or testimonials from friend or teacher – we did this, this happened, it was great, because I worked on my habit of persevering, and I achieved this this and this, and I tried something new, adventurous, I know that good learners are adventurous. We have this – good learners are adventurous, persevere. They use that language to describe their learning."

Conclusions

This brief case study of Wheatfields school is illuminating for various arguments in this book. In the context of this chapter, it illustrates how dis/orderly spatialities are managed to produce particular learning effects and affects, which ultimately manifest in learners as styles of being – as *habits*. The school then asks children and teachers to enter into conversations about how children have developed those habits. Therefore, the example of Wheatfields connects back to the discussion of some of the care farms and forest schools earlier in this chapter, in which I tried to find ways to represent the un-representable – the emotional and affective elements of learning. It also connects forward to Chapter Six, where I enter into a much fuller discussion of learning habits after my analysis of movement/stasis. And, set against John Law's work, Wheatfields represents an example of an educational approach that attempts to engage with and even represent the messy, fluid uncertainties of the ('real') world.

Wheatfields provides a specific 'take' on what I have tried to do in this chapter. In line with the book's aims, I have combined an analysis of space and time to develop my analysis of the 'internal' spatialities of alternative educational approaches. I have sought to stress various combinations of materiality and temporality in the production of feeling. The chapter has played with different combinations of order and mess, to theorise the diverse but overlapping ways in which alternative learning spaces constitute *dis/ordered spatialities*. In some instances, material order is crucial to producing particular learning affects and effects that will appeal to children's developmental stage or enable their creativity. This is particularly true, for instance, in the time taken to manipulate colour, texture and smells in the 'home-like' Steiner kindergarten. In other cases (especially homeschooling houses and care farms), material mess may be valorised in one or more of four ways: in messy play that creates 'wow' moments and accidental learning experiences; in the symbolism of mess, showing that creative learning has taken place; as a resource to be managed; and as a key way to support the non-teleological, non-linear, semi-child-led approaches to learning promoted across alternative educational praxes. Critical here was the *absence* of particular materialities and temporalities. Absence could afford conceptual time and space for reflection, away from the uniformity and ordering that was deemed to be symbolic of the pressurised environments of mainstream schooling. Critically, this did not mean the absence of rules and boundaries. Rather, alternative educators (and learners) recognised the need for the careful introduction of adult-imposed rules at particular junctures – for instance, as children reached the teenage years.

To return to theory for a moment, I am arguing for what we could call a 'weak' version of Actor-Network Theory (ANT) in alternative learning spaces. Like Law (2004) and others (Callon, 1986; Prout, 2005; Latour, 2005; Bennett, 2010), I am seeking to enrol a diverse array of human and non-human agents, specifically into an understanding of educational affects. I have implied that non-human materials might offer particular kinds of affordance: from the texture and smell of paper, to the didactic qualities of Montessori's directed activities, to the playfulness and symbolism afforded by mess. Like Actor-Network theorists, I have tried to place such dis/ordered materials on a more equal footing with human practices. Yet I term this a 'weak' version of ANT because the more familiar versions of that approach tend to foreground the *agency* of non-human materials far more than I have done in this chapter. Rather, my account has foregrounded how educators themselves seek to combine learning materials with what they *do*. Sometimes, those materials may be highly ordered and carefully chosen; sometimes, that order may be present but more relaxed; sometimes, there may be an openness to mess, contingency and the thing-power of material stuff (Bennett, 2010), albeit within carefully negotiated boundaries. As I have shown, each combination of materiality/temporality is geared to the production of particular learning effects and affects. Thus, this is a 'weak' version of ANT because, despite their recognition of mess, most educators cling on to some semblance of order. There is arguably less room in such accounts for materials to elude control, or to exert unexpected agency, than in traditional accounts of ANT. Perhaps that is the mark of good pedagogy and good teaching – exemplary control over the materials and material spaces pertinent to their approaches. Perhaps, then, we should not be too worried (and even pleased) if educators take time to carefully order their material environments so that material objects do *not* have the power afforded to them in some ANT accounts. With this argument in mind, I do, however, return to the agency of non-human processes in Chapter Eight. In that chapter, I explore how certain forms of matter (like food) and processes (like neurological impulses) do not determine, but are acknowledged and carefully enrolled into alternative learning spaces.

This discussion of ANT leads again to the question of the kind of 'alternatives' that are constituted by alternative learning spaces. And once again, this leads me to touch on the concept of autonomy (see Chapter Four). That is, the dis/orderly spatialities of alternative education offer different (but not entirely opposed) ways to conceive of the materialities and temporalities of neoliberalised education. Indeed, it is important not to forget that across several learning types – including Steiner, Montessori, homeschool, forest school and care farm settings – children will progress *to* (or back to) mainstream education. Surely, then these spatialities are as central to the theorisation of autonomy as the forms of 'external' dis/connection I explored in Chapter Four. As I have already mentioned, I am keen that the sometimes divergent, sometimes overlapping examples of dis/orderly spatialities presented in this chapter are taken *together*, as a set. This may run the risk of glossing the obvious differences between particular approaches, some of which I have signalled in this chapter. But my intention is that the overall effect of reading this chapter should be something like that of reading J.K. Gibson-Graham's (2006) work on diverse economic practices. Specifically, it should enable us to theorise the *multiple* ways in which alternative education practices reconfigure the assumptions of mainstream education – in the case of this chapter, in terms of materiality, temporality and affects (on the latter, see Gibson-Graham, 2006; see also Chapter Six). I say 'reconfigure' because, bearing in mind the lessons of Chapter Four, I should repeat that, in their 'internal' workings, few educators attempt to reverse, revolutionise or totally escape mainstream education. Rather, they seek to reconfigure education and follow slightly different, perhaps more relaxed approaches to learning.

In Law's (2004) terms, then, questions of materiality and temporality are as political as those questions of 'dis/connection' I broached in Chapter Four. Read against the notion of autonomy, I think the kinds of dis/order presented in this chapter obtain significant potential political potency. This is because both Law (2004) and Pickerill and Chatterton (2006) promote (albeit very differently) *engagement* with the world, not escape or rejection. They envisage the same world, differently arranged: they envision dissonance, to use Rosi Braidotti's (2011) term. Thus, while this chapter has focused upon the arguably 'internal' affairs of alternative learning spaces, it has once again found – as in Chapter Four – that most educational alternatives are outward looking because they attempt to engage the world in ways that are critical but constructive. They are as much about reconfiguration as revolution (Braidotti, 2011). Arguably, they attempt – to differing degrees – to accommodate messiness far more than do mainstream educators; but they rarely dismiss order. This dis/ordering may mean that they may look *different* from mainstream education systems, but at the same time there is enough to recognise to mean that there could be further constructive debate about how education in general could be spaced and timed. I broach some of the pragmatic implications of this recognition – for mainstream *and* alternative learning spaces – in Chapter Nine.

SIX

Movement/embodiment: learning habits (I)

One of the key arguments of this book is that the spatialities of learning are *lively*. In other words, the seeming obduracy of the physical environment may be brought to life in ways that lend learning spaces a dynamic, complex quality. In Chapter Five I began this argument by attending to temporal and material forms of dis/order. In this chapter I turn to a related but distinct set of ways in which alternative learning spaces may be enlivened: in the movement of human bodies within and between learning spaces. I focus upon movement for two reasons. The first is empirical: because many alternative educators believe that bodily movements are somehow central to their approaches. As I will show, they argue that children in their learning spaces should cultivate different kinds of bodily movements from learners in mainstream schools. In turn, I will demonstrate how some (but not all) educators are engaged in the production of particular learning *habits*, which flow from those bodily movements. The second reason is conceptual. For, contemporary human geographers – like social scientists in general – have been engaged in theorising the centrality of movement to geographical processes (like globalisation). For instance, conceptualisations of movement have heralded the so-called 'mobility turn' in the social sciences (for overviews, see Urry, 2007; Adey, 2009). In a sense, I take these literatures for granted, accepting as they do that an understanding of mobility is crucial to an understanding of contemporary spatialities. Therefore, the mobilities literature is not the principal frame of reference I use in this chapter. Rather, the chapter is situated within an overlapping and more particular series of literatures that has focused on *bodily* movements – on how gestures, dress, performances and habits are central to the experience of social spaces (for guiding examples, see Goffman, 1959; Butler, 1990; Longhurst, 2001). Since these are large literatures, this chapter leads towards discussion of a quite specific kind of bodily movement: of *habit*. And indeed, I want to orient my later arguments around a particular understanding of habit, which centres upon the work of Félix Ravaisson (2008).

The chapter proceeds as follows. Since Ravaisson's work has only (re)gained prominence in the past few years, I first provide a brief introduction to his theory of habit. I also highlight the resonance of his text *Of Habit* with non-representational theories of embodiment. I then turn to an empirical analysis of three kinds of bodily movement: movement between places, through motorised travel; bodily performances, like walking; and the repetition of bodily movements. Finally, I explore how, in certain circumstances, alternative educators translated these bodily movements into particular learning habits (and the learning *of* habits). I read empirical material against Ravaisson's conception of habit. I use Ravaisson's work to show that – despite its failings – it offers a key bridging point for the argument I am developing in this book. This is because, looking back, his conception of habit combines the twin temporalities observed in Chapter Five ('taking time' and 'spontaneity') with the bodily movements witnessed in this chapter. And looking forward, his theory of habit anticipates the discussion of interpersonal relations, the good life and 'life-itself', which I explore in Chapters Seven and Eight.

Of habit

Scholars of education are no strangers to the notion of habit. Here, for instance, the 'habit-forming forces' of education that inculcate practices and (classed) social norms spring to mind (Bourdieu and Passeron, 1977, p 34). Often, the relationship between habit and education is conceived negatively: where 'much teacher action is the product of custom, habit, coercion and ideology which constrain action in ways that the teachers themselves do not recognise' (Carr and Kemmis, 1986, p 189). In this way, habit is often viewed as an unthinking, external, constraining force that limits the capacity for creativity – a view shared by many psychologists and policy-makers (Middleton, 2011). Thus, the role of education can sometimes be to reverse the 'bad' habits that can lead to 'problems' as diverse as laziness and obesity (see Evans, 2010). Such habits always refer to the human body, both because they may designate specific forms of (chemical) addiction, and/or because habits involve the diminution of cognitive reflection – 'laziness'. In the case of the latter, this is when we refer to certain activities (like how we walk) being 'second nature' (Middleton, 2011, p 2857). Habit is viewed as an external force acting *upon* the body, becoming more concretised in that body over time, and over which people may have little control.

There is a long history of understanding habit as an external, negative and constraining force (Carlisle, 2010). But this view tends – rather oddly – to separate the mind from the body and to separate the habitual actions of a body from more intentional kinds of bodily performance. This runs against the grain of feminist, poststructural and non-representational theorisations of the body. Taken generally, each of these schools of thought dismisses the mind/body dualism. They also, in their different ways, emphasise the permeability of human bodies. In this way, human bodies are composed inescapably of relations situated both 'within' and 'without' the envelope of skin into which they are packaged. In poststructuralist parlance, bodies are always already *assemblages*, rooted within (not floating above) 'the *intensive environment* in which they emerge' (Dewsbury, 2011, p 148). Humans are 'body-brain-material assemblages' (Dewsbury 2011, p 150), composed of fleshy, mineral, chemical materials that flow around or through them (and through which those human assemblages may in turn flow) (see Bennett, 2010).

A recognition of the permeability of human bodies has important ramifications for how we theorise life-itself, which I turn to in Chapter Eight. Rather differently, as Gibson-Graham (2006; see also Chapter Seven) so beautifully illustrate, it has ramifications for the kinds of subjects, identities and collective modes of feeling (affects) that might be required to prop up communal economies and other non-mainstream practices. Thus, as Gibson-Graham (2006) explain, it means recognising that bodily performances and gestures are not always reducible to nameable categories (like gender identities) because human bodies exceed such categories. However, in terms of habit though (which Gibson-Graham only cursorily discuss), the main repercussion is that habit is not only an external force acting upon human bodies but always and also *internal* to those bodies (Middleton, 2011). This means that habit cannot be conceived as a simply static, oppressive, anti-creative force where other bodily gestures and affects are somehow more creative. Habit *endures*; habit may change more slowly than other human (re) actions. But if we accept the erasure of the mind/body dualism and the permeability of human embodiment, then we must also accept that habits may be as dynamic and emergent as any other property of the human body (Dewsbury, 2011).

It is here that I want to introduce the work of Félix Ravaisson, to whose theory of habit I will return in several places in the rest of this book. In my mind, his work provides a more appropriate frame of reference for alternative learning spaces than, for instance, Foucault's ethic of self-cultivation (which is nevertheless used to brilliant effect by Gibson-Graham). Ravaisson was a 19th-century French philosopher whose writings have been a source of inspiration for, among others, Maurice Merleau-Ponty and Gilles Deleuze. However, his work *Of Habit*, originally written in 1838, has only recently been translated into

English (Ravaisson, 2008). The historical context of his work means that some of his claims seem anachronistic to contemporary philosophies of embodiment. In particular, he makes (proto-Darwinian) assumptions about the order of things – from material bodies like minerals, which 'persist in [...] inertia' (Ravaisson, 2008, p 27), through plants, to animals and humans, with the latter being the 'most accomplished forms [capable] of the freest activity' (Ravaisson, 2008, p 39).

These caveats notwithstanding, the most striking part of Ravaisson's work is his assertion – against the grain of much other thinking – that habit actually offers the basis for individual human freedoms. It is for this reason that habits are most entrenched and developed in embodied *human* actions – in our bodily movements. Ravaisson's claim is based upon a recursive, dualistic conception of habit: the 'double law of habit' (Ravaisson, 2008, p 37). That is, that in engaging in repetitious tasks, passive 'impressions lose their force the more frequently they are produced' (Ravaisson, 2008, p 37), while, at the same time, 'active, motor movements become more precise and assured' (Carlisle, 2010, p 128). In other words, responses to external stimuli gradually require less thought, less effort, over time; simultaneously, the actions that result become honed. This, I think, chimes with our own embodied knowledge of everyday life: in learning to drive a car, considerable thought is required at first; over time, the manipulation of the pedals and steering wheel become 'second nature' so that we can do other things at the same time – talk, eat, read the traffic, listen to the radio; and, in general, our driving improves over time – our movements becoming more and more precise. (See also Middleton, 2011; Bissell, 2012, for a fascinating exception to this argument.) We also know that sometimes, when we stop to think about a habitual action, it can sometimes be harder to complete it successfully instead of following our (finely honed) instincts and just doing it. Thus, habit can engender human freedom – it allows the development of excellence in fulfilling complex tasks with little effort, and, therefore frees up the body/mind to engage in other tasks not dedicated to the fulfilment of immediate needs.

Ravaisson's work is striking because he too overcomes the mind/body dualism: he too posits that habit is acquired in the dynamic engagement of a body in space. The brain–body–material assemblage is here posited as malleable, or *plastic*, in contemporary neuroscientific terminology (Carlisle, 2010; Dewsbury, 2011). Thus, as much as they can be acquired, habits can be learned and un-learned, taught and un-taught; habits can also be subjected to particular forms of reflection, and hence directed towards particular moral conceptions of the good (Carlisle, 2010, pp 140-2). Yet the implications of Ravaisson's conception of habit for education are, as far as I know, virtually undeveloped. Ravaisson himself says relatively little about education per se, although, I want to argue, one could interpret his thoughts on morality, the undoing of habit and the bringing to consciousness of habit as being all about education. Thus, I will demonstrate that there are multiple resonances between his work and the kinds of alternative approaches to learning I foreground in this book. For instance, Holt's (2004) notion that children do not learn but acquire skills through *doing* them until they become sufficiently proficient is, arguably (but not explicitly), premised upon Ravaisson's positive understanding of habit. Hence, whether one agrees with Holt's radical stance on learning, Ravaisson's work could be re-read as a thesis on *how* learning takes place within everyday life (compare Falk et al, 2009). At the same time, a focus on learning provides an occasion to interrogate moral assumptions about learning habits – for instance, about the extent to which it is desirable to learn or unlearn *particular* habits, and about the extent to which one should aim to subject children's habits to reflection that may orient them towards *particular* conceptions of the good life.

However, I am getting ahead of myself here. For it is first necessary to exemplify some of the forms of bodily movement that constitute alternative learning spaces. Thus, I leave these critical questions about Ravaisson's notion of habit bubbling under the surface of the earlier sections of this chapter. I then return to habit at the end of this chapter and in Chapters Seven and Eight, where I broach some of these questions about morality and the good life.

Mechanised movement between places: the experience of homeschoolers

"I'd say homeschooling is school, but a different place every day." (James, homeschooled young person, aged 15, London)

"We say that we do our learning in a series of three landscapes. [...] So we have firstly what we call our core landscapes, places like our local park, the woods. Then we have industrial landscapes. I suppose IKEA is the best example. It's controlled but it's also free, the children can rest but they can also play in the play area, where other children are playing. And they can come face-to-face with 'another world' [gestures scare quotes with fingers and laughs]. And then finally we have open landscapes. Like the marsh, say.

> With [son's name] at the marsh, I let him run way out in
> front of me, he's nine." (James, homeschooler, London, cited
> in Kraftl, in press, 2013b)

In this section, I look exclusively at homeschooling. This is because, as I have argued elsewhere, homeschooling can be understood as a spatially combinative practice (Kraftl, in press, 2013b). In other words, homeschooling tends not only to take place at home, but in museums, parks, nature reserves, libraries and many other places besides (see also Stevens, 2001). Homeschooling is, thus, predicated on movement *between* places. Homeschoolers follow a conviction that if learning flows from everyday life, children's exposure to the greatest variety of everyday spaces is crucial. In this way, homeschooling can flow, non-teleologically, as much from a broken window as it can from a trip to the supermarket (compare Chapter Five). For more privileged homeschooling families, holidays were an opportunity for learning languages, history and geography. Indeed, some families enjoyed the flexibility – wrought by financial stability – to travel abroad for extended periods of months or weeks.

It was not unusual for homeschoolers to have formulated their own situated theorisations of these "landscapes" of learning, as James put it – different kinds of spaces that would prompt different kinds of learning experience. There is not space here to examine some of the implications of James' statement (the idea that IKEA is "another world", for instance), other than to reinforce the idea that it is movement between places that distinguishes homeschooling from mainstream forms of education. This also marks homeschooling – in degree at least – as something distinct from other alternative learning approaches like Steiner or Montessori education, which tend to centre upon the classroom as the core learning space.

In addition to the combination of different learning sites, several homeschoolers insisted that learning could also take place on the move, 'between-places'. In this way, learning happens in the car, or on the bus.

> "We do a lot of learning in the car. Either discussing, or
> audio books, or learning foreign languages. We drive a fair
> amount, simply because everything we go to is at least half
> an hour away. We've always listened to audio books. We sort
> of progressed from there. We've got tapes on philosophical
> debate that we can listen to and talk about. Might as well.
> Nothing else to do." (Elizabeth, homeschooler, English
> Midlands)

"The children are learning how to read maps, distance, how long it takes to get there. There's lots of things going on and around. Buses. We have a free supermarket bus, sometimes we take that as a change. There's a whole social thing on the bus, we are all fascinated by it. There's a big building project nearby, a big crater, which you wouldn't have seen if you weren't on a double-decker bus. How buildings are created. It's a mobile classroom. It's important to have different kinds of travelling experience. The world is completely different from a double-decker bus" (Dana, homeschooler, London)

"The way I learn stuff is by hearing it. I listen for ages to cassettes. I love them. I could do it for ages. Usually we have a family CD in the car. It's great. My brothers don't so much. It sort of works. We have Harry Potter cassettes in German and English. Some just in German. And that's where I remember lots of different words. On the journey." (Jena, homeschooled young person, aged 10, London)

In each of the above examples, parents and children reflected upon the kinds of learning that could flow from listening to tapes in the car or observing the world from the top deck of a double-decker bus. Learning could be fairly formal and intentional – in the form of foreign language acquisition or philosophical debate; or, it could be informal and emergent from everyday life – observing the gradual process of a construction site. But in each case learning also flows in part from the simple, everyday necessity to travel, to engage in mobile practices – itself a function of the combinative approach taken by homeschoolers and, as has been repeatedly observed, of late-modern life itself (Urry, 2007; Adey, 2009).

In turn, I want also to observe that car and bus travel necessitate *sitting still*, often with little else to do than to look out of the window, talk or listen to a CD. As Elizabeth rather bluntly put it, "[m]ight as well. Nothing else to do." Here, then, we begin to see the kinds of *bodily* comportment and movement that are also integral to learning, and which I explore in detail later in this chapter. Perhaps ironically, the focus here is upon the kinds of bodily *stillness* urged upon the body *by* mechanised movement – having to sit, relatively still, in a car or on a bus. Thus, the process of learning can, in passing, more accurately be conceived as one that involves both movement *and* stasis. Elsewhere, in his wonderful explications of waiting during railway journeys, David Bissell (2007, p 277) has similarly argued that 'waiting [not be] conceptualised as a dead period of stasis or stilling, but is instead alive with the potential of being other than this'. Movement and stasis are combined to offer possibilities on a variety of 'planes' (Bissell, 2007, p 277). Thus, homeschoolers do emphasise the importance of combination and 'the journey'; but those spatialities must be managed – they must be restricted, slowed down, even halted – in order for quality kinds of learning to follow. Several homeschoolers thought that simply "rushing between places" was a mistake. Rather, as I argued in Chapter Five, stillness, taking time and boredom can be *productive* of learning, this time in terms of the relative absence of bodily movement, rather than of 'uniform' materials or timings:

> "We used to go to the museums and rattle around and see everything and come back exhausted. But then I was pregnant and I was slower and we just went to the Natural History Museum with pencils and paper. We went to one room. That was all we did. And we stayed there. For an hour and a half. We sat there, no one else came in – it was too boring. The children loved it. They sat, they walked around, painted and drew." (Hannah, homeschooler, south of England)

> "We try to restrict what we do. So we have a network of spaces that we visit regularly, as much as we can. But we restrict that, so that we're not rushing between places. It's partly in not having a car, which is of course deliberate, but a result of that is that you just can't rush! It takes time. And we usually spend most of the day doing that thing. So that things are slowed and controlled and rhythmical." (David, homeschooler, London)

Whilst these experiences of movement and stasis are fairly unique to the freedom experienced by homeschoolers, the broader implication is that, in some contexts, young people may increasingly be being afforded the opportunity to interact with different, alternative learning spaces. As I indicated in Chapter Four, this is the case in Scotland, where over-16s at risk of exclusion from education and employment enter into an 'Activity Agreement' where they can choose from experiences at forest schools, care farms and other learning spaces. I do not have any data about young people's journeys to or from such learning spaces, but there is certainly increasing recognition of the possible benefits of combining alternative learning spaces, sometimes with mainstream education or referrals from mainstream institutions. This observation resonates with Ferguson and Seddon's (2007) conceptualisation of learning 'bubbles' that overlap in local areas to form diverse networks of learning (Chapter Two).

Bodily movements: distraction, implication, repetition

While the combinative approach to learning spaces is, then, fairly unique to homeschooling, other forms of embodied learning are not. This statement is hardly surprising for educators familiar with diverse learning styles. Advocates of VAK (Visual, Auditory and Kinaesthetic) learning stress the importance of presenting information to children in various ways; with the kinaesthetic approach involving practical experience and movement around the classroom (Knowles, 2010, p 159; Fielding and Moss, 2011). As Knowles (2010) argues, to allow for such diverse learning styles can be to make learning experiences more inclusive. Elsewhere, important work by historical geographers of childhood – such as Elizabeth Gagen (2004) and Sarah Mills (in press, 2013) – has shown how the disciplining of bodily movements through sport or institutional routine can be a core part of education for particular kinds of citizenship. And, indeed, it is recognised in both the mainstream and alternative sectors (in my research, in several Montessori schools and human scale schools) that young children must, ideally, be able to 'flow freely' between indoor and outdoor learning environments rather than have strictly timetabled sessions in each place (see Bilton, 2010, p 91 for an instructive example).

These are all important points, but they have been well developed by academics and practitioners. My argument in this section is rather more selective. Namely, that particular bodily movements can be related to identifiable processes of learning in three ways: first, through *distraction* – exemplified by the practice of walking; second, through *implication* – through training children's bodies to do a task that will, perhaps much later in their lives, foment in their ability to achieve a quite different task (in this case, reading and writing); and, third, through *repetition* – engaging in the same movements over and over again to foster familiarity. These three styles of bodily movement and learning will inform my later discussion of habit.

Distraction

In many settings – and notably forest schools and care farms – physical activity is used to break down a formal 'educational' relationship between teacher and learner. Thus, activities like cleaning, maintenance, fire lighting, mountain biking and walking are important because they require a different configuration of human bodies than that found at school. For a start, many young people are initially referred to forest schools and care farms for one-to-one work, not as part of a larger class. From this starting point, there is an attempt to 're-boot' (my word) the disposition of a young person towards an adult who is still, in some ways, an authority figure. Critically, bodies are configured differently from those in most formal learning situations. Teacher and learner do not face each other but are placed side-by-side. Furthermore, they are engaged in a collaborative task that requires movement around one another, perhaps even the placing of a hand on top of another hand to demonstrate how to saw a piece of wood (as mentioned later in this chapter). Thus, there is an attempt to escape the combative face-to-face arrangement of bodies in space in most formal learning environments. In this way, learning happens more effectively because young people are, initially, *distracted* from any sense that the primary task in which they are engaged is learning. I do not think this is usually meant in a coercive or deceptive sense, but rather to afford a young person some time and space away from the pressures of school (Chapter Five). Let me provide two very different examples.

> "There's an opportunity to come on a tour around Findhorn. They go and look at the wind turbines, gardens, eco-housing, it's all very casual. Very informal, all walking together, side by side. So we don't have a classroom. This whole campus is the classroom – that's a good way of putting it. It's [...] working with those while you're talking and walking. It's being outside, I feel a lot of space outside. And you can just be silent. For as long as you want." (Sarah, education officer, Findhorn, Scotland)

> "Another good place is walking to the station. A lot of learning goes on then. It takes about 20 minutes. We do it a lot. It's one that we're so familiar with that a lot of conversation goes on. [...] It's important to be familiar, because when it's not, then they're taken up with looking at the different things, where we are, what's that, why that's

there. [...] They'll be more inside their heads and they'll go on and on, in these really intricate fantasy worlds that they've made up themselves. And that comes from, the walk, it's an opportunity, really, for them to have that space to ponder and then, oh, it all comes gushing out in these monologues as we're walking [...]. It's purely because they have time to do it, this kind of critical rumination, reflection. Not like the heavy routine at school, and where they're told how to think, and then they're exhausted when they get home. [...] I don't know if it's innate. Or if it's a product of the way they're brought up." (Rowena, homeschooler, London)

Once again, in both of these quotations, we see the importance of 'taking time' and having space, especially compared with what Rowena called the "heavy routine" at school. And again, we witness how, seen in this way, bodily movement begets a kind of stillness, of "silence" (Sarah), of "rumination" that is productive of creativity (compare Bissell, 2007). In both cases, though, I want to point to the significance of *distraction*. For Sarah, the kind of learning that emerges from "walking, together, side by side" is one where some kind of learning is happening, but that learning is informal, as per the proper definition of the term (Jeffs and Smith, 2005) – it is non-pressured, relaxed, and one can "just be silent" at times rather than feel compelled to engage in a formal learning task. For Rowena, fascinatingly, her children's fantasy worlds are a direct product of repetitive, habitual engagement with their local environment through a walk they often take. She, too, emphasises conversation – a crucial element of informal learning. But she also points to how her children are *less* "taken up" with what they are seeing because it is so familiar to them. They are, then, somehow distracted from their environment: but that (semi-)withdrawal does not result in complete inaction or vulnerability, but an opportunity for *further* action (Harrison, 2009). In other words, it proffers up the occasion for precisely the kinds of creative, fantastical deployments of the imagination that are so valorised by play practitioners (for example Bruce, 2011) and apparently lacking in contemporary childhood experiences in some western countries. I return to this principle of distraction later, as it resonates in a significant way with Ravaisson's theory of habit as that which cannot (fully) be subject to thought.

Implication

The second way I want to understand bodily movement is by implication. Again, let me provide a couple of examples before I move on. Both concern the acquisition of literacy skills. The first comes from Steiner schooling, where children do not learn to read and write until they are seven. When they do, they learn to write first, and do so through a variety of active and more concentrated (or passive) means, including dance and story-telling. The second example is taken from Montessori education. Both quotations, however, are taken from teachers at individual schools so indicate their practical interpretations of Steiner's and Montessori's pedagogies.

> "Art and movement are considered to be the realms in which a young child lives [...]. Ideally, in a Steiner school, a lot of subjects are taught, using movement. And, the rhythm of the school day is structured such that a child won't have to sit still at their desk. When we get up [...] then we do some more, heavy, work again, writing or whatever, and then again there'd be physical activity. So, children learning the letters of the alphabet [...], they might spend part of the morning playing different games with straight lines in them, and then you're running in curves. [...] Then we'd have stories about the letter 'b' and the friendly letter 'b' who's a big brown Bear. They would live the whole day with the letter 'b'. So there are as many approaches as you can get, to a fundamental experience." (Beatrice, Steiner teacher, Wales, cited in Kraftl, 2006a, p 499)

> "A lot of parents would get upset. You have to warn the parents. They [children] say 'I spent six months washing a table.' [It helps for] when you are doing your letters. But it [writing] has so many steps. If they can do it [table washing], they show good concentration. They find the table, move the chairs, find the basin, sponge, soap, cloth, brush, lay it out, put on the apron, lay it all out on their towel, go get the water, how much to get, do you fill it to the top and spill it on the way? And if they do – good, a bit of mess – they mop it up. Then they get the brush, scrub the table from left to right, in preparation for writing." (Athena, Montessori teacher, US)

In these examples, movement is, intentionally, meant to prepare children for literacy skills. However (building upon the principle of 'distraction'), the children may not necessarily know this, because the key thing is to prepare their *bodies* to undertake generic styles of movement (from "left to right", as Athena put it) that will later emerge and be honed as they learn to write. They are not, specifically, 'learning to write', but they are preparing their bodies to become proficient at particular movements that will facilitate writing (Figure 6.1).

Figure 6.1 A child preparing to clean a table in a Montessori classroom. Children can spend half an hour preparing the materials to clean a table before carefully wiping the table from left to right.

Arguably, these proficiencies constitute forms of habituation, but, interestingly, these do not immediately lead to the longer-term habits that are desired (that is, learning to write). Rather, they are *deferred*, in much the same way some homeschoolers discussed learning outcomes emerging months after a particular learning experience (Chapter Five). Indeed, we could understand "good concentration" as an attempt to name one of the habitual styles acquired through table cleaning. Moreover, these are both conscious and subconscious learning acts. In the Steiner classroom, children may well know that they are learning to write the letter 'b', although not immediately they start running in shapes. At the same time, Steiner's broader (spiritual) approach is such that children never knowingly engage in certain reflective tasks, at least until they are much older. Hence, learning is again deferred or stored up for a time when habituated styles of being, acting or thinking can be *appopriately* expressed by children – for instance, as 'moral imagination' (Oberski, 2011, p 14; see Chapter Three for details).

Repetition

Beatrice's and Athena's quotes also touch on the theme of *repetition*. Repetition is absolutely central to many alternative learning spaces. In forest schools, for instance, a programme of repeat visits, over a series of weeks, is instrumental to fostering trust and confidence among children in the woodland, in each other, and in adult practitioners (Knight, 2009). One forest school practitioner expanded on how such trust was achieved, specifically through the creation of intimate atmospheres:

> "In the whole 24-hour session over five weeks we only saw one other person. And the group was the same every time. And we do repetition and reflection, repetition and reflection, to embed stuff. We do get close. I think, and I'm not a child psychologist. This lad would come back to the woods for the third time, and it was a display of him saying, I'm at home here, somewhere I feel safe, somewhere that's fun. At the very least he felt comfortable. He knew we could be trusted. He knew the boundaries of the woodland. And that's what made him feel comfortable. And also compared with living on an estate. Maybe that's the bottom line. Freedom, I suppose – he was just free to run around." (Joanne, forest school practitioner, south-west England)

Joanne indicates a relationship between repetition and freedom that is common across many alternative learning spaces, although it may be achieved in very different ways. In the Montessori classroom, the didactic method requires the repetition of tasks like pouring until children are ready to move on to the next task (Carnie, 2003). In care farm environments, I have repeatedly been told that repetition is "better for learning" because it increases independence and a sense of belonging among older children and adults with learning difficulties (Yvonne, care farm practitioner, south of England). Such freedom can lead to many kinds of positive outcomes. For instance, as Helena (a young person attending a care farm) told me, her engagement in repetitive tasks boosted her own mood and increased her capacity to care for animals:

> "I'm cleaning the animals out and letting them out, mucking them out. This afternoon I'm in the flower section, watering them, feeding them. I do it every week, and I really like it. I like having the same task each week and caring for the animals, it makes me feel better and makes me think about how they feel." (Helena, young person, aged 16, at care farm in north of England)

Quite differently, at one human scale school in East Anglia, which takes children who have been severely bullied, the repetition of bodily movement took on critical importance for their rehabilitation:

> "I taught kids how to walk, how to look at you, using drama. It was about confidence. Even if you don't feel it, you can look it. I taught them how to open the door and walk in. They would look down and trip over their feet. Open the door and walk in – 10 or 12 times – walk in here. I'd move around, you wouldn't know where I'd be. Hold onto the door, find the person in the room. If you shuffle, people will think you are not confident. You have to stop, look around and say hello. Things as simple as that." (Anne, director of small school network, East Anglia)

Each of the three quotations above contains some striking resonances with Ravaisson's conception of habit. At this juncture, I simply want to highlight these features, before including them as part of my more general discussion of habit, later in this chapter. First, in Joanne's case, was the idea that the introduction of repetition *with* boundaries could engender 'trust' and 'comfort'. Importantly, it was this particular combination of time, space and emotion that produced sensations of 'freedom'. Second, in Helena's case, was the idea that repetition made her more receptive to her own feelings and increased her empathy to others (in this case, animals). And third, in Anne's case, was the idea that the repetition of bodily movements did not simply create emotions or alter corporeal dispositions for the sake of it. Rather, the inculcation of confidence followed a powerful moral sense of duty: that altering the habituated vulnerability of a severely bullied young person could not only help to 'heal' them but lead to them returning to school, qualifications, a job, and a 'normal' family life. Otherwise, in many cases, severe bullying can preclude all of these outcomes (Hayes and Herbert, 2011). It is the case, of course, that repetition figures in mainstream schools and that in certain guises ('learning by rote') it gets a bad press. But it is important to recognise that few alternative educators dismiss the importance of repetition – quite the reverse. Rather, we can see each of these three examples as a different *configuration* of repetition – in Braidotti's terms as different forms of dissonance with what happens in the mainstream. While this book does not attempt to evaluate the effectiveness of any or all of these forms of dissonance, it is nevertheless worth noting that each kind of repetition may be appropriate for some children but not others. Hence, learning by rote may suit one child but not another, just as much as repetitive visits to a forest school might suit one child but not another.

Channelling bodily movements: articulating habit

> "Targets are not always objective. Sometimes it's about trying to find how someone's *moved* in a direction. Can we say he is more confident?" (Tony, care farm, Scotland, original emphasis)

Building on the previous sections, I chart next a number of examples of alternative learning spaces where explicit attempts are made to channel bodily movements towards particular habits. I also return to Ravaisson's theorisation of habit. In some cases (like Montessori education), the desired habits have been set out by the founder of a particular approach. Conversely, some educators had developed their own rationales, methodologies and evaluation strategies for articulating habits within young people's learning. In other cases, (like the Wheatfields school, introduced in Chapter Five), educators drew on published materials for their inspiration. A recurrent example was Guy Claxton's notion of the accessibility and articulation of 'habit maps': neural and behavioural 'patterns that are most well entrenched and easiest to articulate. It is these well-marked channels of concept, talk and expectation that drive perception' (Claxton and Lucas, 2007, p 101). I should note here that Ravaisson's conception of habit is quite different from Claxton's. Claxton situates habit at the surface level in cognition and talk, *driving* perception. Almost in opposition, Ravaisson sees perception *weakened* through habit, and ostensibly difficult to access via everyday kinds of cognitive reflection and talk (Carlisle, 2010).

I want to discuss several examples, necessitating some relatively lengthy quotations. I see each as a standalone (rather than 'representative') example, but in each case I begin to draw out conceptual arguments inspired by Ravaisson's theorisation of habit. In the first example (from Kilquhanity democratic school), one of the teachers made the observation that teaching embodied habits can be a way to persuade children about *why* they are learning something.

> "A kid would say, 'Why do I have to use this saw?' No, I'll not tell you why you can't use another one. [...] I find myself making a link naturally between how the body moves and what is achieved. I key into that quickest. The Japanese, their saws work when you pull, ours when you push. It's showing them the difference. That explanation, whether verbal or physical, is important. I make the sound of how it should sound. I speak to them and go 'shoo, shoo'. I put my hand on the saw with them, to feel the rhythm of it. Sometimes, you need to see, to hear, to feel." (Harry, teacher and ex-pupil at Kilquhanity democratic school, Scotland)

Harry's point helps us to understand both *how* and *why* the acquisition of habit should figure in learning. For him, the eventual ability to appreciate how to properly pull a saw through a piece of wood was instrumental to understanding what is to be "achieved". The "explanation" of a task was accomplished through feeling "the rhythm of it". This is a seemingly obvious point about the acquisition of embodied skills. However, it speaks to one of the many features of Ravaisson's conception of how habits can be either made or 'undone' (Carlisle, 2010, p 141). That is, in Ravaisson's schema (in contrast to Claxton and others), habits are not easily accessible to cognitive reflection or learning techniques. They are – by definition – hard to see, because they involve the diminution of perception. Thus, 'awareness of habit has to be cultivated at the level of sensations, feelings, involuntary thoughts' (Carlisle, 2010, p 141). Learning to use a saw is not merely undertaken in the visual register but in the aural and haptic registers: that is how the "explanation" of habit proceeds.

My second example expands on the question of 'un-doing' habits, and is taken from a care farm in Scotland.

> "With young people it's mostly about changing behaviour. Getting a break. Seeing the world's not all bad out there. And what I always try to do is they always leave here and leave a mark, that they can say they did that. Mending a stile or a gate, or whatever. Not I've broken this, or I've broken that,

which they have done in the past. [...] It's building up self-esteem. They need something to make them feel good about themselves. [...] Not too much pressure, and reorienting, so that when they see a half-broken pipe, they don't just instinctively kick it, they ask straight away, how can I fix that? It's *channelling the same energy*, you can fix it with the same kind of energy, changing the mindset – using a power tool, if [it] feels the same, you get the same kind of buzz, release, but look at the end result. [...] You can see they become more confident. The way they stand, things like that, their body language, it's the only way you can judge it really. Or, [...] they will become confident to make decisions – how much food for the hens, measuring it out. Say, I'll show them for the first couple of weeks, but then, taking a step back, I won't tell them. They're doing it without thinking that I'm watching them, they just start doing it. Not all of them will get it right, but they will gradually be distanced, from me, and do things by themselves." (Clive, care farm practitioner, Scotland, emphasis added)

Clive's experience resonates with Helena's, the young person who spoke about her feelings of increased self-worth after repetitious work at a care farm (mentioned earlier). On the face of it, Clive's quotation indicates once again how alternative learning spaces view themselves *as* alternative – as remedial, therapeutic spaces that can support young people out of school – giving them "a break", as he puts it. But I think that Clive is pointing to something slightly different, and perhaps more profound. He indicates that the un-doing (or, we could say, 'un-learning') of habit is a process of "channelling" an already-existing "energy" in a new direction – towards an inclination to "fix", not destroy. I want to concentrate here on the idea that (in Clive's own words) there are particular energies that flow through an individual that can nevertheless be "re-oriented" through carefully orchestrated physical tasks and a gradual process of withdrawal by an educator. The processes of distraction, implication and repetition (discussed above) are all present here. All of this chimes with Ravaisson's (2008, p 57) conception of habit 'not as an external necessity of constraint, but a necessity of attraction and desire'. This desire is, I think, the very "energy" described by Clive: the very same "buzz", the same "release", in the brain-body-material assemblage of the young person (compare Dewsbury, 2011; see also Gibson-Graham, 2006, p 130). The question for Clive is one of how a young person can learn to satisfy the very same function of desire through fixing, not breaking. Clearly, he believed that through showing, repeating and then gradually retreating, young people could learn to "do it by themselves" without even realising they had done so. As I have already stated, this non-cognitive undoing of habit is central to Ravaisson's understanding of the term.

The final example I want to take is from homeschooling. This is because – in part in justifying why they do what they do – homeschoolers refer to changes in the emotional and behavioural disposition of their children, as well as their relationships with their children (Lois, 2009; Merry and Howell, 2009). Both parents and young people articulated some of the differences between how they act and how children who attend mainstream schools behave.

> "It's very important to learn ways of being. In my view, homeschooled children are different. When a school kid comes in to our group, they act in a certain way. And it's almost like our children de-school them, and mould them. They might come in to try to impress them and our kids would look blank. They just wouldn't understand. They've not had that competitiveness that comes at school. After a couple of weeks the kid will usually, not always, stop trying and then will just hang around. It can be difficult." (Annette, homeschooler, London)

> "And when you go to educational places [like museums], they [staff] expect them to behave as school children. Like learning to queue up. They're really quite funny. And ours are like lounging around. Sometimes it's funny and sometimes you think oh, they're [homeschooled children] awful. It just doesn't matter to us. Homeschooled children don't know how to sit on chairs. If you give them a row of chairs, some will sit on them, others will turn them upside down, others will sit on them backwards." (Rowena, homeschooler, London)

> "I was told to calm down, because I hug too many people. I was like, yeah. That's not calming down. I'm the calmest person there. They're all the ones who are uptight. I'm like, calm down. It's kind of weird, it makes me cringe, the difference between the seriousness. It's seriousness of two kinds. Like me and my sister and my brother, we are serious about what we do when we're into something. But this is

something else. They're even serious about having fun. Like so competitive. You tell a funny story, and someone has a funnier one that goes even further." (James, homeschooled young person, aged 15, London)

Significantly, Ravaisson rarely considers the role of feelings in the course of learning or undoing habits (Carlisle, 2010). The conclusion we can take from Rowena and James is that particular emotions *flow* from the meeting of different expressions of similar kinds of habit. That is, when the same habitual 'energies' (to take Clive's term) are channelled differently in two different people; but when those two people meet, those differences become evident, and are expressed as emotion. Thus, James talks about two kinds of "seriousness" – calm, concentrated seriousness and competitive seriousness. Each could be taken as a different habituation to seriousness; and when they meet, it makes James "cringe". A similar point can be made regarding Rowena's observation of homeschooled and mainstream-schooled children queuing – differences she finds "funny". It is, then, in this emotional response to differential habits that we see a further example of what makes some alternative learning spaces dissonant, if not 'alternative'.

The second point to make about these quotations concerns Annette's experience of how homeschooling groups "de-school" children who have been in mainstream education. Here, it seems that it is the force of *collective* habit that makes the difference. This is a two-way, collective process about which Ravaisson says little (as he focuses on how individual bodies acquire habits). Rather than emotion simply flowing *from* habit, the changing *of* habit also flows from the affects created *by* collective habits (for instance, homeschooled children "lounging around" (Rowena). Here, in the terms of non-representational theory, affective habits can be understood as a sense of 'push in the world' (Thrift, 2004, p 64); as a more-than-personal force 'through which any situation or event proceeds through a potential filled change in the distribution of background intensities that only subsequently comes to fold into the production of an emotional re-ordering' (Anderson, 2006, p 219). The collective force of habit – how homeschooled children are not impressed by showing off, or sit on chairs differently – is one which acts as this push, this ordering of background intensities, that eventually prompts emotional and embodied changes within a new member of the group.

Annette acknowledged that this process could take time and be "difficult". Significantly, Ravaisson is more forthcoming on this issue. He does discuss how the undoing of habits can take time and cause significant pain for the individual concerned, although that pain does diminish over time. Thus, just as with the acquisition of an earlier habit, '*movements* or situations that are initially most tiring become over time the most convenient' (Ravaisson, 2008, p 67, emphasis added). I do not seek to broach the rather thorny question of whether such pain is worth the effort – of whether the acquisition of these particular habits and the unlearning of 'schooled' habits is always a positive thing. However, it is my view that, in their critiques of mainstream schooling, many alternative and radical educators are at least implicitly concerned by the kinds of habits acquired by children in schools. I leave it to a more open discussion about what desirable, alternative habits might be and how they should be learned: the case studies in this section provide the briefest of indications, but nothing more.

Conclusion: learning habits (I)

In the final section of this chapter I began to sketch out some features of a theory of habit that is at least partly applicable to several kinds of alternative learning spaces. In the context of other possible theorisations of habit (located in education, psychology and elsewhere), I have sought to develop a theorisation of habit inspired by the work of Félix Ravaisson. I chose Ravaisson's work not only because of the resonance with non-representational theory, but because, as I began to show in the last section, his work evokes some of the concerns of educators and (a limited selection of) learners. I fully acknowledge that other theorisations of habit would probably resonate in some very different ways with the experiences of alternative educators and learners. However, this chapter provides a step along the way to a more detailed theorisation of habit and the 'good life' and, thereby, towards my eventual argument in Chapter Eight that some alternative learning spaces present autonomous, dissonant versions of life-itself. In order to progress towards this argument, in this conclusion I tie together what an emphasis upon embodied *movements* has contributed to the arguments thus far. I begin by focusing upon pragmatics: upon the strategies employed in alternative learning spaces to manage and capitalise upon particular kinds of bodily movement. It is these kinds of movement that add further weight to the livelier conception of alternative learning *spatialities* to which I am committed in this book. I then discuss how those strategies were specifically directed towards the learning/unlearning of habit, with a little further reference to Ravaisson's *Of Habit*.

In this chapter I have touched on a range of practical strategies through which alternative educators seek to channel bodily movements and, to a lesser extent, mobilities. It is, I think, helpful to list the major strategies in a quite straightforward way

- *Combination.* This refers to the process whereby homeschoolers seek to immerse their children in as great a variety of 'everyday' spaces – parks, museums, libraries – as possible. This props up the more general idea among alternative (and radical) educators that learning should be imminent and immanent to everyday life (Kraftl, in press, 2013b).
- *Movement-between places.* This refers to the kinds of learning that are made possible through contemporary mobility practices, especially travel by mechanised transport. Again, homeschoolers found that both kinds of learning – informal and formal – took place when travelling in the car or on the bus.
- *Taking time/stillness.* Some educators negotiated forms of mobility and stasis concurrently. For instance, the car is a place where the capacity for bodily movement is reduced; elsewhere, educators tried to find places to just sit. In both cases stasis afforded time and space for reflection.
- *Walking.* Several educators highlighted the importance of walking. The cadence of walking and the non-combative, side by side positioning of teachers' and learners' bodies could provide the opportunity for talk – and equally for silent reflection. Walking in familiar *places* also afforded *distraction* (discussed later), imagination and creativity.
- *Repetition and manual training.* The repetition of tasks is not anathema to alternative learning spaces. In fact, it is valorised across a range of spaces, including homeschooling, care farming, forest schooling and human scale education. Repetition does not always imply learning by rote. Rather, the perfection of particular tasks (including walking through doors, sawing, pouring, cleaning) may be central to the development of creativity, confidence, empathy and freedom (discussed later).
- *Gradual withdrawal.* In selected learning spaces (like care farms), practitioners will show young people how to do a task but gradually, and imperceptibly, withdraw themselves. The intention is that young people will learn skills – like cleaning out chickens – without realising they have done so.
- *Art/play.* In many alternative learning spaces – and in the mainstream educational sector – it is recognised that children learn in different ways. However, art and movement are considered to be 'realms' in

which young children live, and through which skills like literacy can be acquired. It is open to (probably endless) debate about whether those 'realms' are constituted by habits that are 'natural' or 'learned', or whether instinct proceeds via a combination of the two.

In anticipation of subsequent chapters, it is possible to 'map' the above strategies against Ravaisson's writings on habit. That is, it is possible to begin to articulate *how* the above strategies are productive of habit, and of how habits can be learned or unlearned. I would like to highlight four themes in this regard, which both resonate with and extend Ravaisson's treatise on habit.

In the first theme, two of the major *temporalities* at play in alternative learning spaces actually mirror Ravaisson's own position on the temporalities of habit. These are the entwined notions of 'repetition' and 'taking time' (Chapter Five). Ravaisson argues quite straightforwardly that the repetition of a task leads to familiarisation, habit, and the diminution of both perception and habit. I have argued, specifically, that this leads to *distraction* from the habitual task at hand – like walking to the railway station. For Ravaisson, this can open up the possibility of freedom because humans are no longer bound 'servilely to their routines' (Carlisle, 2010, p 129). In my examples, I showed rather more particularly how the distractions afforded by habit provided occasion for creativity, fantasy and imagination. I ask the question, then, in Chapter Eight, whether such kinds of distraction are the necessary precursor for transformative utopian fantasies, which may flow from educational settings (for now, compare Gardiner, 2004; Kraftl, 2008). The second temporality is duration – the necessity for 'taking time' to unlearn habits. The process of taking time may well involve repetition, and vice versa. For it may only be in the repetitive process of attending a forest school, over a period of weeks, that particular dispositions come to be learned or unlearned (Knight, 2009). In supplementing Ravaisson's argument, I have provided examples in this book of the need to take time not only to unlearn 'bad' habits, but also to produce 'good' habits – such as reflective contemplation in the park.

The second theme I want to highlight is how habits may be reconfigured or 'channelled' in and through alternative learning spaces. It is in this sense that alternative learning spaces may reflect a particular mission with regard to their local community, or with regard to the remedial value of what they do for excluded or severely bullied young people – or, less spectacularly, with regard to the negative effects of increasingly standards-driven, neoliberalised forms of education. I have already made the argument that some practitioners (and I have only cited a few specific examples) try to recalibrate the very same energies that make a young person destructive and withdrawn, into an instinct to fix, mend, create, or proceed with confidence. Ravaisson argues that the inclination of habit is always towards the 'good', although in contemporary societies that 'good' is perhaps even harder to define than it was for Ravaisson in the 19th century. What is more certain is that, in the examples I have cited, educators had found success with particular strategies that enabled them to channel young people's bodily movements in ways that *they*, at least, deemed desirable (and with which I suspect some readers will agree). They were trying to foster habits that would lead to greater individual autonomy for children in later life.

The third theme to which I draw attention relates to the second: to the ways in which similar 'energies' or 'desires' (for Ravaisson) may result in different habits, which, when they coincide, may produce provocative effects. By this, I mean, for instance, the different ways in which (some) homeschooled children might use a chair, or queue, or respond to an adult, compared with (some) mainstream-educated children. I also mean the ways in which (some) young people's habits may change over time, after their interaction with the people and material spaces that constitute alternative learning spaces. This is a slightly toned-down version of what homeschooling parents, forest school and care farm practitioners have said to me. Toned down as it is, the point I have made in this chapter is that it is when different habitual reactions to the same event or space *coincide* that something interesting happens, and that the 'something interesting' operates in both emotional and affective domains. Ravaisson neither accounts for these kinds of coincidence, nor, in detail, for their emotional or affective import. At the very least, when mainstream-educated and homeschooled children bump into each other in a museum, there could be immediate emotional repercussions (humour, perhaps). More significantly, such moments might prompt reflection about how what I called the 'force of habit' of a community creates an affective 'push', with the power to change a newcomer fresh from school. While this force may be rare in some learning spaces, we can add it to the list of features through which forms of collective autonomy might be constituted – this time through affective, collaborative displays of habit. More significantly still – and going beyond the examples provided in this chapter – I have argued elsewhere that the coincidence of two similar but distinct entities can provoke effects and affects that, following Freud and Heidegger, are *unheimlich* (uncanny): they may be humourous, but also bemusing, estranging and provocative. In this way, they may create pause for thought, critical reflection, unexpected collaboration or, even, contain a kernel of a kind of unsettling utopianism (Kraftl, 2007). Thus, we might not only understand alternative learning spaces as microcosmic, prefigurative utopian practices, reflective of but somewhat disjoined from the mainstream (Fielding and Moss, 2011). Rather, we might also seek to further understand how the dis/connections between mainstream and alternative spaces (Chapter Four) could productively operate at the level of embodied encounter: in the possible affective provocations that ensue from the meeting of dissonant habits.

This latter observation leads to a fourth and final theme: specifically, the status and kind of interpersonal relationships implied by the cultivation of habit. These relationships are the subject of Chapter Seven, but I do want to make a couple of remarks here in closing this chapter. These are inspired by Helena's experience at a care farm (mentioned earlier in this chapter). She told me that it was the *repetition* of activities that had made her more compassionate and empathetic towards animals – to "how they feel". This resonates with Ravaisson's key claim that habits denude the receptivity of perception but may increase a person's capacity to empathise with others. For if, for instance, one becomes more habituated to the needs of an animal, or, in a medical context, less affected by the suffering of those in pain, Ravaisson argues one is actually *better placed* to care. Hence, 'repetition or continuity makes moral activity easier and more assured [...] the inner joys of charity develop more and more in the heart of one who does good [... and] love is augmented by its own expressions' (Ravaisson, 2008, p 69). Habits are, if you like, not only affecting but infectious, in a positive way. Herein, Ravaisson provides a welcome supplement to the conviction of several educational theorists – bell hooks and Paulo Freire among them – that radical educators should seek to foster relationships of empathy and love. I turn to some of these interpersonal relationships in the next chapter, which also allows me to return in more detail to the concept of autonomy.

SEVEN

Inter/personal relations: scale, love and learning habits (II)

This chapter focuses on some of the interpersonal relations that sustain alternative learning spaces. Drawing on the arguments in previous chapters, it asks what kinds of interpersonal relationships are – in the view of educators – most appropriate for learning. I look initially at how these relationships are characterised – for instance, as 'friendship' or 'family'. I then interrogate the intensity of these relationships, focusing, as in previous chapters, upon feelings, and especially those like empathy, care and love. Finally, I return to the question of habit. However, rather than thinking about how habits are internalised within young people to change their behaviour (Chapter Six), I want to consider how the learning and unlearning of habits can be understood as outward facing. That is, through some detailed case studies, I argue that some educators advocate spiritual conceptions of love, which are integral to the production of habits of generosity, care and responsibility to *others*, rather than the self. Ultimately, then, this chapter is not simply about the roles of interpersonal relationships in learning. This would be a far from original topic in terms of the broader field of education studies, even if a largely untapped area of research for geographers. Rather, this chapter is about what kinds of feeling and habit are emergent from interpersonal relations in alternative learning spaces.

In doing the above, this chapter also provides some reflection on that most geographical of terms: scale. The question of scale is actually an important one for alternative learning spaces. This is because, as I have repeatedly stated, many alternative approaches to education somehow emphasise 'smallness' (Carnie, 2003; Sliwka, 2008). In some contexts, this can mean the physical smallness of the classroom, with bespoke furniture designed at child level (as is the case in many Montessori, Steiner and human scale classrooms). At the same time, most mainstream schools use furniture designed for children, so other than the volume of the classroom itself, we cannot with any confidence claim that it is the physical size of the space that makes the difference. Rather, many alternative educators – take human scale education as an obvious example – adopt a broader definition of smallness. This definition usually encapsulates class size, the intimacy of teacher–pupil relationships, and a desire for a caring community where everyone (of whatever age) knows and trusts everyone else. As I have argued throughout this book, spatiality – in this case, scalar spatiality – implies so much more than physical space.

Given the emphasis on smallness in many alternative learning spaces, it would be quite defensible to end the story there. But, while I do account for the small scale in this chapter, I also want to *upscale* my argument. I want to provide a sense of something *more*, something *beyond*, the small scale and the local. Strikingly, this 'something beyond' is not separated from the small scale. Rather, it is prompted by the very kinds of interpersonal intimacy, empathy and love that smallness (mentioned above) implies. That is, that channelled appropriately, interpersonal love can exceed, or spill over, into a loving disposition that maybe presumptively generous (Connolly, 2008), empathetic, caring or responsible. It is for this reason that, at the end of the chapter, I return to the question of habit (Chapter Six). I will argue that, in some examples, interpersonal love is productive of, and recursively produced by, a more outward-looking, loving disposition, manifested as a kind of readiness to empathise with others. As we shall see, often those others are very often unknown others, located physically and conceptually 'outside' the immediacy of a particular learning space. Indeed, sometimes, they may be situated on the other side of the world.

Thus, my argument will be that loving habits maybe *spatialised* beyond immediacy, in an intermingling of spatial scales (Massey, 2005). I highlight now that I see this as yet another form of *connectedness*, crucial to an understanding of alternative learning spaces as *autonomous* (Chapter Four). I also highlight now that there are overlaps here with the kinds of generosity to others already accounted for in autonomous social spaces (Pickerill and Chatterton, 2006) and diverse economic spaces (Gibson-Graham, 2006). As I will show in Chapter Eight, these overlaps are far from coincidental, and this chapter will flesh out what the role of autonomous learning spaces might be in light of other attempts to exceed neoliberal versions of life-itself. Before I do so, I introduce two important academic contexts for this argument: research on interpersonal relations; and geographical theorisations of scale.

Interpersonal relations, interpersonal scales

The significance of interpersonal relationships to educational research is undoubted. There exist large and overlapping bodies of work that consider different kinds of interpersonal relationships in educational settings. Let me give four brief examples. First, there are those studies that have explored the development of friendship amongst children in different age groups, and their outcomes for participation and attainment in particular subjects (for varied examples, see Corsaro and Eder, 1985; Vaquera and Kao, 2008). Second, much work has been devoted to the role of parents and other family members in supporting (or compromising) children's learning and educational choices (Lareau, 1987; Ball et al, 1995; Brooks, 2003; Moore, 2004). Third, scholars have explored the role of power relations and emotion in teacher–learner interactions (Noyes, 2005; Arnot and Reay, 2007; see also Chapter Five). Fourth, much attention has been paid to the construction of identity through interpersonal relationships in educational settings – particularly in terms of gender, class and ethnicity (Willis, 1977; Reay, 1998).

All four of the above issues have gained increasing prominence in emergent geographies of education, as well as in earlier research on children's geographies that was situated in schools (see Chapter Two). At the same time, geographers have turned increasing attention to what Hopkins and Pain (2007) term 'relational' geographies of age – in particular to intergenerational relations, tensions and collaborations that take place in both public and private spaces. Thus, of late, geographers have begun to turn attention to family relationships (Hallman, 2010), intimacy (Valentine, 2008) and, most recently, friendships (Bunnell et al, 2011). Importantly, many authors pay close attention to the role of intimacy, although not necessarily love, as I do in this chapter (Valentine, 2008; Bunnell et al, 2011). Despite the above advances, geographical studies of family and friendship remain in their early stages. This chapter – indeed this book – makes a key empirical contribution to these literatures, specifically by exploring the role of family and friendships in alternative learning spaces.

Whereas research on education and interpersonal relations is still emerging in geography, the same is not true of scale. Geographers' ruminations on scale have been enduring and diverse. However, it is possible to distil some pertinent differences in approach (see Marston et al, 2005, for a longer review). Some of the earliest understandings of scale viewed scale as a nested hierarchy – from the local, through the regional, national, and ultimately to the global scale. Traditionally, the 'local' has been privileged as the scale at which spaces acquire meaning – as places (Cresswell, 2005). Conversely, the global scale has been afforded most explanatory power (that is, where globally-scaled processes can override lesser-scaled processes). In this conception, scales are viewed as pre-given entities. More recently, scale has been viewed as social construction. In this way, as Taylor (1982) showed, scales could be constructed in the service of a particular mode of political-economic organisation, like capitalism. Hence, the idea of 'globalisation' has been actively narrated by large, multinational corporations seeking to capitalise upon consumer markets in different geographical contexts. The idea that globalisation is a social construction is a particularly powerful one, which, for instance, underpins Gibson-Graham's (2006) analysis that global capitalism is not a monolithic, faceless entity and can be challenged and eluded. This view of scale is also important because, as Gibson-Graham's work suggests, it means that the global scale holds no more meaning or explanatory power than the local, as they are both ongoing constructions, often contingent upon one another. The third – and most controversial – theorisation of scale is that there is no such thing as scale (Marston et al, 2005). Following Actor-Network theorisations of relationality, they argue that even social constructivist notions of scale work *from* the idea that certain scales exist before they begin their analysis. Instead, they prefer a focus on 'sites' – upon temporary constellations of people, things, infrastructures and discourses that come together through events. Sites, then, are produced only by events, and not vice versa. Sometimes certain events endure, and, therefore, particular sites can take forms that are denoted as scales – like nation states or 'big' buildings (Jacobs, 2006). While an attractive idea, some critics have argued that the notion of 'sites' tends to efface the fact that, for instance, less powerful social groups actively use particular scales in order to constitute resistance or protest (witness the Occupy movement of 2011, which was knowingly local and global; see also Jonas, 2006).

Whether one takes things as far as Marston et al (2005), one implication of all this is that, if scales are mutable and dynamic, it becomes more difficult to assert that particular things can or should happen at a particular scale. This goes especially for feelings like care, love and responsibility, which have traditionally been viewed as local, proximate, affective and embodied concerns (Popke, 2006). In this vein, geographers have begun conceptualising the theoretical and empirical possibilities for care at a distance. One response has been to see care as a universal ethical disposition that binds each human being to every other – a feature of Emanuel Levinas' work (Barnett, 2005) and one element of the spiritual conceptions of love I attend to below. Another response has been to try to explore how people in one context can actively demonstrate at least a disposition for caring for distant or unknown others – for instance in work on giving to charity or the consumption of fair trade foods (Bryant and Goodman, 2004). In this way, if scales are mutable and constructed, there is no necessary moral foundation for caring for those who are closest *before* those furthest away (although, equally, there may be justifiable reasons for doing so) (Whatmore, 1997).

These ideas are not incontrovertible, but this is not the place to debate their relative merits any further (see Popke, 2006, for more). Rather, I want to set up my subsequent analysis in this chapter with two final points. The first is that, whereas in Chapter Six I saw habit as something that was located within an individual or shared by proximate individuals, for the sake of those individuals (as does Ravaisson, 2008), in this chapter I want to ask *what else* and *where else* habit might be for. In other words, I ask how the effects and affects of particular habits might exceed the individual human body and its proximate surroundings to engender care, love or responsibility at a distance. Thus, the effectiveness and affective-ness of a body may not simply reside in that body literally, seeing or being seen, touching or being touched. The second point is that this chapter sets up the analysis in Chapter Eight because it anticipates alternative/autonomous forms of life that, according to their proponents, could be 'good' forms of life if allowed to *endure*. This means a key role for habit as one among several aspects of life that take hold through duration. Other forms include the kinds of 'sites' that, for Marston et al (2005), last longer than others and may acquire a status as 'scales'; or, constellations of life matter that obtain seeming coherence as human bodies, buildings or plants (Jacobs, 2006; Coole and Frost, 2010). In this chapter I examine what are the 'bigger' goals towards which alternative educators aim by fostering interpersonal learning habits that might endure both within children's bodies and beyond. I build towards this argument via an empirical consideration of two kinds of interpersonal relationship: friendship and the family(-like).

Friendship: intragenerational and intergenerational support

> "My worry was that home-educated [HE] children would be unusual, that my children would be. Especially because my eldest was so sociable and I knew he wanted to be able to mix with lots of children. I knew I didn't want him to end up strange. I wanted to see how sociable it could be, and I could see that HE groups were very sociable. I went to a couple of home-ed groups. One of the things that struck me was the mix of age groups and the opportunities for play and activity that weren't segregated. *It looked very family-like.* Big families, all together, very natural, including older teenagers. We have lots of activities where older girls

nurture younger girls and older boys teach younger boys. I can see the benefits for all ages. The older ones can play for longer because the younger ones are still playing." (Hannah, homeschooler, emphasis added)

As Hannah indicates, a key concern for parents who choose to homeschool their children is whether they will have opportunities to make friends. This concern is not unique to homeschooling. A key question asked about human scale education is whether – given the smallness of class sizes – children will have an adequate mix of classmates to find friends of their age (Carnie, 2003). The same observation can be made in many Steiner and Montessori schools where – as I discovered during my visits – similarly small class sizes can mean a greater mixing of age groups than one would find in most mainstream schools. A further concern for parents and critics alike has been one of whether children attending what are often independent, fee-paying schools are exposed to social difference – for instance in terms of social class, ethnicity or religion.

In this section, I offer just one way to address these questions and concerns, by focusing on the kinds of friendships that children forge. I do not have space to address issues of class, ethnicity or religion here. I would observe, in passing, that many educators indicated that they felt their learning spaces were characterised by significant social diversity – especially at urban care farms, London-based homeschooling groups, and human scale schools. However, further research on this specific issue would be required to substantiate these claims (see Rothermel, 2003; Collom and Mitchell, 2005, on homeschooling and social diversity). Instead, drawing on recent work in geography, my focus will be upon *age* relations (Hopkins and Pain, 2007). My essential argument is that fears about making friends are often addressed by what appears initially to be another fear – around the mixing of age groups. The upshot is that many alternative learning spaces provide greater opportunities for both intragenerational friendships (with other children, of different ages) and intergenerational friendships (with adults) than do mainstream schools. Indeed, one can argue with relative confidence that a distinguishing feature of alternative learning spaces is that they pay less attention to categorising children by age group.

I will argue that educators view these intra- and intergenerational friendships as crucial for the foundation of trusting, caring and loving communities of learning. I will also begin to tease out the importance of habit within these interpersonal relationships. As Hannah indicated in the quotation that began this section, mixed-age friendships can provide all kind of outcomes: they can be very nurturing; they can afford older children the chance to teach and mentor younger children (teaching being an important way to reinforce learning); and they can allow older children the opportunity to "play for longer", rather than reinforce the idea that playing is not acceptable amongst teenagers or adults.

The implications for young people themselves can be profound. Rebecca – a young person about to go to university, having been home educated until the age of 16 – reflected upon her experiences of friendship with older children:

> "It's really weird. I found people my age who go to school, I don't get on with as well. We have completely different interests. But people who are older, the ones who go to school and the other home-ed kids, I get on better with. I am older than them [people in her age group]. It's been the same – going to home-ed groups, you grow up surrounded by older kids. And I've always been attracted to them more than making friends my age." (Rebecca, homeschooled young person, aged 18, London)

I observed during several visits to social gatherings organised by homeschoolers that children were usually free to mix with anyone they wanted to, of whatever age. However, at care farms and forest schools, the situation can be very different. As I indicated in Chapter Five, many care farms and forest schools have to set careful boundaries between different learners. Therefore, usually, new learners work on a one-to-one basis with a practitioner. One-to-one learning is deemed important for several reasons. First, it offers the opportunity for non-threatening, practical-based work, through which a young person's (somehow 'problematic') relationship with adults and with learning can be recalibrated (Chapter Six). Practitioners are often viewed more as 'mentors' than teachers. Second, it provides a smallness of scale – an intimacy – that is meant to remedy what may be lacking at home or school. And third, their safeguarding measures dictate that individual learners must be kept apart until they are 'ready' to interact with others.

Clearly, in many cases, during a six-week, one-to-one programme of perhaps three hours per week, young people may not forge friendships with their 'mentor' or anyone else, although they may successfully reintegrate into school. But in some cases, if one-to-one work has led to enough of a shift in a young person's disposition to others, they may start to work in small groups, from which inter- and intragenerational friendships might ensue:

> "If you think about it carefully, you manage it carefully. You introduce them at the right time. You can spark off all kinds of new relationships, sometimes friendships, between some very different youngsters, and young people and adults."
> (Daniel, care farm practitioner, English Midlands)

At a different care farm, from a young person's perspective, the opportunity to work with other learners *had* led both to friendships and a sense that she was cared for:

> "Another thing about having the same task each week is that you build up over time. I've got some of my best friends here, who are a lot older, they're old men basically, and they are amazing, they can do it all on their own, really easily, without thinking [...] and, so, like, they buddy up with the younger ones, like me, caring for the younger ones." (Helena, young person, aged 16, at care farm in north of England)

Helena was the young person quoted speaking about repetition and care for animals in Chapter Six. Again, she returned to the question of *habit*: she focused upon the ability of the "older men" to fulfil their work at the farm "without thinking". For her, this meant that they had the time to teach her, to "buddy up" and, in this way, they had become her "best friends". In this way we can see at least two kinds of habit entwined at a place like a care farm. Whereas in Chapter Six, I documented how Helena's habitual work with animals had made her think about "how they feel", here, I am emphasising how older men's habituated work made *Helena* feel cared for. In fact, this captures the essence of a care farm: they are not *simply* spaces in which young people may experience 'therapy' by cleaning out some rabbits for an hour a week, but in which multiple, interrelated forms of caring habits foster a kind of caring atmosphere (Berget and Braastad, 2008). I am suggesting that interpersonal relationships – and intergenerational friendships, specifically – are a crucial element of this atmosphere.

In the above way, we can see interpersonal friendships as just as important an element in the production of learning affects as material dis/order (Chapter Five). If we turn to *intra*generational relationships again, it is possible to see something similar happening amongst much younger children in the Montessori classroom. Maria Montessori was adamant that children must feel 'most comfortable' in order for free, creative learning to take place (Maria Montessori, cited in Hainstock, 1997, p 83). On the one hand, as documented in Chapter Five, this meant that the material environment must be right for the child: 'the room must be dedicated to him [sic]' (Maria Montessori, cited in Hainstock, 1997, p 83). On the other hand, and in tandem, children had to learn to respect others, not because they have been told to do so by a teacher, but:

> "[t]he child comes to see […] this is a reality that he meets in his [sic] daily experience […] waiting one's turn, becomes an *habitual* part of life […]. The charm of social life is in the number of different types that one meets […]. What matters is to mix the ages […] [o]ur schools show that children of different ages help one another." (Maria Montessori, cited in Hainstock, 1997, p 83, emphasis added)

Thus, taken together, the material and social spatialities of the Montessori classroom are productive of a caring learning atmosphere in which, as Montessori herself explicitly recognised, respect becomes *habituated*. To some readers this may sound quite remarkable, but, in the contemporary classroom, teachers still put this into practice with very young children. One teacher put this process in terms of 'trust':

> "Trust is taught and learned. They start at age three. They learn it's a safe environment. They come at two and three, the older children are helping them. Even the toddlers help each other with their coats. They can hardly wait until they can be the helper, because they think they are the big kids then. Trusting comes because there is always someone there helping them in a nice way. So you feel good about yourself. Not just your friend – it can be anybody. It can also be when some of them are being too harsh with some equipment, they take care for equipment, care for community […]. When they go to public school and they are assigned a seat, they can't get up. The Montessori children *know themselves*." (Athena, Montessori teacher, US, emphasis added)

Athena's quotation begins to highlight the way in which I want to understand habit in this chapter. That is, that Montessori education is – like many other alternative approaches – at least in part about the learning and happiness of individuals. It is therefore in part about children acquiring individual habits – about 'knowing themselves' (which I interpret in Athena's quotations as being both about self-confidence and simply knowing what to do in a situation as a matter of habit). This conception of habit resonates with Ravaisson's. But there is something more here: a sense that individual learning habits work recursively with outward-looking dispositions of care. That is, that in 'knowing oneself', one is able to help produce a learning atmosphere in which others feel cared for (and vice versa): so that toddlers "can hardly wait until they can be the helper" – not just for friends but for "anybody".

Whether children appreciate that they are (or are not) learning such habits, it would be virtually impossible to tell. What I did glean at one Steiner school in Wales, where I spent a considerable amount of time, was that the kinds of interpersonal relations (and friendships) recounted above were engrained into children's *memories*. In the Steiner kindergarten, as in the Montessori kindergarten, children embark (albeit unknowingly) on the first stages of acquiring loving habits that will eventually awaken them as 'autonomous' human beings (see Chapter Three). During a painting class, I asked older children (aged 12 to 14) to paint the kindergarten from memory. This process sparked several unanticipated conversations wherein children reminisced about how their friendships had developed in the kindergarten. Two of the children replayed the conversation they had had with each other when they joined the kindergarten aged five, remembering how the older children had showed them how to play particular games and 'looked after them'. Another group of children worked forwards through time, talking about how their friendships had changed since they had left the kindergarten. Instead of painting in the kindergarten, one of the boys – Ethan – chose to paint the school gate instead. I asked him about this and he said:

> "It's very important. I sit there every morning before school. I always have, since I was in the kindergarten. When I'm waiting. I just watch people. And talk to anyone who walks past. I'll talk to anyone me! I know everyone in the school now, all the teachers, all the children, all the parents, and I like to just watch people, see them every day, say hello, and I know they will always say hello back. It's my favourite place really. It makes me feel good, like, to just sit there." (Ethan, young person, aged 13, Steiner school in Wales)

Thus, at this Steiner school, children were very positive about the friendships they had developed with both other children and adults, and about the kinds of interpersonal relations that, as Ethan put it, "make [them] feel good, to just sit there". Whether these feelings had become habituated I am not sure; certainly, they had become engrained in children's collective memories, and had prompted Ethan's desire to sit outside the school every day for several years, just watching and talking to "anyone who walks past".

Despite all of these positive experiences, the picture is not a completely rosy one, of course. It goes without saying that children of different ages (and children and adults) will not always get on, let alone become friends. As one 12-year-old boy at the same Steiner school put it:

> *Derek*: "Steiner school, there's this thing about not being competitive. Apparently we're not supposed to play football. But we do. We play everyday. And people get kicked in the shins."
>
> *Author*: "How come?"
>
> *Derek*: "Err – that's usually me. I don't do it on purpose. But sometimes it causes, like, little fights. But we usually sort it out between us."
>
> *Author*: "Without the teachers?"
>
> *Derek*: "Yeah, usually, if we can. I say we. It's usually me."

Derek's account mirrors young people's experiences of minor skirmishes and fights across several of the kinds of learning spaces I visited. At one homeschooling social club I witnessed a fight between two boys in which a parent had to intervene – at which point several parents openly started to talk about how important it was that homeschooling *not* be seen as a somehow 'perfect' solution to school. There is a residual question about what happens when things go wrong – when there are fights, arguments, and simmering tensions (and I saw a fair few of each at various sites I visited). Responses to this question tended to vary quite widely:

> "Their attitudes and dispositions do change. They do learn alongside playing with the other children, especially the different age groups, which often want to do very different things in the same space. How to take themselves away, sometimes, if they're feeling angry. It's a major part

of learning. They learn to deal with situations, without anybody else stepping in. In broader society, you see parents always stepping in. And the key thing is, it's not just the thinking about it, the theory, that they might learn in citizenship ed at school. It's the immediate thing, the immediate, *impulse* response, almost emotional. They do have to learn how to challenge each other but also how to react in a way that's going to smooth things out, you know." (Maura, care farm practitioner/play worker, East Anglia, emphasis added)

Within reason, at Maura's care farm adults took a step back and allowed children (especially older children) to resolve their own arguments. Maura argued that the resolution of such tensions, as much as the smooth running of friendships, was precisely a matter of habit. She talked of disagreements being resolved through learning "dispositions" (*without* "adults stepping in"); of that "immediate, impulse response" to "challenge" one another but also to "smooth things out". As I documented in Chapter Five, Maura viewed the care farm at which she worked as a space between home and school, which worked with a high proportion of children experiencing socioeconomic disadvantage and disenchantment with school. Strikingly, rather than working on a one-to-one, remedial basis, like other care farms, her care farm offered an open space in which young people could arrive and leave when they wanted and mix with whomever they wanted. But the effect was more or less the same as at other care farms, as mentioned previously: of altering a young person's 'immediate' response from being one of lashing out (a destructive tendency) to one of resolution (a constructive tendency).

Mary's experience of social tensions at homeschooling groups mirrored Maura's, to some extent.

"Yeah, so we educate in a kind of fishbowl here. All the mummies are around. So, they don't always sort their own stuff out. Everyone's the judge and the jury. I don't know, school grounds can get violent, you know. But if you're not careful [in homeschooling], they're not able to sort out the things that we shouldn't even *hear* about." (Mary, homeschooler, talking at homeschool social group, London, original emphasis)

I have suggested thus far that positive, intergenerational relationships between adults and children may form an important element of learning in alternative settings. But both Mary and Maura suggest that this should be carefully managed. As Mary states, with "all the mummies around", the children "don't always sort their own stuff out". Thus, at homeschooling groups, children are able to learn from and care for children of different ages: but the presence of parents means that the resolution of sometimes minor disputes can be unnecessarily painful. Mary's experience inspires two broader points about friendships, intra- and interpersonal relationships in alternative learning spaces. The first is a widespread acknowledgment that the provision of greater freedoms for children to interact with different age groups is something that must be carefully managed. The benefits of interaction with diverse age groups can be many – for learning, for fostering caring friendships, for acquiring particular habits. But the second point is that the presence of adults – especially family members – is something that equally has to be managed. There is a difference between a space being "family-like" (Hannah) and parents intervening where educators feel they should not (Maura, Mary). This is an important distinction because a tendency to loving or presumptively generous dispositions is not the same as 'let's all just get along'. Instead, such a disposition is as much one of acknowledging, working with and challenging differences that may arise (hooks, 2003; Gibson-Graham, 2006). This is something I consider in more detail in the next section, where I explore the significance of family(-like) relationships to alternative learning spaces.

Family(-like) relations: on intimacy, love, but "not being too involved"

At the end of the previous section I argued that the presence of family members (especially parents) within learning environments could be viewed negatively, especially in terms of children's learning to deal with social tensions. However, at most settings, educators did see a role for the family, in some guise, within children's learning. But I want to conceive of 'the family' in a slightly unusual way. Here, I am not talking about the relationship between home and school, or the role parents can play in supporting children's learning (see, for instance, Holloway and Pimlott-Wilson, 2011). I am also not talking about the family as a (nuclear) unit. Rather, I am pointing to a range of what I want to call *family-like* relations that are intended to be productive of particular kinds of feelings. In the previous section I introduced some of these feelings, like trust and care. In this section I emphasise further feelings, centred around intimacy and love. I argue that these latter kinds of emotion characterise relationships that feel more like 'family' than 'friendship', although the distinction between the two can often be fuzzy. Let me be very clear that I am not exploring whether the family per se provides a good framework for learning; and I am certainly not seeking to privilege the (nuclear) family as a distinct unit, as do some homeschoolers (compare Conroy, 2010). Rather, my emphasis is on kinds of relationships and feelings that, in being characterised as family-*like*, purport to offer something that mainstream schools do not.

It is with this distinction in mind that I turn first to homeschoolers. For reasons of balance I must first acknowledge that around a third of the families I spoke with *did* believe in the primacy of the family (over the state) as the environment in which children should be brought up and educated. For various reasons – political, pedagogical, practical, religious - many of these families promoted the role of the nuclear family in children's learning. I say more about this in a separate publication (Kraftl, in press, 2013b). It is not my place to criticise these beliefs. Instead, in this book, I want to highlight that the remaining respondents placed less emphasis upon the family as a social unit, and more upon the kinds of relationships and feelings that supported their children's learning. Thus, they provided a helpful introduction to what I am calling 'family-*like*' relationships.

> "It's not important to have a word to describe who I am, a parent, a teacher. When people ask what we do, I say we home educate. It's much more about the relation, relationship than about who is who. I didn't think about who taught him to talk, or walk, or how. And it's the same with education. And anyway, I like [son's] company. And he's independent enough to have time away from me. I love time away from him. But his umbilical's not there. But I enjoy his company. He's a nice, interesting kid." (Beatrice, homeschooler, English Midlands)

> "The parent-as-teacher and child-as-student dynamic becomes much harder as you get older. And you're setting the work. People would say, are you the teacher? And I thought about it more along the lines of, we're on a path together. And that if something got in the way, we would learn about it and figure it out together. So we would do it as a family. Our approach was kind of [...] that learning was

a family *ethos* for us. We would be a learning-rich family."
(Mary, homeschooler, London)

Several studies have demonstrated that a key parental justification for homeschooling is a desire for greater and continued intimacy with their children (Merry and Howell, 2009). The quotations above seem to reinforce these studies – Beatrice, who "enjoys" her son's company; and Mary, "on a path together" with her children. However, later in this section, I will highlight how a degree of intimacy, which may be expressed as love, is not something unique to learning environments where educators and learners are blood relations. Significantly, Beatrice and Mary actually allow for this possibility, albeit in a subtle way. This is because they both characterise the family as something *more* than the representational categories of which a family is comprised (see Valentine, 2008). Beatrice argued that it was not important to "have a word to describe who I am" – rather, it was about the "relationship" itself. Equally, Mary did not think about who was the "teacher" and who was the "pupil", but stressed being on a path together. For her, this was about having a "family ethos". The difference is a subtle one, because in both cases a family 'ethos' is clearly bound up in being part of a family. But that ethos – what I am calling the *family-like* relation – is one that is based around particular *ways* of relating to and feeling about one another. As Beatrice states, this does not mean she always has to be with her son, acting *as* a family – "the umbilical's not there" – but she still enjoys being with him, acting *like* a family, when that is appropriate. Her reason for continuing with homeschooling was, in fact, that she simply got on extremely well with her son and would probably have stopped if she did not.

I began with homeschooling families because they help, I think, to clarify the distinction between the family and the family-like. To repeat, in distinction to some work on age relations (Hopkins and Pain, 2007), I am less interested in the nameable roles or identities taken on within a family, than in the *non-representational feelings* that characterise the family-like. These latter kinds of feeling were evident across several learning spaces, but especially alternative *schools*. I note that forest schools and care farm practitioners did not articulate any notion of family(-like) relationships, largely, I think, because educators and learners only saw each other for a few hours a week for six or seven weeks. By contrast, it was in human scale schools that family-like relationships were key. Let me provide two longer examples, from Kilquhanity and Wheatfields (introduced in Chapter Five), to illustrate what I mean.

First, at Kilquhanity, Christopher discussed the various ways in which teachers and pupils "connected" with one another, which made the school feel "*like* a large family".

> "Some people say it was *like* a large family. I never felt I had any particular relationship with [teacher], but with [another teacher]. I think what it was, was people had a special relationship – not sexual – in relation to what they needed. I came from a very loving nuclear family, incredibly supportive, so I didn't need a surrogate Dad or Mum. Kilquhanity would be very caring and loving for those who needed it. But very accommodating for everybody else. There were staff who I enjoyed more than others. The maths teacher and the science guy for me. Because we connected." (Christopher, ex-pupil and current teacher, Kilquhanity democratic school, Scotland, emphasis added)

In Christopher's experience, the school provided a caring and *loving* environment. This is one thing that in my mind distinguishes the caring/trusting relations of friendship discussed in the previous section from the notion of family-like relationships that I consider here. For Christopher, this was a "special relationship" that held the potential to be "supportive", depending on what children needed. Christopher's understanding of love – as a feeling of being "accommodated" – resonates in part with those of pedagogical theorists like bell hooks (hooks, 2003). Given that her work focuses upon post-18 education, hooks does allow for romantic and, on occasion, sexual relationships between teachers and pupils (whereas Christopher does not). But it is in the idea of love as a willingness to reach out to another (learner or teacher) that hooks' work interests me more. Citing Parker Palmer, hooks writes of love: 'the act of knowing is an act of love, the act of entering and embracing the reality of the other, of allowing the other to enter and embrace our own' (Palmer, 1983, p 8: cited in hooks, 2003, p 132). For example, Christopher discussed the weekly community meetings at Kilquhanity. This being a democratic school, run along similar principles to Summerhill, the meetings were chaired by children, and children and adults had an equal vote on most (but not all) issues (Cooper, 2007).

> "[There was] love in community meetings. It's a kind of intimacy you don't get in most settings. It takes a certain kind of disposition in yourself, if you're being bullied, to

put that out there in a public meeting. You would find a significant number of kids who found the transition from Kilquhanity to society quite difficult. What that means is that there's something about mainstream society that doesn't understand being trusting, open, honest, trusting and sharing feelings. There is an atmosphere. Something shared. Everyone has as much right to speak as everyone else. Kilquhanity must take some credit for affecting the adults as much as it affected the kids, in positive ways." (Christopher, ex-pupil and current teacher, Kilquhanity democratic school, Scotland)

Once again, the sense I am trying to convey here is that intimacy and love are not feelings tied to the family but constitutive of a family-like "atmosphere" that Christopher felt was lacking in mainstream societies. That atmosphere was constituted by a series of feelings, which Christopher listed, that could predispose members of the community to accommodate others and deal with tensions (like bullying). Whether those feelings are indeed lacking from mainstream societies is a point for debate beyond this book. Certainly, several educational theorists I have cited elsewhere in this book (hooks, Freire, Fielding and Moss) agree that they are missing from most mainstream educational environments. Rather, my point is to observe the connectedness between individual habits ("disposition[s]", as Christopher put it) and the loving, accommodating "intimacy" of the *setting*. As I have been increasingly arguing, habit is personal but also more than personal. As per the title of this chapter, it is *inter/personal*: "something shared", something that affects "the adults as much [...] as the kids, in positive ways". And, specifically, it is something predicated upon a quite particular interpretation of *love* – 'love spatialised' – to which rather odd term I return in the final section of this chapter.

It is in turning to my second example – the human scale education at Wheatfields school – that I want to attend further to the importance of space. At Wheatfields, the younger children are in a 'double class' of 24 children aged four to six, comprising a reception class (usually the first year group in mainstream schools) and Year 1 (the second year group). Previously, as Judy (the headteacher) told me, the children had been in a much smaller classes:

"There were six kids per class – it was too precious, too small. Actually, I think one-to-one teaching is overrated. We are clear about what we do. Not having more than 100 kids

– I don't go for the idea of schools being more than that.
But very small, that's limited and precious. The smallness
is the *intimacy* of the relations between the children.
Us all knowing each other. When there's a new person,
the children say 'hi, how are you?' But enough to have
connections with [others] and different interactions." (Judy,
headteacher, Wheatfields human scale school, England)

The first point about space, then, is how educators articulate exactly
what it means for a school to be 'small' in scale. As Sliwka (2008)
acknowledges, plenty of alternative educators privilege the idea of
'smallness' in some guise; but, as Judy argued strongly, at Wheatfields,
they were "clear" about both the upper *and* lower limits of what 'small'
meant. In effect, a very small class or "one-to-one" situation would
be as inappropriate as a larger (100-plus pupils) setting. Echoing the
kinds of social constructivist (and even abolitionist) conceptions of
scale I discussed earlier, smallness is a situated and relational concept
(Marston et al, 2005). Just like the family-like relations espoused by
homeschoolers, smallness was a feeling as much as something that
could be hierarchically categorised. Although Judy did put some rough
numbers to the term, smallness was as much about "the intimacy of
the relations between the children". Thus, just as I argued in Chapter
Five that 'taking time' was not simply about absolute 'slowness', we see
here that smallness is not simply about making a learning environment
as small as absolutely possible.

The second point about space is connected to the fact that
Wheatfields – like most Steiner and Montessori schools – is meant to
feel *like* a home, but not *be* a home (see Chapter Five; see also Kraftl,
2006a).

"The nursery [for the Reception/Year 1 children] is a haven,
a safe place – it's the first step from home. The parents say
it feels like home. That feels important to us. We value that
continuum. Materially, the mess in the nursery makes us
feel at home. The teachers are a nurturing, gentle presence
with kids, a maternal energy. But not overly – sometimes
you can be overly protective. We are not their parents.
They don't need cuddling all the time, unless they hurt
themselves. That's important, that distinction – it's not a
care space. It's the next step up, daring to be in the bigger
group, but helping kids to be with that. That's what makes
this a learning environment – there's enough to feel safe and

easy, but there's a robustness." (Judy, headteacher, Wheatfields human scale school, England)

Judy articulated perfectly the key to the kinds of family-*like* intimacy and love that I am trying to theorise in this chapter, and which were evident not only in Wheatfields but also in other alternative schools. These could be conceived as further kinds of dis/connection (Chapter Four) that must be carefully negotiated and managed. Thus, for one educator, speaking about his experiences of alternative *and* mainstream schools, good teachers connect with pupils but "the good teachers don't become *too involved* with the pupils" (Harry, ex-pupil and current teacher, Kilquhanity democratic school, Scotland, original emphasis). Or, for an experienced Steiner teacher: "we worry about them being too bound up with their parents – education is about *freeing* children from home. It's another phase – of weaning – a part of nourishment, not of withdrawal" (Michael, Steiner school teacher, English Midlands, emphasis added). It is this that, in Judy's terms, makes a family-like learning environment a *learning* environment, not "a care space". It is not a surrogate home, and teachers are "not their parents". At the same time, there is an attempt to embrace in some particular ways what might be deemed emotions proper to the family – being "nurturing" or "maternal". As Michael put it, this is a form of "weaning" that is meant to nourish children, not force them to "withdraw" from the home. This is, in other words, yet another form of *autonomy* – an egotiation through emotional dis/connection, not a rendering of learning spaces as alternative in a detached sense. Seen in this way, some (and only some) alternative learning spaces are meant to instil a family-like atmosphere that will enable children to become autonomous human beings. It is to this grander aim that I turn in the final section of this chapter.

Habit (II): love scaled, love spatialised

"I think love is extremely important. Clearly not romantic love. Not a sentimental kind. Where you're doing something because you know it's what the children need to do. I would hope that the connections that the teachers have to their own inner lives, their spirituality, and what we share together as teachers in our meetings – I would say that love of what we do, that enthusiasm, that sense of purpose, the future of the individual children – that it might be an atmosphere that might nourish them for the rest of their life. And that is done with a gesture of love. Towards the world, to

> humanity. You can't make them becoming loving people by
> preaching to them but by developing that relationship over
> time." (Michael, Steiner school teacher, English Midlands)

In this quotation, Michael summarises a conception of love that I think
resonates with many alternative educators. While many educators would
not use the term love (and some I interviewed actively resisted it), they
would, I think, recognise the distinct spatiality at play here. That is, as
I observed at the beginning of the chapter, they would acknowledge
at least a weakly *outward-looking* philosophy. By this, I mean a sense in
which intimate interpersonal relationships, and individual habits, could
and *should* manifest themselves positively beyond the small scale of a
particular learning space. Michael encapsulates what I meant when I
said earlier that *interpersonal love is productive of, and recursively produced
by, a more outward-looking loving disposition*. This is love *scaled up*; it is
love *spatialised*. It is not only a love *of* humanity but a love "*towards*"
humanity, as Michael puts it. It is *spatialised* because it combines three
distinctly spatial elements, which reach across spatial scales. First, there
are the individual habits learned by a young person, and which dispose
them to act in certain ways towards others – their "gestures of love"
(Michael). Second, there are the affective, material and interpersonal
spatialities of the school environment – the "atmosphere that might
nourish them" (Michael), the material dis/order (Chapter Five), the
family-like relations of love and intimacy. Third, there is the way in
which this combines with a "sense of purpose" (Michael) to individual
people and humanity, which may be spiritual, political or philosophical
(or any combination thereof) (see Oberski, 2011).

In the rest of this section I provide some further, selective examples
of how other educators explain this 'sense of purpose', and its recursive
relationship with embodied learning habits and family-like relations. I
do so with relatively little analysis at this point, in order to try to give
a fuller sense of what are some complex, multi-scaled dis/connections
between habit, love and the 'wider' world, as one might put it (see also
Ansell, 2009).

At Kilquhanity, Harry suggested that what was required across
all learning settings (alternative and mainstream) was a pragmatic
'cultivation' of responsibility (Gibson-Graham, 2006). He was keen
to impress that neither Kilquhanity nor any alternative learning space
provided the ultimate answer in this regard, but that the kinds of habits
and interpersonal relations fostered at the school could form a step
along the way:

"I think we're going down the road of 'you can't blame me'.
A fear factor. Instead of use your own blinking instincts [in
mainstream schools], follow this programme of work and,
as long as they do it, it's not my [teacher's] fault. *You must
let those instincts rise.* Cultivating those instincts, the self-
belief, which leads eventually into a responsibility. *There's
no one correct way and I'm not saying there's an endpoint.* But
it's cultivating that sensibility that will go in different ways
but always allow you to take more responsibility for yourself
and others. Not 'don't blame me' but 'what can I do and
why?'" (Harry, ex-pupil and current teacher, Kilquhanity
democratic school, Scotland, emphasis added)

In Montessori schools, the rather unfortunate terms 'normalisation'
and 'obedience' are used to describe how children acquire habits that,
ultimately, could form the basis for a more peaceful society (Chapter
Three). Maria Montessori argued that children developed obedience
in three stages: first, through being able to obey, but not each time
they are instructed to do something; second, when they always obey
an order; and, third, when they 'can absorb another person's wishes
and express them in [their] own behaviour. And this is the highest
form of obedience to which present day education ever aspires' (Maria
Montessori, cited in Hainstock, 1997, p 73). Critically, normalisation
comes *in practice* through the habits learned through didactic, material
activities in the Montessori classroom – such as taking out mats at the
beginning of the day:

"From the beginning you would teach them lessons of
grace and courtesy. You would take a mat out, the teacher
would talk about how you take it out, walk around the
mat, do it herself., Then everyone can have a turn if they
want. Then the next day, or you have to give it other
times – usually everyone gets it from day one. As a teacher,
[Maria Montessori] calls her a directress or a guide – you
give them the preparations – the grace and courtesy lessons
help them move around the class and be independent – you
teach them and then allow them to do it. And we do that
every day. It could be control of movement. How to turn
a doorknob. The epitome of the class is if you can do the
silence game. When they are really ready. Every child is told
to sit quietly. It's a game not a punishment. The teacher goes
outside the door. She quietly whispers each child's name.

> They don't move either. Then each stands up and comes to you quietly without making a sound, until they all come. They are doing this for each other really. They are being quiet because they want to do it for each other."(Athena, Montessori teacher, US, emphasis added)

At Findhorn, the connections between habit, materiality, love and the 'wider' world are understood through spiritual teachings (there is not space here to discuss the latter, but for details, see Caddy and Platts, 2004). In these teachings, '[l]ove is compassionate acceptance of and respect for our self and others. Thus choosing to love means learning to take our self as we are and others as they are'(Caddy and Platts, 2004, p 9). Love is both a virtual energy waiting to be actualised *and* something learned: love 'is waiting to be drawn forth' (Caddy and Platts, 2004, p 9) in relations of respect and mutual learning. In practice, this allows for people to love each other in the seemingly contradictory sense I indicated earlier – to get on just fine, while broaching tensions ("our lumps and our bumps and our faults"):

> "[I]t is very much down to the space. You can say your dreams, and no-one will disrespect them. Everyone that comes here comes for some inner healing. To take a breath. And be yourself, it's a place for that. These young people can come up with whoever they are. With their anger, their disconnectedness, not knowing. Love has everything to do with that. This is a wonderful place. This whole place is about love. Ultimately we all want to love each other more and ourselves more. This feeds into the 12-week programme I run. The desire to create it is for the love of our children. The love of humanity. The love and support we have in this community, this family of ours, is just lovely. We all have our lumps and our bumps and our faults. It's a very special place in that sense. It is this place." (Sarah, education officer, Findhorn, Scotland)

Whilst Findhorn was a "special place" because of the interpersonal relationships that sustained love, some of its material spaces were also integral to these feelings.

> "We brought some street kids into the nature sanctuary [see Figure 5.5] as part of the tour. A lot of them are disconnected from society, like I was when I came here – 17

or 18 [years old], hoodies. One of them looked around and said, 'Wow, feel the tranquillity!' And I never even knew they would know that word, let alone what it means. So there's a lot you don't need to do in this place. The foundations, the buildings, the feeling, the people, it just does it for you. If you want the magic of this place to land, go and sit still in the nature sanctuary. It's the unseen world, which is very much part of this place. And we have four sanctuaries on site, open to everybody. In that one you really feel like the earth, you're being pulled into the earth. The original one is like a big green duvet in a caravan. It's very much a love space." (Sarah, education officer, Findhorn, Scotland)

At Findhorn, these mixtures of people and place combine formally as the "education of consciousness":

"My interpretation of education of consciousness is me being conscious of how my actions affect myself, others, nature and the world around us. I could sit here and be very dry and cold and limited in my answers to you. That will have an affect on you, on how you feel about this place, and on others how it reflects on the place. Or I can answer them with love. And that will affect in a positive way your interactions and the people you meet today. And then there is an element of critical reflection. It's like, why is the planet going through a rough time at the minute? But it's not saying it's happening over there, it's saying it's my greed that's doing it, for wanting to go into a supermarket that takes energy out of my community. Or I can go in and pay for whatever I want around the world with a bit of plastic, there's no accountability. It's a consciousness about if I buy this bit of fruit, is this person from Zimbabwe getting paid? It's very simple. It's not about internalising guilt or shame. That's wrong. It's not inward looking only. It's what I see reflected around me, but that's also coming from me, what's around me. It's a level of transparency. Yourself spills out into others. It's seeing too that you're all connected, locally and at a global level." (Sarah, education officer, Findhorn, Scotland)

My final example comes from a human scale school in England. The school was started by a group of teachers inspired, in part, by Ananda Marga philosophies and practices. Ananda Marga is one of the world's largest yoga communities with branches around the world (http://www.anandamarga.net/). Ananda Marga combines classical forms of yoga with a commitment to social service, and has gained prominence through relief work following several large natural disasters in Asia and elsewhere. As a form of neohumanist education, Ananda Marga follows the 'rings of sentiment' model, which 'can be employed to convert narrow [self] sentiment to universal [global] sentiment' (Bussey, 2009, p 13). The 'rings of sentiment' are an explicitly spatial model of human attachment to the world at different scales. The rings radiate more or less concentrically outwards from the body: the ego, the family, geo-sentiment ('attachment to territory'), socio-sentiment ('attachment to race, religion or class', and neohumanism itself ('love and respect for all beings, animate and inanimate, in the universe') (Bussey, 2009, p 14). Each of these rings provides a call to service and responsibility.

> "The ethic [of Ananda Marga] is to combine yoga with social service. The self-expression of the bodily dimension is in its social mission. We do the physical yoga with a meditation process. *Social service flows from care of yourself.* The most well known is the relief team that operated after the Tsunami in India – it's had a presence in relief work. It works at different scales." (Helen, small school practitioner, England, emphasis added)

The school makes no attempt to 'convert' children to Ananda Marga but encourages forms of 'mindfulness' among children, designed to activate reflection at both the most intimate, bodily scale and the global scale. Indeed, many of the school's teaching practices only look loosely like yoga; although inspired by Ananda Marga, they are more redolent of the kinds of family-like intimacy I have been trying to capture throughout this chapter. Helen continued:

> "Some of the guidelines we have to follow in health and safety have almost gone against what we had a feeling for. The children used to answer the door. We had to let that go. The climate of security, safeguarding. A close relationship with the home. An affectionate kind of relationship, [that] is, feeling that you're [teacher] their equal, your brother or sister. Bending your knees and coming down to their level. Trying to use approaches where you repeat back what they're saying, so that they feel you're listening. [And] some sort of hugging, not uptight about physical contact, a lot

of interaction between ages of the children, which uptight families might find hard to deal with. In this way love is a precondition for learning. Getting children to express themselves, how they feel, some children find that hard, but especially it can be a key way of opening out bullying when it's talked about through the group – a positive attitude between the adults, children and other children."(Helen, small school practitioner, England)

In fact, Helen's description resonates with Christopher's picture of the community at Kilquhanity, where bullying was dealt with in a similar way – "through the group", as Helen put it. And like Wheatfields, forms of physical contact are encouraged, reinforcing a sense that this is a family-like space – for instance in feelings that teachers and pupils are "brother or sister". A key part of "getting children to express themselves" is the teaching of mindfulness via meditation, in a way which subtly reinforces the 'rings of sentiment' model:

"Children take some responsibility for reaching targets. They decide what their target is, on their own or with me. We have circle time every day, our meditation, story and yoga time, and talking time, sharing time. That's important. And if an important discussion or issue comes up, it will be the right atmosphere for trying to resolve that. Underlying that meditation is the pattern of the year, [which] is based on subtlety to crudity and back again. It's based on the idea of family, love, space, air, fire, water, solid, plants, the earth, animals, then humans, an idea of coming to consciousness. Of realising and embodying what your place is in the world. That we have responsibility." (Helen, small school practitioner, England)

Conclusion: from mindfulness, to consciousness, to the good life

Beyond the example of Helen's school, it is worth noting that the teaching of mindfulness among children can take numerous forms, but is becoming increasingly popular in mainstream and alternative settings around the world, despite scientific uncertainty about its effectiveness (Greenberg and Harris, 2011). Inspired by Buddhist meditation texts, mindfulness is a form of 'mental silence' gained through meditation, involving the 'passive observation of internal and external stimuli without mental reaction [...] attain[ing] a state of no mental content at all, while remaining in full control of [one's] faculties (Manocha, 2011, p 47). It is also understood as a 'way of directing attention [...] a state of consciousness that incorporates self-awareness and attention with a core characteristic of being open, receptive and non-judgmental (Schonert-Reichl and Lawlor, 2010, p 143). Other than the examples given by Helen, emergent pedagogical research reveals that several kinds of learning activities have been used with children, in education settings, to try to foster mindfulness. These include focused breathing, listening to a repetitive chime, reflection upon feelings and thoughts, managing emotions and concentrated attention to the feelings of others (Schonert-Reichl and Lawlor, 2010). The key principle is that mindfulness must be 'trained' and habituated – so students practise three times daily, usually for a period of weeks.

I am not citing the example of mindfulness because it is in any way 'representative' of any or all alternative learning spaces: Helen's school was the only school that explicitly advocated mindfulness. Indeed, I encountered several religious and spiritual belief systems, from Christian and Muslim homeschooling families, to paganism at one forest school, to the complex anthroposophy that undergirds Steiner education (see Woods et al, 1997). And many alternative learning spaces are guided by no religious or spiritual belief at all. My point is, rather, that the principles and practice of mindfulness encapsulate my arguments in this chapter.

My first argument has been about *scale*. As I mentioned above, a key implication of the idea of interpersonal relations is that they appear to be resolutely microspatial, intimate and/or physically proximate in nature. As I have shown in this chapter, intimacy between children of different ages (and adults) is often viewed by educators as the foundation for both friendships and family-like relations, from which care, trust and love may flow. In distinction, several recent studies *have* highlighted how contemporary forms of mobility and information exchange mean that intimate family relationships and friendships can be sustained at a distance (Holmes, 2006; Bunnell et al, 2011). In the case of 'small-scale' learning spaces, however, the emphasis is not upon sustaining existing family or friendship relations at a distance, but upon constituting intimate relations *locally* so that a disposition towards often *unknown*, distant others can be forged. In both cases, there is an attempt to collapse *scales* into one another. In the former case, it is more a pragmatic matter of eliding distance – of trying to reproduce intimacy by compressing space and time through technology (Harvey, 1991). In the latter, it is the conceptual and moral distance usually presumed to follow from physical distance – the assumption that 'charity begins at home' – that is deliberately effaced. In the 'rings of sentiment' model – just as in the other examples I cited in the previous section of this chapter – the local is no longer privileged as the scale at which human responsibility, care or love should take place. Interestingly, this is done by first reinforcing the primacy of smallness, of human scale, of proximate body-to-body relations; but, simultaneously, those relations of proximity produce and are recursively produced by their constitutive outside. This mirrors what William Connolly (2008, p 5) terms a 'presumptive generosity' to strangers both near and far, who are not part of their immediate learning community. In a sense, the concept of scale recedes in significance – because the relationship is really a recursive one between bodily intimacy and everything else, not between the local and the global, or the national. The issue, then, is not so much one of whether scale exists or can be effaced, but of how two scalar conceptions – interiority (body-to-body relations within learning spaces) and exteriority (people, places, non-humans beyond that learning spaces) – can be *related* through feeling (Marston et al, 2005). Because they are simultaneously concerned with inward- *and* outward-facing forms of love, which help some alternative learning spaces to be both self-organising and offer support to diverse publics, this is yet another principle underlying my conviction that alternative learning spaces be understood as *autonomous*.

My second reason for ending with the example of mindfulness relates to my building argument about *habit*. We can see mindfulness as just one among many intentional activities at alternative learning spaces designed to raise *consciousness* in some form or another. All of the examples in the last section wanted to instil among children some kind of awareness about the world – about peace (Montessori), freedom (Steiner), responsibility (Findhorn and Kilquhanity) and so on. Many alternative educators have some kind of world view, some kind of philosophy for how what they do could make the world a better place. The relationship between education and utopianism is, after all, a long and complex one (Halpin, 2003). But in the examples I have given I have emphasised the primacy of feeling, atmosphere, materiality and the creation of family-*like* spaces and relations, as constitutive of consciousness raising. I have sought to emphasise how the habits of individual children and groups might be affected and effected by non-representational practices like meditation. There is resonance here with Ravaisson, who argued that in the search for the good life it was important to 'deal with [...] tenacious unwanted habit [by leading it] back to the sphere of consciousness' (Carlisle, 2010, p 141). This, however, could not be done by simply thinking about habits but

> cultivated at the level of sensations, feelings and involuntary
> thoughts [...] deliberately cultivated in certain therapeutic
> and spiritual exercises – for example, in psychoanalysis or
> cognitive behavioural therapy, and in *Buddhist meditation
> techniques.*' (Carlisle, 2010, p 141, emphasis added)

Ravaisson, then, emphasised the bringing to consciousness of habit,
through practices like mindfulness. For him, if good habits could do
more than simply forge individual freedom (in the ways I explored
in Chapter Six), then such indirect, non-representational forms of
consciousness raising were crucial. To do so would produce desirable
effects that Ravaisson named through a lexicon of terms that have
appeared throughout this chapter: 'freedom', 'intuition', 'love', 'grace',
and so on (Carlisle, 2010, p 142).

Other than these brief thoughts, Ravaisson says little more about the
possible connections and disconnections between individual habits and
any conception of the broader moral good. It has been the purpose
of this chapter to expose – via empirical material from alternative
learning spaces – some ways in which some educators seek to make
these kinds of connections. There exist relatively substantial bodies
of research around spirituality in education (for instance, on Steiner
education and spirituality see discussion, in Chapter Two, of Woods
and Woods, 2006; Oberski, 2011). My perhaps narrow contribution to
this work has been to demonstrate how particular kinds of habits are
spatialised. That is, I have argued that particular kinds of habits produce
feelings – named as trust, care and love – that take place through and
constitute the very spatialities of alternative education. I have explored
the recursive relationship between intimate love and a loving disposition
that is meant to be universal. Moreover, building on the previous two
chapters, I have argued that the material *and* interpersonal relations
that make up alternative learning spaces create 'atmospheres' that can
gradually move children towards particular dispositions. The nature
sanctuary in Findhorn was a prime example of the ways in which
material and interpersonal relationships combine to produce particular
(spiritual) atmospheres, which in turn are supposed to 'educate for
consciousness'. Thus, spaces themselves – understood as spatialities –
can be as productive of habit as attempts to 'train' the individual to
learn or unlearn particular dispositions. Indeed, one could argue that
the mindfulness meditation done at Helen's school is a *collaborative*
exercise: mindfulness does refer to an individual state of mind, but in
her school, meditation is carried out by the whole class, during circle
time, and meant to be a social as well as individual endeavour.

My third point, then, is that I have sought to emphasise the importance of two overlapping kinds of interpersonal relationship: friendship and the family-like relation. Once again I have characterised these through particular feelings, considering a relatively narrow constellation of emotions around love, trust and care. Clearly, I could have explored other feelings (anger, hate, joy, sadness). However, as an eternal optimist, my rather more affirmative aim has been specifically to chart how such feelings could be productive of 'good habits' and, ultimately, quasi-utopian visions of the good life. Once again Ravaisson has little to say about the kinds of *inter*personal relationships that could engender good habits, retaining in his analyses a focus upon individual desires, sensations and forms of consciousness. I have argued that such interpersonal relationships are, according to some educators and learners, an important conduit for learning. Thus, in forest schools, young people work one-to-one with adults, sometimes forging intergenerational friendships that will enable them to gain enough trust in adults to return to school. In homeschooling settings, older children may teach younger children about particular skills or knowledge. In human scale schools, children engage in emotional learning by living with particular affective atmospheres. At Helen's school, these atmospheres are explicitly promulgated through the idea of the family-like – where teachers are like brothers or sisters, where children of different ages interact closely with one another, and where physical contact is encouraged, within reason. In turn, that family-like atmosphere is meant to be conducive to mindfulness and the kinds of consciousness raising about "your place in the world", as Helen put it. Thus, I have argued that habit is spatialised through friendship and family-like relations, because those relations are meant to be productive of outward-looking dispositions of trust, care and love. Understood this way, habits can be produced individually *and* in relation with others: in *inter/personal* relations.

As a fourth point, once again the idea of *autonomy* has been bubbling under this chapter. I want to retain the notion from Chapter Four that alternative learning spaces are involved in different degrees of dis/ connection with the mainstream. For it was far from the case that every learning space I visited held such clearly articulated, 'outward-looking' visions about the connections between embodied learning habits and the good life as those I have discussed in this chapter. Some educators did not speak about habits at all; others focused on individual habits in a relatively instrumental sense (for instance, in getting children back to school or building their confidence); others invested in more or less intense versions of the notions of care and love I have outlined in this chapter. Thus, *habitual* dis/connections between alternative learning spaces and the mainstream may vary in kind, intensity and duration. But in several cases, learning habits are meant to produce individual and collective forms of autonomy: of conscious, emotional empowerment. It is *through* those habits that is envisioned the power to forge possible connections – whether conceptual, pragmatic, with the local community or with someone/someplace else (Chapter Four). More broadly, my focus on love has – like Paolo Freire's work – a resonance with other, more politicised forms of autonomy. For instance, in Sitrin's theorisation of the horizontal forms of interpersonal relation that constitute autonomous spaces in Argentina (2006) she shows how love is a key driver for non-hierarchical, self-sufficient communities of action. While she explores very different kinds of interpersonal relations, in a very different geographical and political context, nevertheless love is viewed as something productive, which can create effects and affects both within and beyond a small-scale community. Clearly, many alternative learning spaces may not share the political goals of autonomous collectives in Argentina (although some might, at least at an abstract level). Nor do they propound the same notions of love or autonomy – indeed in some learning spaces, which I have not included in this chapter, these notions did not figure. As I have emphasised throughout this book, alternative learning spaces are very diverse. Yet, in several of the very different examples I have cited in this chapter, love is a crucial element, both in terms of what makes those spaces different, and what connects them to their 'outsides'. In these cases, in variegated ways, the dis/connections I explored in Chapter Four *interact* with loving relations, in the production of autonomous learning spaces.

Finally, the notion of habit implies a certain kind of *endurance*. That is, for habits to take hold they must endure: as meaningful, lasting interpersonal relationships (friendship, the family-like); as more obdurate affects that come to characterise a particular material space (like a nature sanctuary or homely classroom); as a lasting potential within a person's disposition to act with care, love or grace (as in Montessori, Steiner and human scale schools). Indeed, the very definition of habit implies endurance as well as it does contingency (Dewsbury, 2011). This may mean, in a negative sense, that habits may be stubbornly inflexible to the shifting demands of life – some readers may find some of the conceptions of love and trust outdated or irrelevant to their contemporary situation. On the other hand, we could – and should – remember that each of the examples I provided in this chapter attempts to produce *different* kinds of habit. None of them attempts to create exactly the same habituations of trust, care or love within young people, nor for precisely the same reason. There are similarities, and these similarities rest in part, I have argued, in the ways in which habits are spatialised, and in which they are dissonant from the 'uniform' habits of mainstream schooling. But these are nevertheless *diverse* learning spaces, promoting different forms of autonomy, different dis/connections, different kinds of friendships and family-like relations, and different kinds of love.

All of this anticipates my argument in Chapter Eight. It is important to recognise that alternative learning spaces are not only microcosmic, prefigurative, often temporary 'experiments' (compare Fielding and Moss, 2011). Rather, they are productive of a series of overlapping yet also distinct forms of *life* that *endure*, to some extent. Some schools may open, close and open again (like Kilquhanity). But that does not mean that they cannot produce or attempt to produce other kinds of lasting effects (and affects). Moreover, for some teachers and learners, in some spaces, at some times, those effects matter – they are viewed positively, they make a difference to a young person's life, they make people feel cared-for, or they support communities near and far. It is crucial to understand this because the neoliberal governance of life-itself is predicated upon the endurance of (very) particular forms of life and the belittling of alternative forms of life as escapist, ephemeral and thus irrelevant (Jacques, 2002). Neoliberal agents pursue increasingly exacting ways of doing and knowing the economy, politics, science, nature and, no less importantly, *habit*. The latter (habits) are in turn propped up by mainstream forms of neoliberal education, and it is important to recognise (as I do in Chapter Nine) that theories of mind, neuroscience and the malleability of habit are being deployed *by* neoliberal governments too (Dolan et al, 2010).

Having said all this, then, a comparative stance should urge careful thought about *which* habits are deployed, by whom and for whom, when, why and where. For, if the 'wrong' habits are most clearly exposed when a subject displays habits that do not conform to neoliberal governmental expectations – when a person does not complete a routine journey on the underground, or when they act 'suspiciously' enough to provoke the idea that they are 'terrorists' (Amoore and de Goode, 2008) – then, equally, we must question what happens in alternative learning spaces when the 'wrong' habits are exhibited (on this I have no empirical material, unfortunately). But neoliberal attempts to govern habit and produce mindfulness are also set into relief, I would argue, by the defamiliarisation writ by exposure to alternatives – like alternative economic practices (Gibson-Graham,

2006) and like alternative learning spaces. In different ways, to differing degrees, the learning spaces in this book attempt to create forms of life that endure, and it matters that they endure if we are to take them seriously rather than as 'simply' escapist, alternative or utopian fantasies. Their endurance – not least through habit – means that they *must* both rub up against *and* connect with the increasingly neoliberal mainstream in some provocative ways: it is up to readers to make sense of where they stand on the particular examples of habit and mindfulness reported in this book. However, these autonomous forms of life are not simply about habit. Returning to Helen's final quotation, she said about mindfulness that "it's based on the idea of family, love, space, air, fire, water, solid, plants, the earth, animals, then humans, an idea of coming to consciousness". Understood in this way, habit is but one (human-centric) way of conceiving life-itself. Therefore, I turn to broader notions of life-itself in Chapter Eight, which posit versions and visions of the good life that are dissonant with, if not autonomous from, neoliberal mainstreams.

EIGHT

Towards the 'good life': alternative visions of learning, love and life-itself

Our biological life itself has entered the domain of decision and choice [...]. This is what it means to live in an age of biological citizenship, of 'somatic ethics', and of vital politics. [...T]hose who I have termed 'biological citizens' are having to reformulate their own answers to Kant's three famous questions – What can I know? What must I do? What may I hope? (Rose, 2007, pp 254-7)

A maxim is just another word for a secular prayer. It is a statement of expression in our shared desire in the sense of *potentia*. It is also an act of faith in our capacity to make a difference and as such it is an expression of generosity and love of the world. It is also a plea, an open question, a reaching out, or an invitation to the cosmic dance. It is an imperative, an injunction to endure in the sense both of lasting in time and of suffering in space, but it is also a spiritual gesture, a declaration of love. It is a political act of defiance of social norms and resistance against the inertia of habits [...]; an act of politics as autopoesis, or affirmative self-creation, not of an atomized self [...] but rather as a collective, multirelational nomadic subject [who is] active in the world. (Braidotti, 2011, p 360)

Are there more everyday tactics for cultivating an ability to discern the vitality of matter? (Bennett, 2010, p 119)

"For me, life is learning. If you stop learning, you're dead."
(Dana, homeschooler, London)

Throughout this book, I have tried to provide a sense of the liveliness of alternative learning spaces. From the outset, I have not wanted simply to discern the role that physical, bounded spaces (the classroom, the forest, the farm) might play in directing children's learning. I have continually insisted upon the importance of the *spatialities* of alternative education, which, bearing in mind the previous chapters, can be understood as entanglements of materiality, habit, feeling, temporal rhythm, interpersonal relationships and much more besides. I have tried to build up a sense that alternative learning spaces are constituted of multiple, complex and dynamic spatialities. In my mind – writing, of course, as a geographer – these provide one (but just one) series of ways in which to understand what makes alternative learning spaces 'alternative', and what kinds of learning go on within them.

In this chapter I begin to tie together my arguments about the spatialities of alternative learning spaces. This will constitute my final attempt to enliven the spaces of alternative education. Or, rather, more properly, it represents my last effort to witness the ways in which alternative learning spaces attempt to enliven life-itself. My argument – which seems rather simple on the face of it – is that alternative learning spaces offer alternative versions and visions of life-itself. That is, they do not just proffer alternative approaches to education, but to the very *thinking* and *doing* of life. As the four introductory quotations to this chapter imply, as well as further empirical material from my research, this task will be very much inspired by a trans-disciplinary series of thinkers who have propounded distinct but overlapping theories of life-itself. Their theories have in some circles come to be termed 'vital materialisms' – inspired both by poststructural theories of materiality, like Actor-Network Theory (Chapter Five), and ongoing developments in biology, neuroscience and social psychology. Significantly, these theorists say little about education explicitly (although Jane Bennett, for instance, references select works by John Dewey on art, experience and collective social endeavour). Meanwhile, despite the enduring deployment of social and environmental psychology (and more recently, neuroscience) in education studies, theories of vital materialism have not yet provoked much discussion within educational research. Nor, beyond use of William Connolly's work on neuroscience, do scholars like Gibson-Graham (2006) explicitly use wider vital materialist theories in mapping alternative/autonomous spaces – despite, for instance, Braidotti's (2011) use of terms like 'autopoesis' and 'affirmative self-creation' (see quotation at start of chapter).

In this chapter, then, I am once again guided as much by empirical material as I am by the theoretical perspectives afforded by vital materialists. I proceed through some vignettes taken from across the range of case studies included in my research. I use each vignette to develop some of the introductory points I made about vital materialisms in Chapter Two. But my intention is not merely to demonstrate how neatly some aspects of vital materialist theorising resonate with what alternative educators (say they) do. Rather, I want to extend the well-known maxim in the education world (especially the alternative education world) that the division between learning and everyday life is a blurry one – indeed, that much 'good' learning flows from everyday life (Falk et al, 2009) and that 'good' learning can prepare humans 'for how to live one's life' (Curren, 2007, p 13). I do not discount this maxim at all; but, rather, in juxtaposing the experiences of alternative educators with vital materialists, I attempt to complicate the kinds of *autonomy* that it presupposes. That is, throughout the course of history, theories of education have repeatedly contended that the purpose of education is to educate for *individual autonomy* – the freedom to evaluate and make choices about one's life course (Curren, 2007). Of course, such individual forms of freedom are nearly always predicated upon some kind of social relationship or community with others.

Notwithstanding this conception of autonomy, and building upon previous chapters, my argument is that we could and should allow for additional kinds of *matter*, and of other kinds of *relationships*, towards an understanding of alternative learning spaces as alternative versions of life-itself. While Pickerill and Chatterton (2006) emphasise that autonomy is a collective, social practice, to understand alternative learning spaces in this way is to push the concept of autonomy still further. It is to argue that some alternative learning spaces may prefigure, experiment with, or envision, alternative constellations of the diverse things and flows that *constitute* life. This chapter provides a highly selective list of some of these things and flows: love, nature, food. Eventually, this leads me to theorise steps towards a broader and more accommodating notion of educational autonomy as *more-than-social, collaborative autonomy*. Through some further vignettes, I will focus on some diverse efforts to sustain life at alternative learning spaces – to somehow envisage and perform forms of life that *endure*. These are collaborative efforts in a broader sense than the collective forms of *human* sociability articulated by most notions of autonomy (for example Pickerill and Chatterton, 2006; Sitrin, 2006) – hence the slight change in terminology. I call them collaborative (rather than collective) because they involve diverse, multiply scaled communities of people, things, chemicals, electrical flows and expressive feelings, as well as the pragmatic, conceptual, financial and other concerns I explored in Chapter Four. They encapsulate and seek to channel some of the many ideas I have covered in this book – habit, materiality, love, interconnectedness. Finally, and inspired by the political convictions of vital materialists like Braidotti and Bennett, I argue that these enduring forms of collaborative autonomy are utopian in a specific sense, and that it matters to see them as such. Running both with and against the grain of contemporary utopian thought, I argue that alternative learning spaces seek both fluidity and endurance. This makes them more obdurate than the prefigurative, experimental spaces favoured by Fielding and Moss (2011), and more so than the emergent, contingent, processual utopias favoured by poststructural and/or feminist utopian theorists (Sargisson, 1996, 2000). This, I will argue, is an important political point of departure, *if* we want to see alternative learning spaces as but one form of dissonance (Braidotti, 2011) or diverse performative practice (Gibson-Graham, 2006) that could both engage with and extend beyond the spaces of contemporary neoliberal governance.

Love

> "For their first two or three years I practised a continuum method of being with them. Which means that you carried them a lot of the time. I don't know if that's created that bond of speaking and being together. It sounds awful but on the other hand it's not literally being here all the time together. I consider now [time of interview] being together, even though my son's not physically here. He's around somewhere, he's a teenager, with his friends at the moment, but we came here together. He probably doesn't want to know me. But I think it's had some nice results. I'm very close to my daughter. We see each other as equals. They've never had a fear of speaking to me. They've always been children and I've been an adult, but whereas in schools some children have a problem speaking to adults, mine don't."
> (Annette, homeschooler, London)

In the previous chapter, I showed how love and intimacy are considered vital interpersonal relations that can sustain learning. Across many case studies I was repeatedly told that these kinds of relationships were, in fact, somehow '*natural*': that they had been lost in many mainstream settings, and that particular learning habits could re-install such relations (and vice versa). At one Steiner school, a parent told me that she didn't "have much sympathy for people who don't think children *deserve* to be cuddled". At Helen's human scale school, hugging formed part of the premise that "love is a precondition for learning, it's only natural".

Unsurprisingly, perhaps, the idea that love was a *natural* predicate for learning was most prevalent amongst homeschoolers, who practised child-led approaches to both learning and parenting. Initially, this led to the common observation – mentioned earlier – that "there's kind of no line between our life and what we learn" (Rowena, homeschooler, London). As I have shown elsewhere (Kraftl, in press, 2013a), several homeschoolers used this assumption to criticise their experiences of mainstream education – arguing that (in part) the lack of love and intimacy in schools had caused children to develop behavioural problems, depression, anxiety, nosebleeds and several other medical problems. They argued that the separation of parents from children was artificial, breaking a natural, affective bond (see also Merry and Howell, 2009; Conroy, 2010). Simultaneously, like Annette (quoted earlier), several parents advocated 'natural' styles of parenting – what Annette terms the "continuum method" and what others call 'attachment' styles of parenting. These parenting styles (which are often *mothering* styles) include long-term breastfeeding, carrying toddlers in papooses and several other practices (Kraftl, in press, 2013b). In this way, many homeschoolers view homeschooling as a 'natural' extension of attachment parenting.

At this point, most social scientists will observe that these kinds of feelings are largely socially constructed. By now, it goes without saying (virtually) that childhood is a social construction, that emotions and affects are learned, and that parenting styles that appear natural vary by socioeconomic status, geographical location and historical epoch. Indeed, several mothers recognised how their attachment styles of parenting had actually developed through engagements with mothering groups like La Leche League (www.laleche.org.uk). And, repeatedly, in the last two chapters I have argued for how alternative educators attempt to *foster* habits and dispositions so that they become 'second nature' – not somehow pre-social instincts. However, as part of what Papoulias and Callard (2010, p 33) call the 'affective turn' in philosophy and social sciences, these social constructivist accounts have come to be questioned (or, at least, tempered). For instance, renewed theorisations of the construction of childhood have attempted to make room for non-human objects (Prout, 2005) and natures (Taylor, 2011) in the constitution of childhood experience. More radically still, affect theorists (including vital materialists) have foregrounded

> the importance of biology [...] as a creative space [...] that, crucially, *precedes* the overwriting of the body through subjectivity and personal history [...] to address

intimate aspects of life through attending to an enfleshed understanding of action and thought. (Papoulias and Callard, 2010, pp 33-4)

Let me be clear that affect theorists do not aim for a return to deterministic understandings of agency, emotion or interpersonal relations. In a sense, we can view this as a reassertion or re-balancing of the role of biological processes in the constitution of human life after decades of exclusion from social-scientific explanation. However, the implications of affect theories are more profound than this. My discussion of habit (Chapter Six) began to address some of these implications. There, via Dewsbury's (2011) discussion of the 'body-brain-material' assemblages, I argued that borders between a seemingly 'individual' human body and its outside are in fact porous. The body is constantly subject to minerals, pollutants, bacteria, feelings and energetic forces that enter, cross, and exit the thresholds marked out by its fleshy exterior. In this way, feminists and poststructuralists have diminished the idea that 'the body' is a sealed unit, and that subjectivity corresponds precisely to that unit. Taken crudely, the implication is that there are indeed what I term *more-than-social* (both social *and* biological) elements to what makes us human. Whether or not, in their conceptions of attachment parenting/learning, homeschoolers are *accurately* accounting for these elements is not the point. Rather, the point is that it would be tremendously arrogant to assume that everything that they feel *can* be reduced (and, it could be argued, dismissed) by the explanation that they are *socially* constructed. Note that I am very carefully *not* terming these non-social elements 'natural' – this would be disingenuous given that the very point of much vital materialist philosophy is to blur the boundaries between human and non-human. Thus, we can see homeschoolers' feelings as an entry point into the idea that there are more-than-social forces at play in the constitution of learning-as-life. The argument is not that social construction does not happen but that social processes channel and are mediated through more-than-social processes. It is, if you like, an ethical argument to acknowledge (but not to comprehensively account for) an expanded range of actors and processes within human lives. This, for instance, is how Ravaisson (2008) accounts for habits – as inclinations that are learned, can be changed, but that also help us to fulfil desires over which we do not have *complete* control.

I will return to other versions of these more-than-social materials and relations in this chapter. In the rest of this section I flesh out what these more-than-social forces might look like in relation to the specific questions of love and attachment. It is here that we require a very brief foray into neuroscience – an area of biological research much-favoured by affect theorists (Papoulias and Callard, 2010). Neuroscientific research has attempted to provide explanations for the neurological bases of human experience – how genes, brain proteins, and neural pathways can account for criminal behaviour, empathy, fear, love, obesity and much else besides (Kandel, 2005; Vrecko, 2010). Yet within the contemporary neurosciences themselves is mirrored a conviction that neuroscientific processes are neither wholly natural nor wholly predispose a human to act or feel in a certain way. Thus, compare two accounts of the brain from neuroscience (first) and philosophy:

> The brain is sculpted [...] in a close interaction between genetic conditions and environmental stimulation [...] development progress follows a highly complex choreography that integrates and coordinates the neuroanatomic and neurobiological development with the infant's experiences through close interpersonal relationships. (Hart, 2006, p xii)

> Neuroscience describe[s] a fluid materiality of excitable neural networks, capable of disturbing the role of foundations in general and the distinction between nature and culture in particular [...] depending instead on a novel micro-geography of synaptic connections, cellular interactions and electrochemical flows that operate in a dispersed fashion and below the level of consciousness. [...But] neurons, cells and signals have emergent qualities; that is, their scope and connections are not simply there at birth, but [...] incomplete and [...] must therefore plug into the social world to function. (Papoulias and Callard, 2010, p 36)

Seen in this way, neuroscientific and social processes *only* operate in collaboration with one another. Thus, it is arguably in these collaborations between 'biology' and 'society' that habits can be learned and unlearned in the ways I described in Chapters Six and Seven. This is what I think Clive, at a care farm in Scotland, was talking about when he discussed channelling the "same energy" from the impulse to destroy into one to create.

Beyond the question of habit, the insights of contemporary neuroscience (especially in combination with social psychology) have led towards re-theorisations of person-to-person attachment. Known as 'attachment theories', these more-than-social explanations of affect have three implications. First, observational studies have shown how multiple inter- and intra-bodily processes are at play when humans bond with babies (the following examples are taken from Music, 2011). Thus, some babies are able instinctively to find their mother's breast in order to feed, but can also adapt and refine that instinct to find the breast more quickly. Simultaneously, 'in skin-to-skin contact a mother's body maintains an unclothed baby at just the right temperature, forming a two-person homeostatic system' (Music, 2011, p 24). And at the same time, breastfeeding reduces a mother's stress, releasing oxytocin, which increases 'protective feelings and attentiveness [and], present only in mammals, [...] is released in pleasurable moments such as [...] when we fall in love, or have sex' (Music, 2011, p 25). Thus, multiple biological and social processes – more-than-social processes – are entwined in the production of affectionate bonds between mothers and babies, with flows of materials (milk), chemicals (oxytocin) and energies (heat) moving between and within bodily boundaries.

Second, there are implications here for the development of habit. The same chemical – oxytocin – is part of the *deactivation* of receptivity when people enter into a loving relationship (compare Ravaisson, 2008; see also Chapter Six). Bartels and Zeki (2004) studied how, when experiencing feelings of love, the activation role of vasopressin and oxytocin receptors in the brain's reward system

> deactivated[...] networks used for critical social assessment and negative emotions [whilst] bonding individuals through the involvement of the reward circuitry, explaining the power of love to motivate and exhilarate [...]. The neural mechanisms suppressed here might be the same that, when active, are responsible for maintaining an emotional barrier towards less familiar people. (Bartels and Zeki, 2004, pp 1156, 1164)

The implication is that love can become a form of habit that reduces our receptivity to critical appraisal. This means that two people in love can sometimes (although, as we know, not always) gradually learn to ignore one another's foibles and faults. This occurs particularly in the relationship between mother and baby (Music, 2011). Whether this means that there is always a more-than-social explanation for the development of loving habits in alternative learning spaces (Chapter Seven) and in pedagogical theory (for example hooks, 2003), I could not say. But it is entirely possible that the activation of oxytocin may in part be responsible for what Ravaisson views as the relationship between habit development and desire fulfilment. That is, specifically, that humans are programmed towards 'good habits' – directed towards helping others – in order to fulfil biological desires, *but* that those good habits can be developed, unlearned, or relearned (Carlisle, 2010).

The third point is a political one. That is, few neuroscientists assume that attachment has to occur between a child and the natural mother (although some homeschoolers do assume this). As Music (2011) points out, humans can potentially bond to any baby, not only their own biological offspring; wet nurses have been and remain prevalent in different historical and geographical contexts; and adoptive relationships can lead to incredibly strong feelings of attachment (on biological and social explanations of alloparenting, see Bentley and Mace, 2009). There are therefore grounds to promote intimate, family-*like* relationships if those are settings in which attachment can be fostered – but these neither have to be between biological family members (that is, mother–child), nor have to take place within the home. What I am saying, then, is that the family-like relations that occur across different alternative learning spaces (Chapter Seven) constitute not only particular kinds of learning *relationship* but particular ways of channelling the interpersonal, human and non-human flows of life-itself in the constitution of learning *spaces* themselves.

In turn, this recognition has potential ramifications for social constructions of childhood and the family. In essence, James Conroy (2010) – in his stinging critique of mainstream neoliberal educational policy in the UK – argues that the state has increasingly intervened into intimate, family(-like) spaces in which it has no justifiable role. But, for centuries, state governments have *mobilised* the idea that the family is a social construction (not natural) as a way to validate their intervention into the domestic realm. For, if the family is not viewed as 'natural' it is therefore easier to justify the removal of children into state-controlled institutions (schools). Clearly, this is but one particular reason for why schools exist, but, across my case studies, I encountered a sense – sometimes vaguely defined – that love (or at least intimacy) could play some role in children's learning, and that there could be some biological bases to this feeling. I am not arguing that any of the family-like, 'loving' relationships discussed in Chapter Seven are any more 'natural' than those in mainstream schools – just that mainstream schools and diverse alternative learning spaces attempt to manage and/or promote more-than-social forms of attachment in some strikingly *different* ways. The question – which is political and ethical, and which I do not propose to answer – then becomes one around which forms of attachment one deems 'good', and whether burgeoning knowledge about more–than–social processes (like attachment) should be incorporated to prop up such judgements.

Nature

> "People who come here see this as coming to work. But the work we do here is always therapeutic too. Our ethos is to give people a worthwhile working day. So that's therapy and work combined. Grooming, barrowing, potting up plants, mixing compost – can have both elements. The touching, the smells, the sounds. A lot of therapeutic work is done with the animals. To be fair, most of ours are more able, because of the environment that we're in. It is a working environment." (Ursula, care farm practitioner, East Midlands)

> "You can see the difference when the kids come here. The ones – it's usually the boys – who are loud and aggressive in the classroom, who are the ones at the centre of any trouble, they come here and they are different children. There's no ceiling, they calm down, they work better with the other children, they talk to other children I've never seen them talking to before, they just relax. There's more space, but it's more than that, it's something about being out here in the woods. We've [teachers] all been trying to put our finger on it every since we started coming here but we still don't know what it is. But it works. Well, at least as long as they're here!" (Ella, mainstream primary school teacher accompanying class to forest school, south–west England)

In this section, I build on and exemplify the argument in the previous section that there could be *more-than-social* components to the forms of learning – and life – that take place in alternative learning spaces. The first consideration – inspired by these two quotations – is a desire among many alternative educators to validate the importance of being *outside* the classroom. In some contexts, this specifically means interaction with 'nature'. At once, we run into a problem here: that is, that there exist relatively few validated studies about the effects of interaction with 'nature' upon children's learning or their wider wellbeing (Knight, 2009). At the same time, many forest school and care farm practitioners struggle to represent how children 'have moved'

– what they have learned – because these changes may be subtle, hard to represent, or not correspond with usual measures of learning (Chapter Six). A further problem is that – in the vein in which I started this book – there are stark differences in opinion about the extent to which a person's feelings or actions can be determined by a physical space. On the one hand, high-profile texts like Richard Louv's (2005) *Last Child in the Woods* argue that the results of 'nature-deficit disorder' are many, ranging from obesity to attention deficit disorder. On the other hand, such texts have provoked cynicism, particularly because certain kinds of 'nature' (like woodland) tend to be privileged in these writings – environments that for various reasons may not be accessible to or even attractive for some groups of children.

This is a difficult set of arguments to navigate and my aim here is certainly not to prove or disprove the *effects* of nature or outdoor space upon children. On that point, it is interesting that recent studies from neuroscience and environmental psychology have begun to demonstrate some of the more-than-social effects of being outdoors. For instance, it is becoming accepted that being in 'natural environments' (the definition of which remains a little vague) may lead once again to the release of oxytocin, with associated positive impacts upon wellbeing and trust (O'Brien, 2009; Knight, 2011). Elsewhere, psychological research on outdoor educational environments has found positive impacts of being outside upon test scores, willingness, adaptability, self-esteem and stress, sometimes more so amongst boys than girls (see Gustaffson et al, 2012; compare with Ella's quotation). I certainly do not want to question this increasingly large and robust body of research. Once again, the point is to understand these as more-than-social elements of life – the *interaction* and blurring of the 'natural' and the 'social'. Thus, Knight (2009, p 107) recognises that the impacts of forest school are *diverse* – including increased confidence, social skills, physical skills and new perspectives. Similarly, Gustaffson et al (2012, p 64) acknowledge how 'macrosystems' (school district, funding of school, special educational needs) and 'microsystems' (teachers, school ethos, peers) interact with environmental systems (being outdoors, among nature) in the production of particular psychological effects.

Hence, we can understand such research as effectively espousing learning (and life) as an ongoing series of collaborations between the 'natural' and the 'social'. Rather than either validate or dismiss the relative 'power' of nature and natural processes to influence children, it is perhaps more helpful to explore – as per attachment theories – how they are constitutive of learning, and how they are mobilised by educators in alternative learning spaces. This also reflects what I termed the 'weak' Actor-Network approach I took to non-human materialities in Chapter Five. The implication is to move beyond social constructivist theses to allow some more *active*, but *not determining*, role for nonhuman agents, viewing the latter as entangled within, not a sphere separate from, human activity. Thus, 'nature' neither operates 'outside' the social, and nor can it be fully accounted for in processes of social construction. So, as Joanne put it:

> "We only go for smells when we specifically want them to use all their senses. Clearly that does have an impact on them. A general ambience, though, is just, calm, and, fun, if that's not too separate and distant. One thing I will never forget, with a group in the woods, just a group of six. And this was a group with lots of behavioural and emotional problems. All physically very capable. Most of them capable of flying off the handle at any time. So we had to be careful about introducing sharp instruments. [...] So when we finally got to using the very sharp penknives and the bow-saws, we remarked when we finished that day that when we got onto them using that stuff, all we could hear was birds. Silent. They were all just completely absorbed and engaged, with their little penknives. All doing it absolutely by the book. You know, the way they're meant to hold their body, where they hold the knives, wearing their gloves, and all that kind of stuff. They just took it, listened, did it, loved it. And all that we could hear was the birds. That's just one of those moments that I never forget. And everything turned, then. Those sessions sort of became *theirs*. And from then on, they defined all the sessions, they told us what they wanted to do. What they told us they wanted was what would help them." (Joanne, forest school practitioner, south-west England, original emphasis)

Here, then, multiple, more-than-social elements combined to produce a moment through which young people with emotional and behavioural needs became empowered in a forest school environment. In Joanne's account, we see several of the kinds of elements I have attended to elsewhere in this book: smells, materials (knives), birdsong, acquired habits (using a knife), timings (repetition), feelings ("they loved it") and much more. The point is that these elements were all combined: sometimes passively (like bird song), sometimes actively (knowing when to introduce the penknives). These elements faded in and faded out in the more-than-social constitution of a learning *spatiality* that had the kinds of effects upon a group of boys that psychologists like Gustaffson et al (2012) are increasingly able to measure. In the next section, I provide a slightly more concrete example of what I mean by this.

Food

"We maintain the bushes, the pens, all that kind of thing. But we also collect the eggs, and then eat them. We make jams and all kinds of things. One chap picked up an egg and it was warm. He got such a fright, threw the egg and ran away! But eating our produce is really important – some of them have never had that kind of food before. That's actually really important to changing their behaviour, getting into a different groove, like. It's not so much the fact it's 'natural' – it's just trying something different, seeing where it comes from, having worked on it themselves, following that whole process again. So a big thing here is from seed to cooking, things they can pick, just pick them up and eat them. *Internalising the process*. It's all supermarket kids. A lot of them don't know where food comes from, how to care for it, once you get the end product, what to do with it. And the thing they like is taking it home with them. And taking the recipe back and showing mum at home." (Clive, care farm practitioner, Scotland, emphasis added)

"When I came here, I was these kids I was going to work with. Totally disconnected. And I gardened for two years. And it just changed things for me. I haven't a clue why! I remember the first day I went into the garden, I was asked to harvest these lettuces. I felt so much pride. I got to harvest these beautiful lettuces. And got to eat them at lunchtime. You can put a seed in the ground with anger or love or resentment or trust and at the end of the day you get this abundant food from it. It's giving life." (Sarah, education officer, Findhorn, Scotland)

"All the teachers say it. It [Coming here] brings them out of themselves. Schools have so many constraints. Here it's a real world, a real working environment. It's messy. It's muddy. It's gritty. At the same time the direction's quite strong, up here, we don't dress it up as something it's not. It's a real working environment. When it rains the work has to be done. When the manure is flowing through the yard they have to get on with it. All these things are just part of life here. It's structures of life and how we deal with it, which is both dealing with mess and dealing with what you have to do when someone tells you because if you don't then life doesn't just go on, there are implications to what we do. We can't have a lamb dying just because some kid is acting up. Simple.[...] We explain fully why we get them to poo pick a field. Go and poo pick it because our paddocks are small and they get over-grazed. We follow the system through because we know that's how the system works." (Yvonne, care farm practitioner, south of England)

In this section I want to exemplify the *material* elements of life that constitute alternative learning spaces – and learners themselves. These material elements are – combined with those I discussed in Chapter Five – just some of the materialities that constitute alternative learning spaces. However, I want here to make a relatively basic observation: that some materials *flow through* learning spaces in a way productive of some overlapping, but distinct, notions of life–itself. My focus is upon material stuff that at some moments in life we call 'food' (the reason for my slightly evasive wording should become clear in a moment). In Clive's example, part of the process of learning at a care farm is to grow, care for, harvest, cook and eat different foodstuffs. The critical thing is that the engagement is not simply one that should foster awareness about where food comes from and where it goes. Rather, as Clive puts it, learners should "internalise the process" – through feeling the warmth of an egg, through tasting, in food passing–through their bodies. For Clive, this process is as much part of the changing of habits as their learning to fix, not kick out at, a broken fence-post. In Sarah's case, "giving life" – the seemingly mundane act of planting and then eating lettuces – was tethered into a growing spiritual self-awareness. Specifically, she viewed the practice of planting a seed as one as much imbued with the potential for 'love' as any of the other forms of learning that take place at Findhorn. And finally, Yvonne acknowledges the by-products of food that literally flow through care farms, and must be dealt with by learners: manure and "poo". For her, these gritty realities are the ways in which young people are exposed to and learn to negotiate the "structures of life", which can be very messy (Chapter Five). Crucially, as at Joanne's forest school (mentioned in the previous section), the management of animal waste is a more-than-social process. The physical act of cleaning is combined with an acknowledgment that animals may die if that management is not done properly: that, left alone, the excessive properties of animal waste may cause those animals harm, especially if they live in small enclosures.

Taking the last example, and without wishing to cause offence, this is an apposite moment to re-read Jane Bennett's (2011, p 140) explication of the common phrase 'shit happens':

> to say shit happens is to express a sense that life includes processes and identities more ontologically diverse than those recognisable within the binary logic of *either* decisive acts of agents *or* passive objects that express or resist them. It is uttered when the speaker has sensed that agency is *distributive*.

Bennett's own task is to try to find a language that expresses life 'beyond the default grammar of [human] agency' (Bennett, 2010, p 119). Thus the phrase 'shit happens' is, as she explains, one that can help us to witness the flow of manure through a farmyard on a rainy day: it just happens. To repeat, as Joanne pointed out, manure is a part of the "structures of life". But, I would add, as much as all of this happens, it doesn't mean that *any* shit can be *allowed* to happen – that a lamb can be allowed to die because manure has not been cleaned up properly. Thus, Bennett's is not a fatalistic position that somehow advances human passivity to the suddenly acknowledged vital activity of non-human life. Rather, she calls for the careful, thoughtful, moral negotiation of activity and passivity. As she says about ecological justice:

> [i]f I live not as a human subject who confronts natural and cultural objects but as one of many conative actants swarming and competing with each other [...then] eco health will [sometimes] require individuals and collectives to back off or ramp down their activeness, and sometimes it will call for grander, more dramatic and violent expenditures of human energy. (Bennett, 2010, p 122)

In this way, Bennett (2010; see also Chapter Three) asserts the agency of edible matter *within*, not beyond, a series of politicised debates about obesity, commercialisation and the slow-food movement. We can thus understand the lively matter of food as being enrolled into forms of life that we usually understand as 'society' (see also Latour, 2005). However, in some learning spaces (especially Steiner and Montessori classrooms), it goes without saying that there is considerably more thought about active human control over the enrolment of materials like foodstuffs into the learning environment. It would be unfair (if not offensive) to suggest that 'shit happens' where there the material configuration of the classroom can be a key constituent in the affective atmospheres of learning (Chapter Five). For instance, the nature table in a Steiner classroom (Figure 8.1) represents a carefully choreographed micro-space in which seasonal objects collected by teachers, parents and children are displayed to foster children's tacit learning about the rhythms of life. Seasonal foods – nuts, berries, fruits – are often included on the table more for their symbolic and spiritual value than as 'edible matter' (Bennett, 2010, p 39).

The nature table represents a microcosm of Steiner pedagogy – its engaged, spiritually inflected, outward-looking worldview (Chapter Seven). On the one hand, the nature table is utterly different from manure in the farmyard, which is different again from the "seed to cooking" approach at Clive's farm. For the concept of the nature table is, like Sarah's experience at Findhorn and other versions of spirituality present in several of my case studies, animated by a longer-standing, vitalist conception of life. That is, of life as 'élan vital' – a life force, possibly ordained by God or some other spiritual force (Bennett, 2010). There is not space to consider the concept of 'élan vital' here. Rather, on the other hand, my point is that in just a few examples,

Figure 8.1 A nature table at a Steiner school.

it is possible to understand the multiple ways in which more-than-social processes around what we call 'food' are negotiated in different alternative learning spaces. For beyond sensationalist debates about obesity (critiqued brilliantly by Evans and Colls, 2009) and artificial additives (Palmer, 2005), we can also (at least)*appreciate* that alternative educators try to manage the flow of foodstuffs in some very different ways from what happens in the neoliberal mainstream. I return in the final section of this chapter to some of the broader implications of Bennett's work for a theorisation of collaborative autonomy.

Utopia and endurance: towards a theorisation of collaborative autonomy in alternative learning spaces

Building upon the previous examples, I want to provide some examples of what could conceivably be understood as utopian visions and versions of life-itself (not just particular aspects thereof), at a cross-section of my case study sites. These are not meant in any sense to be representative but to give an indication of the diverse, but overlapping ways in which educators conceived life-itself. I will present these 'visions' (for want of a better word) as parallel but, as far as I know, unrelated attempts to articulate what I am calling 'collaborative autonomy'. As I indicated earlier, I understand collaborative autonomy to extend educational theorisations of autonomy beyond both the individual and immediate community to encapsulate forms of life that transcend scale (Chapter Seven) and accommodate non-human materials and flows (this chapter). These visions should therefore be read alongside the 'outward-looking' and arguably equally utopian forms of love and responsibility that I explored in the last chapter. I will provide relatively little analytical commentary, providing instead an extended conclusion to this chapter that draws out some key arguments.

My first example comes from a single mother, who described herself as being of modest financial means, who lives in North London, and who home educates her only child. She sees homeschooling as part of a commitment to a micro-community of action that is also involved in food growing, sustainable house building, alternative energy, and a range of outward-looking 'solutions' for a more sustainable future.

> "This draws in what we do at [local food growing cooperative]. I'm involved in the Transition movement as well. So resources are not infinite. In terms of taking care of the world [...] at the end of the day she [daughter] will be the next generation. We're about to do a community

self-build. And we did some straw-bale building, and she was there and will be right the way through the process. So, in terms of the way you live, not just what you have. We've been looking at alternative energy, and that kind of stuff. Not just sitting out in a wood and appreciating it, but really just thinking about what could we do. Not about blame for our generation and pressure for hers. Just going out and looking at what we can do. Micro-communities, growing locally. So doing home education fits into ways of imagining alternative worlds, if you like. She hears all of this, she's involved in it, asks about it, is part of the events. So it helps her look at things, question, imagine how things might be. We're not planning to go off and live in a yurt but we can make small differences at the local scale too." (Charlotte, homeschooler, south of England)

My second example comes from a care farm in East Anglia. In this poignant quotation Maura talks about the withdrawal of funding from community facilities, following the Conservative-Liberal Democrat government's 'austerity measures' – large-scale 'cuts' to public services designed to deal with the UK's enormous public debt. She argues that, under New Labour (the previous government), communities like hers (experiencing high levels of socioeconomic disadvantage) had come to rely, habitually, upon publicly funded services, like children's centres. She argues that the service deficits created by recent cuts were falling upon poorly funded, non-state facilities like her care farm, which relied on charitable donations and a small entrance fee. She talks about overlapping, more-than-social ways in which life at her care farm – and in the community that serves it – has been stripped back to a matter of mere survival (for its animals, for the space itself, for the community). She says that the community is starting to pull together in this regard – but questions whether it *should* have to. Maura's experiences reflect broader questions about the role of alternative learning spaces in respect of service provision in times of austerity (perhaps not just in the UK), to which I return in the book's conclusion.

"But the parents don't want the children out on the streets any more. We've got a management group made up of parents and local businesses. And parents volunteer. It is about the community for us. And I think we're going to have to step up, I'm going to have to do that work now that the children's centres did, as they're closing down. It's a burden. I will have to do it. But it is the burden that's going to fall disproportionately on this kind of place. We're already seeing it [summer 2011]. Parents have come to expect provision, with a free place. But now not all places can. I think, now it's harder, they will bring them - it's their right. They will get involved, but it's become everyone's stepped back and it's become professionalised. But now the money's being pulled back again, it's reinventing everyone's expectations. They will have to support, to keep even us open. The parents have been brilliant – we've been asking them to provide money for flour, for biscuits. We rely on that almost completely now. One woman, she sponsors our pig, who's going through some bad times at the moment, and she is basically paying for all the vet's fees, to keep him alive. I think people will increasingly rely on this kind of place. We are getting more and more families in. I think it will be a community-based thing, what it used to be years ago, more people doing voluntary work. That doesn't make it right. But these places will become vital for community life, for propping up community life around here, otherwise the community will die, I think – what else is there for people round here? We have to work through this transitional period, where parents have to change their mindset. Just to keep the lights going." (Maura, care farm practitioner/ play worker, East Anglia)

My third example comes from a forest school practitioner in south-west England. Guided by Marxist and feminist politics, she saw that her mission went beyond fostering learning and wellbeing in forest schools. Rather, she wanted to make a difference to life at a variety of scales, in a variety of contexts – from supporting children with 'real tough lives', to creating a national or even international "community of enquiry", to making a difference to standards and practices in mainstream schools.

"What I'm keen to do is to see how much - be part of - a whole community of enquiry about how do we support children who, for whatever reason, have got real tough lives – even families later down the line – we're quite keen to make sure that what we do makes a difference. We can all talk about it. A lot of people now, from the National Trust to the National Health Service, say this is good stuff, but we want to prove it and make sure it carries with them. I suppose the only way we can do that is to make sure they come back and do it weekly or monthly. I guess we'd have to work with others to facilitate that. Although one afternoon can put a child on a high and give us a sense of wellbeing for an hour or two, if there's a number of hours, then in the woods, and you build up all of that, then it can transform behaviour. And I want to be part of a community of people who are working to that. Until we can make a difference to Ofsted results at school, though, we're not going to be taken seriously. Not as a profession. As an outdoor, natural space. We will always be seen as fluffy. Well, we're not fluffy. Well, we might be, but we are definitely making a difference to *your* Ofsted results, headteacher and board of governors. To be taken seriously." (Joanne, forest school practitioner, south-west England)

My fourth example comes from a care farm in the English Midlands. Although located in a similar community (a relatively deprived suburb of a large city), Ursula's vision was very different from Maura's. She viewed her care farm as a "resource"', a hub, a knowledge base, and a springboard for all kinds of people and organisations who were considering or even experimenting with the "good life". Referring to a classic BBC TV comedy series, she took a specific interpretation of the term 'good life': as a kind of self-sufficiency in which households and communities grew food and reared animals for their own consumption, thereby reducing their reliance upon global commodity chains for food and other everyday items. Since the number of care farms in the UK is growing rapidly – as is the number of mainstream schools seeking to grow food and raise animals – Ursula recognised that they could and should be a key resource for a diverse range of local groups.

"A lot of people want to live the good life at the moment – like the [classic BBC comedy] TV series. So we see ourselves as a kind of resource, just for the public, if they want to find out what it's like first, learn whether they can do it. And some schools now have animals, which they have on-site, so they will come to us first to learn. It's becoming bigger and bigger. The outdoor care onto the doorstep – because it's harder and harder for schools to get out. In which case we still have a role to play – about setting boundaries, guidelines, we'll be used more to educate people to go on and do it themselves. It's a new role for care farms and care farmers. Actually, most care farms are set up for that purpose really, when you think about it. It's not just about the space you have, but about just existing as a resource, and having a connection with *other* places. Developing that relationship, thinking outside the farm boundaries. We're a porous place really, diverse and open in lots of ways." (Ursula, care farm practitioner, East Midlands)

Finally, in perhaps the most expressively utopian (and, true to the original meaning of the word, slightly satirical) style, Tony nevertheless expressed a vision of life that resonates across many of the case studies included in this book:

"Ultimately, there's a vision, which we almost never come close to realising, but there's a vision. That is, if you come here on any given day, you'll find the sun shining, you'll find butterflies flying about, lambs baaing in the field. You'll see elderly people, you'll see young children. You'll see black people, white people, green people, people with one leg, three legs, all working together in this atmosphere of utopia. A community that want to work together, that work towards something. That's the vision. At essence, this business is driven by the heart." (Tony, care farm practitioner, Scotland)

Conclusions

In essence, I am arguing in this book that some alternative learning spaces do more than simply provide 'alternatives' to mainstream education. In addition, across a diverse range of educational 'types', they constitute and provoke reflection about alternative visions and versions of life-itself. It may sound rather grand to say this – and I am certainly not arguing that everything that happens at alternative learning spaces is concerned with the production of utopian visions of the good life. However, I have charted several overlapping elements of alternative learning spaces in the preceding chapters that can, in part, be re-read as constituent elements of life-itself. For I do not think it is profitable merely to see these many forms of dis/connection, of material dis/order, of habit, and of inter/personal relationships as simply confined to the realm of learning. Beyond the rather glib acknowledgment that 'learning is life' (and vice versa), my task has been to show how the constituent spatialities of alternative education spill over into alternative versions and visions of life. Thus, they do not merely challenge (or complement) the predominance of neoliberal thinking in mainstream educational systems, but posit alternatives to neoliberal forms of life writ large. That is, they begin from the *premise* of learning, but, in some places, at some moments, they offer distinct challenges to dominant assumptions we hold about bodily habits and dispositions, about mess, about interpersonal love, and about life-itself.

In the examples that ended Chapter Seven, and this chapter, I have in many ways returned to the question with which I began my analysis in Chapter Four. That is, I have once again broached the issue of what kinds of dis/connections there exist between 'alternative' learning spaces and their 'outsides' ('mainstream' societies and educational systems). I repeat that the styles, qualities and intensities of these dis/connections vary hugely, both within and between different approaches to alternative education. But in several places, across several approaches, it is at this point in the book justifiable to argue that – when viewed comparatively – some alternative learning spaces offer a series of overlapping versions of life-itself that I have termed *collaboratively autonomous*. Building upon Pickerill and Chatterton's (2006) definition of autonomy in relation to social centres (Chapter Two), I have charted how some alternative learning spaces are characterised by multiple forms of dis/connection, which nearly always encapsulate but go beyond the idea that education spaces constitute autonomy for *human* subjects.

In the concluding chapter, I summarise these forms of (collaborative) autonomy in a more straightforward sense, outlining some possible implications for practitioners and policy makers. There, I also summarise the role that geography – that *spatiality* – plays and should play in making sense of alternative approaches to education. In the final paragraphs of this chapter, however, I want to say a little more in conceptual terms about the versions and visions of *life-itself* that are prompted by the latter examples in this chapter. As I have mentioned, these versions of life-itself, I am arguing, are *collaboratively* autonomous. I will discuss three things: endurance, dissonance, utopia. Each point is inspired by the recent work of Rosi Braidotti (2011), in her writings on life-itself.

My first point is about *endurance*. Braidotti (2011) argues that neoliberal (and other advanced, global) capitalist formations are founded upon a *fear* of life. She says that attempts to govern and know life (whether through genetic manipulation or the securitisation of potential terrorist threats) have produced a 'society that acts as if it was traumatized' (Braidotti, 2011, p 295). Moreover, this is a society that habitually takes redress for, prevention of, or empathy with *pain* as starting point for collective endeavour; from such a beginning, '[t]he yearning for solace, closure and justice is understandable and worthy of respect' (Braidotti, 2011, p 292). Her view of an affirmative or dissonant ethics – of life-itself – is not one that avoids pain, or such a search for 'justice', however. Instead of protecting oneself from pain (or risk), 'one has to endure' pain (Braidotti, 2011, p 289). For Braidotti, endurance requires a subject to open themselves to being affected by others; to bear pain without being destroyed by it; to working through pain in order to facilitate a 'mode of empathic copresence' that transforms 'negative into positive passions' (Braidotti, 2011, p 290). Returning to my own arguments and empirical material, this understanding of endurance encapsulates what I have tried to highlight. I have addressed how alternative educators attempt to foster habits that channel negative into positive 'energies', that embed changes of habit, that create interpersonal affective atmospheres, all of which are, it is *hoped*, meant to provoke a radical sense of care, openness, responsibility and *love* that collapse spatial scale. Often, they have to work through pain: through social disadvantage, with teenagers with impossible home lives, with children who have been badly bullied. Sometimes, in dealing with such pain, these formations may stutter; they may be, for-the-moment, affective intensities (like the experience of the boys with their knives at Joanne's forest school, quoted in this chapter). At other times, they may solidify into formations that take the form of social and more-than-social relations that become 'sites' (Marston et al, 2005): they may endure. Endurance may be understood in terms of an individual subject who acquires particular 'good habits'. Endurance maybe understood in spiritual terms, as in the Ananda Marga 'rings of sentiment' model, radiating outwards in terms of a presumptive consciousness about responsibility at overlapping spatial scales – through the body, the learning space, the 'local' community and the globe. In utopian terms (which are no more and no less 'grounded'), I have shown in this chapter that the outward-looking visions and versions of life-itself propounded at some alternative learning spaces seek enduring kinds of more-than-social relation. Recall, for instance, Charlotte, who as a homeschooling mother, is involved in all kinds of local projects designed to solidify local communities around alternative food, energy and housing solutions. Or recall, for instance, Maura, who argued that care farms like hers had to *rely on* voluntary community support in order to sustain themselves, in order, recursively, to sustain the local community. Herein, endurance matters to the dis/connections through which alternative learning spaces can support life-itself: it matters to their autonomy. This is a striking conclusion because some theorisations of autonomy (like those of utopia, to which I return below) argue that autonomous spaces gain their radical or prefigurative 'edge' precisely because they are ephemeral: the more they endure, the more the possibility that they can be incorporated into a neoliberal mainstream order, or the more they are beset by governmental surveillance (financial regulations, health and safety rules, and so on) (Brown, 2007). Yet, as Chatterton (2010) points out, the ultimate goal of autonomous social spaces (like squats) might be to draw attention to and act upon the increasing precariousness of life for those disadvantaged groups displaced from city centres by processes such as gentrification. At the same time, autonomous collectives have been involved in long-term projects (such as co-housing initiatives) that aim to solidify alternative ways of living that endure. Thus, the notion of endurance is by far from anathema to the concept of autonomy: autonomy does not only come about through experimentation and ephemerality. This is, as I have suggested, especially the case for some alternative learning spaces. It is just that their concerns differ from those of autonomous collectives and intentional communities (these are learning spaces, after all). Moreover, those concerns can usefully be understood to be more-than-social – to be about food or brain patterns that create autonomous spaces that endure, or whose effects upon learners might take the form of habits.

My second point is about *dissonance*. Braidotti's (2011) work turns on the argument that negativity (especially pain) can be turned to positivity. She does not always advocate direct resistance, opposition or revolution against advanced capitalist formulations of life-itself (and this is where, although they do not discuss 'life-itself' in such terms, her work resonates with that of Gibson-Graham [2006]). Rather, she questions what it might take to sustain

> the subject in his [sic] quest for more interrelations with others [...]. It affirms life as distance-at-work and as endurance. [...] Part of the answer lies in the formulation of the project: 'we' are in *this* together. This is a collective activity, a group project that connects active, conscious, and desiring citizens. (Braidotti, 2011, p 294)

Braidotti's work chimes with several other affect materialist and vital materialist theorists who seek new collaborations between what might seem to be surprising elements (for example Connolly, 2008). Hers is a call to work not only across *social* difference but to think carefully about how more-than-social 'citizens' are enrolled in the formulation of the 'we' who would posit alternative forms of life. As Bennett (2010) shows, the 'we' could involve foodstuffs, base metals, dead rats, and many matters besides. Bennett also argues (as mentioned earlier) that this recognition also allows for the activation of agency among those human *and* non-human agents who typically are unable to voice their concerns – from disadvantaged teenage boys to the materialities of 'mess' that I suggested were so important in Chapter Five. The very last examples provided in this chapter afforded a snapshot of some of these diverse, possible collaborations – Maura's care farm, Joanne's "community of inquiry", and Tony's (knowingly, satirically) utopian community of diversity that "wants to work together". For all of these vital materialist theorists, in this way, a patchwork of sometimes prefigurative, sometimes enduring collaborative spaces exists wherein the seeming obduracy of neoliberal/global capitalism can be challenged without necessarily overthrowing it. I remember (as just two, very simple, examples) that both Joanne and Tony run their learning spaces as businesses, both in spite of and in order to forward their visions of life-itself. Thus, these examples remind us that alternatives – dissonant alternatives, collaboratively autonomous, dis/connected alternatives – *are* possible (Fielding and Moss, 2011). Critically, it is in looking *across* such diverse, but overlapping, visions and versions for collaborative autonomy – as this book has always tried to do – that these visions gain weight. Indeed, it might be possible to forge conceptual, if not political and practical common ground *between* such visions, although clearly a book such as this one is not really the best conduit for forging such connections in practice.

My third point, which draws upon the two previous ones, is about *utopia*. I think it is quite appropriate to frame alternative learning spaces in terms of utopia. One reason for this is that alternative visions of the good life (utopias) – including those propounded by alternative educators – have been ridiculed in recent decades (Jacques, 2002). Thus, as Fielding and Moss (2011) argue, it is a critical task to map and affirm practices that involve some kind of utopian impulse but which too are grounded in real-world practices (see also Halpin, 2003). It is this combination (of vision and real-world practice) that affords a sense that alternatives are possible, and not merely desirable. A second reason is that (in a somewhat ironic manoeuvre), the language of utopianism has been taken up in recent education policies in the UK and other countries. Nowhere is this more apparent than in the grand languages of aspiration, transformation, promise and legacy that have characterised recent nationwide school-building projects in the UK, Australia and Portugal (to name but a few examples). I have argued elsewhere that we need to unpick this utopian languages with great care (Kraftl, 2012).

In these two contexts, then, I think that it is appropriate to reclaim the term 'utopia' in the construction of alter-narratives that expose far more *diverse* kinds of utopian longing than those represented in *Building Schools for the Future* and other school-building policies. Despite (and because of) these contexts, I have always been convinced about the continued importance of utopian visions, feelings and spatialities, particularly in the course of everyday life (see, for instance, Kraftl, 2007, 2008, 2010). I *had* also been convinced by the wonderful work of utopian theorists like Lucy Sargisson (1996, 2000) and Ruth Levitas (2010), who argued for processual, unthinkable, sometimes ephemeral versions of utopian desire rather than the stultifying, often exclusionary utopias of form that are traditionally indicated by the word. I am not seeking to radically move on from their work but merely to qualify it: to slow down their speedy temporalities; to *take time* with utopia (Chapter Five), and to make it endure. Braidotti (2011, p 295) does not see her affirmative thinking as utopian – other than 'in the sense of the positive affects that are mobilized in the process: the necessary dose of imagination, dreamlike vision, and bonding without which no social project can take off' (see also Anderson, 2006). I agree. But I disagree that a 'politics of affirmation [that creates] the conditions for endurance and hence for a sustainable future' (Braidotti, 2011, p 295) is not utopian. At the same time, I also disagree, therefore, with Fielding and Moss's (2011) account of the prefigurative and hence rather temporary utopian status of radical sites of education. This may be a matter of semantics, but, based upon the kinds of vision and collaboration in the vignettes that ended this chapter, I prefer the middle ground. I prefer a utopianism that *is*, indeed, grounded in the present, for the very reason that it works from dissonance with the present, with dis/connection, with the materialities and flows of life-itself, with habits that are spatialised as love and care (and not as static utopian spaces), but in a way that is outward looking and forward looking, and contains a *vision* of life that is inherent to the *version* of life that is currently being practised. In this way, then, the spatialities of learning are productive of collaborative, dis/connected forms of autonomy. Those forms of autonomy may sometimes spill over into alternative versions and visions of life-itself that are so powerful because they can endure through habit or increasingly solidified, more-than-social relations. And – for me at least – those versions and visions of life-itself may be powerfully utopian because they open out onto dissonant versions of the good life.

NINE

Conclusion: geographies of alternative education and the value of *autonomous* learning spaces

The beginning of the 21st century was characterised by both striking changes and significant continuities in the UK educational landscape. From 2010 the role of the state in providing education came under particular scrutiny, with a new coalition government intent on implementing 'austerity measures' after the global economic downturn of 2008 onwards. At the same time, many of the underlying assumptions of neoliberalism inherited from the previous government persisted, albeit in an 'intensified' form (Grimshaw and Rubery, 2012, p 105). For instance, the previous New Labour administration's grand, nation-wide school-building projects had been replaced with discourses of austerity and local control (especially under the flagship Free Schools policy for England and Wales, which, incidentally, was first suggested by New Labour). Elsewhere, in Scotland, a new curriculum afforded the opportunity for pupils at risk of school exclusion to put together a suite of activities taken from a range of learning providers, such as forest schools and care farms. Significantly, a controversial proposed reform of special educational needs provision in England (announced in May 2012) would do something similar – providing parents the control over funding to choose learning provision that would suit their child. It is also notable that several of the fifty or so schools approved to become free schools in the second wave of that programme expressly follow alternative educational philosophies – from a Steiner school in Frome, to schools in disadvantaged areas of Bradford and London that advocate ostensibly human scale values and personalised learning. Outside the UK, the neoliberalisation and marketisation of education also continues apace. In different ways, in different national contexts, a shift from 'largely national and state-focussed control' has created 'contradictory forms of coordination and control, played out in different policy spaces (Brooks et al, 2012, p 10). Notably, looking across different national contexts, alternative forms of education are treated in highly variegated and similarly contradictory ways (Woods and Woods, 2009).

Against this backdrop, this chapter reflects on some of the potential, broader implications of the *spatialities* of alternative education, with a particular focus upon the UK learning spaces that have formed the case studies for this book. Taking my two main aims together, my central argument has been that we see the spatialities of alternative education as *autonomous*, in all sorts of significant ways. Therefore, this chapter does not review all of the arguments in the book, but rather summarises the most significant features of what I have termed autonomous learning spaces. It also explores what might be the ramifications – for policy makers, educators in the mainstream and alternative sectors, and academics – of theorising alternative learning spaces as autonomous. My intention is not simply to replace one word ('alternative') with another, nor to dismiss several excellent and nuanced theorisations of alternative education (especially Ferguson and Seddon, 2007; Woods and Woods, 2009). Rather, with a geographical lens, I have sought to add further complexity and subtlety to this research, in order to account for an even greater range of ways in which alternative learning *spaces* are constituted. As I have shown, a theory of autonomy allows us to account not only for a diverse array of pragmatic, conceptual and political dis/connections with other alternative learning spaces and those people and places named 'mainstream'. In addition, it can help us to understand the ways in which diverse, more-than-social processes (like habit, messy materialities, and flows of foodstuffs) can be part and parcel of the spatialities of alternative education. In Chapter Eight, the culmination of this argument was in recognising how alternative learning spaces can, sometimes, provoke alternative versions and visions of life-itself. I argued there that *these* dissonant versions of the 'good life' are not merely autonomous but *collaboratively autonomous*, because they seek to enrol a greater range of feelings and (more-than-social) agents than was the case for the more overtly 'social', representational concerns outlined in Chapter Four.

In this conclusion, then, I proceed to summarise first and foremost the key features of autonomous learning spaces, turning to notions of collaborative autonomy at the very end. I begin with the arguments outlined in Chapter Four, but tease out elements that cut across several chapters. I should also point out, of course, that the theory of autonomy I am about to outline neither explains every alternative learning space, nor can every feature be found in each setting. However, in the process of generalisation, I tease out some potential implications for policy makers, practitioners and academics, with potential resonances within and beyond the UK context. I hope that, in so doing, the chapter will not merely provoke thought and critical reflection, but inspire and inform readers about the manifold political and practical ramifications of autonomous learning spaces.

Autonomous learning spaces and 'the mainstream'

There exist very few alternative learning spaces that actively seek to isolate themselves from mainstream societies. Rather, most learning spaces are constituted by a fuzzy, dynamic, but carefully orchestrated process of negotiation between connection and disconnection. In a fundamental sense, this is why – inspired by Pickerill and Chatterton's (2006) theory of autonomous geographies – I have generally preferred to term them 'autonomous', and not 'alternative'. But, in focusing upon the rather different realm of alternative education, I have tried to extend, question and open up for debate previous understandings of autonomy. In several chapters (but especially Chapter Four), I demonstrated how the management of connections and disconnections involved many considerations. These considerations encompassed, but extended beyond, the separation/engagement/activism triad advanced by Woods and Woods (2009). They also encompassed, but extended beyond, the idea that 'alternatives' do more than provoke thought or offer prefigurative kernels of inspiration (Fielding and Moss, 2011). I am arguing that the notion of autonomy affords a sense that 'alternatives' are *more* than simply symbolic or affective provocations that, in a rather patronising sense, exist in order to make 'us' (those not able, brave, well-resourced or willing enough to be different) realise that life could be otherwise. That may be the point, but, I have argued, alternative learning spaces are, in variegated ways, so much more *engaged* with multiple mainstreams than this – albeit not always successfully or in ways that every reader would find desirable.

It is vitally important to repeat that I am not saying that all alternative learning spaces are autonomous, all of the time, or in the same ways. Nor am I saying that alternative learning spaces are autonomous in ways that directly mirror the complex, contested and often radical politics of social movements and solidarity groups (for example Sitrin, 2006). To argue in that way would be to undermine my conviction – drawing upon Gibson-Graham (2006), and detailed in Chapter Four – that alternative learning spaces are dis/connected from multiple mainstreams, in diverse and ever-changing ways. Nonetheless, I am also persuaded that the notion of autonomy is important. I mean this in a pragmatic sense, for understanding the ways in which alternative learning spaces draw upon and inform government policies, local education authorities, local communities and so many other elements of 'mainstream' society. And

I mean this in a political sense, because – as I demonstrated at the end of Chapter Eight – *some* alternative learning spaces are involved in visions and versions of life-itself that either implicitly or explicitly connect with the kinds of creative resistance to neoliberal/global capitalism practised in autonomous spaces (Pickerill and Chatterton, 2006). However, even in those vignettes, educators/practitioners struggled with the necessity to sometimes rely on capitalist forms of financial organisation (such as becoming a private business) – just as Gibson-Graham (2006) argue that some non-capitalist, economic cooperatives must sometimes rely on capitalist trade relations in order to survive, and that some groups do so more than others. Following Gibson-Graham, I emphasise that alternative learning spaces represent a diverse and shifting patchwork of connections and disconnections, let alone the diverse ways in which they deal with mess, habit, love or life-itself. Thus, the following should not be seen as a catch-all theorisation or model of 'autonomous learning spaces'. Rather, some (and sometimes all) of the following elements were present across several 'types' of learning space.

De-schooling spaces

Inspired in part by theories of un-schooling (Illich, 2002 [1970]), and by recent variations on that theme popularised online (for example *www.thersa.org/events/video/archive/sir-ken-robinson*) several educators wanted to get rid of the 'artifice' of schooling. Many viewed school as a 'uniform' space, characterised by particular smells, rhythms, dress, forms of behaviour and architecture (school uniforms, classrooms, corridors). As I outlined in Chapter Five, this meant that they had tried to manipulate material spaces in order to create alternative atmospheres – of home, for instance – in which children would feel more comfortable. Some educators (like homeschoolers) articulated a kind of spatial dualism between school-like and home-like spaces, preferring the latter. While the impulse to 'de-school' spaces seemed 'anti-school', the vast majority of alternative educators were not *anti-school*. Instead, they were engaged – to differing degrees – in attempts to radically re-conceptualise schools. They sought to use their experiences to provoke discussions on what schools should do and, especially, what they should look and feel like. In my experience, many teachers in mainstream schools nod along when they view Ken Robinson's critiques of schooling, yet struggle to see how, individually or collectively, they might have the means to change what schools look and feel like. I return to the design and feel of schools later on.

Engaging in dialogue

Whereas my previous point emphasised the *potential* impact of an impulse to radically re-think schools, I have repeatedly highlighted a more *active* impulse among educators to engage in some kind of dialogue with mainstream education systems. Looking across the gamut of alternative educators, these kinds of conversations are highly variegated. In some cases, alternative educators had worked or trained in the mainstream sector, and were inspired by historical practices that had once been prevalent in mainstream education but had now been lost (like vocational science studies). In other cases (as for homeschoolers), the mainstream was a moral guide or touchstone for monitoring their children's progress. In still other cases, educators viewed their learning spaces as 'resources' or 'hubs' through which could be (and was) fostered dialogue about the possibilities of doing things differently in all kinds of settings. An examples of the latter was the care farm in Chapter Eight that saw itself as a central resource for individuals, families, schools and other care settings wishing to keep animals and live the 'good life'. This book has, therefore, highlighted that even the most ardent critics of the 'artifice' of school want to engage in productive, if sometimes critical, conversation with mainstream educators. Not all of these approaches will work in all contexts. But I have traced in some detail a series of ways in which these forms of dialogue might proceed and educators – both mainstream and alternative – might take inspiration from these or, indeed, try something different again.

Engaging with mainstream regulatory frameworks

It is common knowledge that almost all educators – mainstream or alternative – sometimes despair about the 'cultures' produced by health and safety guidance, standardised testing, league tables and outcomes-orientated curricula. But, strikingly, the majority of educators talked about the ways in which they tried to negotiate (rather than avoid) the dense, evermore bureaucratised legislative frameworks that impinge upon children's education. For instance, homeschoolers and teachers at Kilquhanity talked about the on/off relationship they had had with state school inspectors, but were clear that in some cases that relationship could be supportive and productive. In several forest schools and care farms, practitioners were grappling with whether their courses should be accredited in some way, so that young people's learning could combine intrinsic with instrumental outcomes. Since they wanted young people to return to school or get a job, they had also tried to develop ways to account for the non-representational ways in which children had 'moved' that would be recognisable to teachers and employers. Perhaps most importantly, several learning spaces were not designed as permanent alternatives *to* mainstream education. Rather, young people were somehow referred for remedial work, in order to learn specific skills, or with a view to channelling their habitual dispositions in ways that would enable them to take a fuller part in society. While this would not be so true of alternative schools (like Steiner schools) or homeschooling, one must remember that many children educated in those contexts go on to study A-Levels at mainstream schools, study at university, or enter into a whole gamut of 'ordinary' jobs. In any case, the key message – for *all* educators – is that bureaucracy may not necessarily be a bad thing per se. This book has tried to exemplify several productive ways in which alternative educators negotiate, manage, reframe and in some cases capitalise upon regulatory processes, from which some readers may take inspiration.

The dilemma of funding

The majority of alternative educators hold pedagogical, political, spiritual and/or philosophical beliefs for which the *funding* of their activities poses a particularly problematic question. Since many learning spaces cannot rely solely (or in part) upon state funding, they must make difficult decisions about charging learners and their families. Some alternative schools are ostensibly fee-paying, independent schools, although they will offer reduced fees for lower-income families. Some care farms charge small entry fees for members of the public to cover their costs; others have become businesses that charge on a per-head basis. In all cases, educators committed to a broader social and/or community vision have found it difficult to charge for what they do. All of these concerns were heightened by the fact that several learning spaces I visited had been indirectly affected by the austerity measures introduced by the UK government (for instance, a large reduction in funding for play workers that had had a knock-on effect at some urban care farms). Common conceptions about alternative education are either that they offer forms of privatised education for the wealthy minority, or that they naively scrape by through goodwill, volunteer work and the strength of their vision. The point here is that *both* of these facets may be present, but that the status of funding is far more complicated than these conceptions would allow. What is more certain is that the majority of educators are neither set on privatisation, nor naive about their own survival: in fact, in the production of autonomous learning spaces, educators carefully manage complex moral and economic terrains.

Being 'open'

Underpinning all of the above dis/connections was a widespread belief amongst educators in remaining open to engaging with anybody who wanted to engage with them, in whatever form. Thus, as part of their community mission, several urban-based care farms have a more or less 'open gate' policy on entry, dealing with whomever walks in once they are there. Others stressed the need for some basic rules and boundaries so that the interaction between (for instance) care farm clients and public visitors could be as 'realistic' as possible. Very differently, homeschoolers spoke about how they – sometimes reluctantly – remained open to explaining why they homeschooled their children when they were challenged by members of the public. Differently again, several forest school practitioners emphasised being distant but *near enough* to local communities. Locating themselves in this way meant three things: their learning sites could be accessible to communities who 'needed' their services; they could foster a sense of belonging among communities who had not previously identified with a local patch of woodland; and yet they could provide a space sufficiently different from 'everyday' settings that it could be somehow transformative. Across several different learning spaces, educators indicated that, in harbouring such an open disposition, sometimes 'surprising', unanticipated forms of learning could take place. Thus, it is not only important to consider how alternative educators enter into dialogue with mainstream *educational* systems (Woods and Woods, 2009). Rather, alternative learning spaces are constituted by all kinds of relationships with their wider publics – publics that could be diverse and unpredictable. In this sense, being 'open' was a key part of what made some of them *autonomous* learning spaces that, as I indicated in Chapter Eight, tried to operate in an outward-looking, presumptively generous, *collaborative* manner. However, it is also the case that, at each site, the rules, boundaries and everyday practices that framed that openness had to be very carefully negotiated.

Implications

The preceding paragraphs indicate just five kinds of dis/connection, each of which entails a highly variegated set of political, pragmatic, financial, pedagogical and other concerns. In every case, autonomous learning spaces are constituted by careful negotiation and management of such concerns in ways that confirm that what they do is somehow *different*, but in a way that is connected with multiple 'mainstreams' – schools, legislative systems, local communities, visitors and more besides. These dis/connections may harbour all kinds of implications, but I will confine myself to three.

First, in the UK context, schools have been encouraged to offer a range of 'Extended Services' to their local communities – homework clubs, health services, parenting support, sports facilities and more besides. At the same time, for a variety of (sometimes good) reasons, many mainstream schools appear increasingly 'closed' to the local community – physically fenced off to visitors. The impetus for Extended Services has, in my mind, reinforced the disconnection between schools and local communities, simply because those services have been specifically named as such. In other words, one implication (among many) is that schools did not or could not offer such services in the past and that they now need to 'reach out' – albeit in some very particular ways. Clearly, a mainstream primary school is not the same as an urban care farm. Yet, my question for alternative *and* mainstream educators is whether they could enter into a productive, collaborative dialogue about how mainstream schools *could* engage with local communities in some of the ways exemplified in this book. Similarly, because my intention has not been to reify alternative education above the mainstream, I wonder to what extent alternative learning spaces could actually offer some 'Extended Services' – perhaps in partnership with local mainstream schools, and/or perhaps inspired by them (for a critical account of the latter, see Holloway and Pimlott-Wilson, 2011). More broadly, it has been observed that the relationship between schools and their local communities is being reconfigured under certain forms of neoliberal educational restructuring that are globally widespread (for example in New Zealand, see Witten et al, 2003). Thus, this is a consideration that goes beyond Extended Services and the UK context, and one where the role of alternative education spaces in providing for and linking up with state schools in supporting local communities could be of vital importance.

Second, taken together, the regulatory and financial frameworks surrounding alternative education in the UK (as in several other geographical contexts) remain uncertain. There remain both opportunities and challenges. In the UK, the free schools initiative may provide state funding for certain kinds of alternative schools – although I know that at least two of my case study schools unsuccessfully applied for free school status. It remains to be seen whether the state funding of at least two Steiner schools will mean that they must do anything significantly different from other Steiner schools. Indeed, there is a pressing need for research here. In Scotland, and likely in England, changes to curricula and Special Educational Needs funding may provide greater opportunities for a range of alternative learning spaces, as parents are allocated funding to choose learning activities for their children. Once again, this may entail some difficult decisions for alternative educators – not least about whether and how to charge for services for which they had previously only asked for voluntary donations. Furthermore, alternative learning spaces may find themselves being repositioned in light of current austerity measures and Prime Minister David Cameron's vision for the 'Big Society' (wherein, crudely, local communities, businesses and volunteers take greater responsibility for previously state-funded service provision). To be sure, the massive rise in forest schools and care farms in the UK will make them increasingly visible as possible sites through which care, learning and other services for young people could be provided. At the same time, they are losing some of the funding that has enabled them to be so 'open' to local communities, and are themselves increasingly having to rely upon volunteer labour and on communities 'pulling together' to keep them open. Critically, some care farm practitioners openly questioned whether they *should* be repositioned as a replacement for previously state-funded services: arguably they are well placed to do so and should be encouraged to take up this challenge. Conversely, to take on such a role might be to compromise the very forms of autonomy that I have already described, and which many practitioners deemed to be highly effective (for a more detailed and balanced critique of the Big Society's impacts upon local community organisations, see North, 2011).

Third, then, in the policy contexts I outlined at the beginning of this chapter, there needs to be ongoing discussion about the possible incorporation of alternative learning spaces into more mainstream provision, whether through free schools or as loci for the rolling out of the 'Big Society'). It is here that UK practitioners may want to look to other countries to learn broader lessons. In New Zealand, for instance, alternative *schools* are more visible within state policy making, but are more highly regulated than in the UK. For instance, from 2011, alternative schools are required to employ registered teachers as 'pedagogical' leaders (http://alternativeeducation.tki.org.nz). Each school must also enter into a memorandum of agreement if they receive Ministry of Education funding – an agreement contingent upon the satisfactory outcomes of reporting and ongoing evaluation by the Ministry. This runs against the grain of what happens in Canada, for instance, where formal teacher training is deemed less important than certain character traits in the delivery and legitimation of alternative learning approaches (Quirke, 2009). In the US, 'alternative education' has a double meaning. On the one hand, the term 'alternative school' refers to fee-paying, independent schools (including Montessori and democratic schools), similar to the examples referred to in this book. On the other hand, the term 'alternative education' refers to the provision in most states of a specialist service, located outside public schools, for children with special, emotional or behavioural needs. Indeed, an increasing number of such children are being educated outside public schools in the US, with very mixed results (Wasburn-Moses, 2011). There is no suggestion that, in the UK, care farms become incorporated into a US-style system of alternative schools for children struggling in mainstream schools, nor that a funding or regulatory framework like that in New Zealand be introduced. However, as different alternative learning spaces become repositioned with respect to mainstream, public service provision, these international examples could provide a series of important lessons for future research and policy making. How a country treats its alternative learning spaces could have profound implications for the kinds of spaces that exist – and the kinds of autonomous dis/connections that those spaces can forge with the mainstream(s).

What's different about autonomous learning spaces themselves?

Cutting across the chapters in this book was a sense that alternative learning spaces looked and felt different from mainstream educational settings. That is, that the 'internal' spaces – the buildings, the decor, the interpersonal relationships – were underpinned by a different set of assumptions from those of mainstream schools, for instance. Of course, the notion of autonomy implies some distance and alterity (if not separation) from the mainstream, as much as it does connection. I argue that it is in some of the materialities, feelings and interpersonal relationships internal to alternative learning spaces that the differences with mainstream education are most visible. However, I will also indicate some possible implications for alternative *and* mainstream settings. Again, I focus on the UK context, but note that because all of the educational 'types' I have considered in this book are more geographically widespread (if not global) these implications will have relevance outside the UK, even if they may be expressed somewhat differently.

Taking time

A well-known facet of the 'de-schooling' critique is that contemporary forms of mainstream education pressurise children: that mainstream education is based upon a 'flawed' developmental model of childhood that places children into narrow age-classified groups (year groups), and does not allow time for children to follow their own learning styles or interests in ways that might diverge from a linear, teleological model. Interestingly, some alternative approaches retain developmental models (like Montessori and Steiner schooling). But there is, across most alternative learning spaces, an insistence upon taking time to observe and be with children, attuning to their 'needs', however defined. Crucial here are the material spatialities of the learning environment – how, for instance, learning activities in the Montessori classroom are highly regimented in order to allow children the freedom to choose which skill they wish to develop next. Crucial here also are the 'atmospheres' that can be created by careful combinations of textures, colours, materials and smells – such as in the home-like atmosphere of the Steiner kindergarten. The influences of Montessori and Steiner approaches on the mainstream (especially early years) curriculum are well known (Knight, 2009). But, given what some see as the 'schoolification' of the proposed new early-years curriculum in the UK, there may be scope to revisit critically whether the material and practical elements of Montessori and Steiner schooling that have been translated into schools have become somewhat divorced from their underpinning imperative – to take time to attune to what individual children need, and to allow children to take time themselves.

Mess

Drawing on Actor-Network Theory, I argued that several learning spaces (including care farms, homeschooling and human scale schools) valorised mess in various guises. The most obvious example was the inescapably excessive presence of material mess – glitter, glue, paint, twigs, skulls and all manner of other objects. The presence of these objects was both desirable (because it symbolised 'good learning') and viewed as something that simply could not and should not be controlled – the desire for material order was seen as something that could constrict learning and diminish learning atmospheres. But rarely did educators simply valorise mess alone; rather, they attempted to negotiate between mess and order, between contingency and design. The role of mess is something that has gained increasing attention in other settings. For instance, UK children's centres have allocated times for 'messy play' that can involve children and parents. In the playwork sector, the original 'adventure playgrounds', which originated out of post-war urban bomb sites, tended to be (and have often remained) messy, chaotic spaces (Sutton-Smith, 2001; Russell, 2012). Like the learning spaces in this book, each of these approaches represents a different way to account for, manage and incorporate the excessiveness of mess in children's lives. Thus, my feeling is that while mess may be a key constituent in what makes alternative learning spaces different, the difference is not so great. It is, rather, a matter of contrasting *how* mess is dealt with in different learning settings. It may be, then, that mess – and all it entails – may be a critical and productive point of connection in the kinds of dialogues and engagements between the mainstream and alternative educational sectors that I highlighted earlier. I also believe that playworkers have an important role to play in these kinds of dialogue – a point I return to later.

Immanence/imminence

A key feature of virtually all approaches to alternative education is that learning is both immanent and imminent to life itself. This represents an extended theorisation of the sense in which informal learning can take place in any circumstance in everyday life (Falk et al, 2009). My key contribution has been to be argue that learning is viewed not only as temporally imminent but *also* as spatially immanent: that is, that the dis/orderly materialities of parks, museums, homes, forests and farms themselves afford learning potential. Educators and learners acknowledged this in two ways: first, in terms of the affordances – the *feelings* – that could be created through smelling freshly-baked bread in the Steiner kindergarten, or through caring for the same animals, in the same pens, everyday; second, in terms of the ways they managed the *movement* of children through and between different learning spaces. For homeschoolers, for instance, it was vitally important to move between learning spaces to take advantage of the different, immanent learning possibilities afforded by combination. And at Findhorn, for example, I demonstrated the crucial importance of walking-through spaces side by side: the embodied act of walking entailed different kinds of conversation and engagement with the material (and 'natural') world than simply sitting still, face-to-face. I acknowledged that educators in mainstream schools are acutely aware of the different ways in which children learn, and it is far from the case that children in mainstream schools simply sit still all day. Indeed, it is for this reason that forest schools are becoming increasingly well visited by groups of mainstream primary school children, and that mainstream teachers are beginning to take up forest school qualifications themselves. The question is, then, not so much of making teachers aware of what alternative educators do – many of them already are aware, and, anyway, to do so would again be to reify alternative learning spaces as prefigurative examples of how the world could be otherwise (and, by implication, 'better'). Rather, if we follow the argument that alternative learning spaces are autonomous, then the broader question is of how the 'internal' processes that constitute them could be made more accessible to children in mainstream schools, or form a part of what happens there (and this is as relevant to other geographical contexts as it is to the UK). Increasingly, some children in some schools are accessing forest schools and care farms through referrals and school visits. The questions are whether all children should have such possibilities and whether other forms of connection (for instance between a Steiner school and other local primary schools) would be valuable. I hope that this book might give a small sense of what kinds of affordances and movements are deemed to be both possible and desirable in alternative settings, and therefore *may* be incorporated into mainstream settings.

Rules

A longstanding assumption about alternative approaches to learning is that they have very few rules. As I indicated in several places, this is simply not true. At Kilquhanity (as at Summerhill and other democratic schools around the world), there are often *more* rules than there are in mainstream schools. At most care farms and forest schools, practitioners set out careful boundaries – in terms of the physical extent of the learning space, expectations for behaviour, and the ways in which children themselves should deal with interpersonal tensions. Moreover, one can view the careful consideration of learning activities and the rhythms of the school day (for instance in Montessori classrooms) as a series of spatialised rules that make the classroom environment immediately 'legible' to children. And, indeed, older homeschooled children recognised the need for careful rule setting so that they could continue their commitment to learning as they became teenagers. The key point here is that, in each instance, it is a matter of balance. That balance is different not only in terms of each 'type' of learning space but in each individual learning space. In this way, rules are, in general, interpreted to achieve some very particular goals: to engender children's participation in the creation of those rules; to encourage children to deal with their own problems, without the intervention of adults; and to act as a framework (even it is a 'rickety' framework, as one care farm practitioner put it) within which children can be freer than in mainstream settings. Once again, there is a parallel with many playwork settings here, where the seeming chaos of an adventure playground may be (barely) contained by a set of rules negotiated by children and adults. There are two implications for a theory of autonomy here. The first is that in all but the most permissive homeschooling families (of which there are very few) rules are crucial to the development of children's individual autonomy. It is only through such frameworks that children are able to develop towards a kind of freedom that recognises their interdependence with and responsibilities towards others. The second is that, since the 'uniformity' of mainstream schools is so universally criticised, it may be here that alternative and mainstream educators (and, again, playworkers) could engage in productive dialogue. That dialogue would not be directed towards a continuation of despair about mainstream schools, nor making them look more like alternative settings by changing a few rules. It would, rather, be a dialogue about how rules are deployed and what the relationship between those rules and different forms of learning (and learning spaces) might be.

The human scale: friendship, family and love

It is well documented that alternative educational approaches value meaningful, personalised, small scale or human scale relationships between teachers and pupils. Notably, such relationships are also a feature of many autonomous social movements (for example Sitrin, 2006). There is also significant research about the role of friendships and the family in children's learning, and an increasing recognition (especially in the UK and the US) in the mainstream educational sector that the 'small scale' can foster such relationships (for example Harland and Mason, 2010). But, extending these arguments in this book, I have shown that alternative learning spaces are constituted by particular kinds of interpersonal relationships. I have shown how mixed-age friendships are viewed by several educators as opportunities for informal and formal learning, and for caring, nurturing relationships both between children and between children and adults. More importantly, I argued for the significance of family-*like* relationships across a range of settings. Once again, I want to be careful to state that I am not privileging the role of the *nuclear* family, nor necessarily of learning spaces representing a kind of surrogate family. For instance, in Steiner schools and human scale schools, educators were quite clear that their early-years classrooms were *like* homes but were not homes – they were learning spaces.

From the foregoing examples, and drawing upon a range of educational theorists, my aim was to point to the role of love as something that could be promulgated through more intimate, family-like relationships, and which could form an important affective basis for learning. Once again, this is a key feature of some autonomous social movements (Sitrin, 2006). I showed how certain forms of affection and bodily contact could, for instance, be as constitutive of a 'home-like' learning atmosphere as the smells and colours of a Steiner kindergarten. But my most important contribution was to argue that such relationships and feelings were *outward looking* as much as a facet of the inward-facing spatialities of a particular learning site. That is, I dispelled the notion that 'human scale' education is simply about the very small scale: instead, family-like relations are a basis for a 'scaled-up' kind of love. Read this way, love takes the form of a presumptive generosity and sense of responsibility to those both near and far. Ultimately, especially across those approaches that involve a spiritual element, that responsibility was understood at a global scale – as a responsibility to life-itself. Albeit not in these terms, selected scholars of alternative education have also observed these 'scaled-up' notions of responsibility, care and love across several educational 'types', in different geographical contexts (for indicative examples, see the collection by Woods and Woods, 2009). But I am arguing specifically that this 'scaling up' is a key facet of what makes alternative learning spaces *autonomous*. Importantly, this 'outward lookingness' underpins the desire for engagement, dialogue and conversation that I mentioned earlier in this chapter, as much as it is articulated in the rather more spiritual, global commitments of Ananda Marga and other belief-systems, which themselves are globally widespread. This all may appear a little intangible, and seem based upon a premise of potential rather than actual responsibility. At times, this may be true; but at others it may not (and it is certainly not my place to judge). The point is that all of the 'internal' elements that constitute the spatialities of alternative learning spaces are often simultaneously 'external'. The impulse to connect is *driven by* the interpersonal feelings and materialities that make up those spaces – but which very deliberately exceed them. And finally, in a more prosaic sense, I reiterate a question asked by bell hooks and several other theorists: what can we learn *from* alternative learning spaces about the role of friendship, the family-like, and love 'scaled up' from the local scale? And could and should mainstream educators seek to learn from the specific conceptions of those terms that I have attended to in this book?

(Collaboratively) autonomous learning spaces: habit and life-itself

My argument in Chapter Eight was that some autonomous learning spaces present visions and versions of life-itself that do not (entirely) prop up the versions of life-itself increasingly designed and regulated by neoliberal governmental regimes (Rose, 2007; Hansom Thiem, 2009). I argued that the notion of autonomy could be expanded still further because many (but by no means all) educators sought to enrol more-than-social elements into their learning spaces. Thus, we can understand 'autonomy' as a more explicitly *social* process: but we can also understand autonomy in an expanded sense – *collaborative autonomy* – as one in which are enrolled a yet more diverse range of actors. I retain the 'social' in this conception as I do not want to imply that collaborative autonomy simply means attending to non-human agents and flows – like food or neurological processes – to the detriment of human action. Rather, it means extending the remit of autonomy to acknowledge an expanded range of collaborations. This means recognising that the role of foodstuffs in learning spaces is, in some instances, tied into interrelationships between homeschoolers who are also part of food-growing cooperatives. Or, it means acknowledging that those educators who seek to instil loving habits in children see themselves as part of a broader 'community of practice' that could include scientists, psychologists, other alternative educators, mainstream educators, and 'natures' that do not so much 'impact' on children but are carefully enrolled in the process of learning. I argued that these visions of life-itself, which we could at times term utopian, are so powerful because they *endure* and because they are *dissonant* (and it is important that they do both in order to have any purchase). In this way, I see collaboratively autonomous learning spaces as outward looking – as Hansom Thiem (2009) puts it – because they do not prop up or reflect the imperatives of neoliberal global capitalism, but seek to engage, reframe, extend beyond or even (incrementally) to change them. Let me recap my argument in Chapter Eight briefly, focusing on two of my main concerns in the later chapters of the book: habit and non-human natures. In both cases, love, which I introduced at the end of the last section, bubbles under the surface.

Habit

A central argument of this book has been that many alternative
educators attempt at some level to intervene into the habits of young
people. They want to foster alternative learning habits that, initially, are
aimed at individual behaviour change. However, in developing the work
of Félix Ravaisson, and drawing on non-representational theories of
affect, I argued that habit could also be felt and produced collectively
– through the very dis/orderly materialities and interpersonal
relationships I have already discussed. Recursively, those affective,
collaborative habits could have effects upon the habits of an individual,
so that a homeschooling group could gradually 'de-school' a previously
mainstream-schooled child simply through the *force* of group habit.
Once again, I argued that there was then an interplay between the
internal affects created within a learning space and the desired effects
of such habits *beyond* that learning space. Thus, to become loving was
to acquire a particular habitual disposition to the world that made one
open, welcoming, generous and responsible to strangers near and far.
More pragmatically, at care farms, channelling a young person's habits
could provide the foundation for their ability to return to school or
work (because their habitual instinct would be to mend, rather than
kick, a broken fence). And, in the words of one young person who had
been homeschooled and been to mainstream school, it was possible to
discern similar registers of habit (like 'seriousness') in both alternative
and mainstream settings. However, those habits could be manifested
in some particular ways, such as how mainstream pupils were 'even
serious about having fun', or were committed to their studies in
different ways and for different reasons from homeschooled children.
In these senses we can see habit as truly collaboratively autonomous:
promulgating and promulgated by individuals, groups, materials, feelings
and dis/connections between alternative and mainstream settings. We
also encounter the importance of *endurance*: the formation of habits –
directed towards the achievement of the 'good life', however defined
– that exceed momentary, ephemeral moments of hope that could
so easily be dismissed as 'escapist' (thereby diminishing the idea that
alternatives *are* possible). Politically, as a form of life that endures (and
there are others), habits are important to the production of alternative
versions and visions of life-itself.

Notwithstanding the theoretical advances of these findings, what
could be the pragmatic and policy implications here? My argument is
that these implications rest with contrasting the different ways in which
learning habits reflect different versions of life-itself. And here there *are*

some profound implications, which have to be treated with great care. The first is that while mainstream schools have also (arguably always) instilled particular learning habits among pupils, the select examples I provided in Chapter Six afford room for critical reflection about the necessity of those particular habits for learning. In particular, again, I raise the question of whether and how *loving* habits could figure more prominently in mainstream education. The second point is that intervention into children's habit formation is becoming increasingly intensive under neoliberal modes of governance (Dolan et al, 2010). For example, Jessica Pykett (2012) points out how contemporary neuroscientific advances may increasingly be deployed in schools – for instance via 'brain gyms', where the teacher becomes a mere cipher for neuroscientific knowledge about the bodily habits that will foster 'good learning'. Similarly, at the time of finishing this book, a new centre for research in the formation of character was opened within the University of Birmingham's School of Education (http://www.birmingham.ac.uk/news/latest/2012/05/15May-Jubilee-Centre-Press-Release.aspx). The centre will aim to understand the kinds of character traits and virtues crucial to 'modern Britain', asking how 'good character' could shape social futures and public service, and foster more optimistic dispositions to the future. Part of the centre's remit will be to consider the implications for 'teaching character' in schools. And, similarly, in the US, the UK, Australia and New Zealand, there has been significant interest in teaching 'Habits of Mind' – like 'persistence' and 'managing impulsivity' (www.habitsofmind.org). Through reflexive training activities, the Habits of Mind are intended to make children lifelong, flexible, autonomous learners where 'certain patterns of intellectual behaviour that produce powerful results' are acquired and then 'drawn forth' when they are required in daily life (www.habitsofmind.co.uk).

One could read each of these as attempts to inculcate children, whether drawing upon the lessons of contemporary neuroscience or not, with habits that will make them into the flexible subjects apparently required by neoliberal, capitalist economies (Katz, 2008). But my response is a little more sympathetic than this. I am not saying that any of these developments is necessarily bad, nor that intervening into children's habit formation (whether in these examples or those given in this book) is underpinned by an insidious scientific or political agenda. Rather, I am calling for fuller consideration of the possible moral implications (and ends) entailed in intervening into habit formation in whatever way. On the one hand, we might see such interventions as the three already listed as yet more attempts to govern and anticipate life-itself (Anderson, 2010). Read this way, the kinds of habit formation exemplified earlier in this book might be read against this grain – as realistic and desirable alternatives to neoliberal habits. On the other hand, if we retain a focus upon autonomy, it would be more productive to place these different forms of habit intervention alongside one another, because there are certain resonances between the values underpinning the Birmingham research centre and those in some of my case studies. For example, like several human scale educators, the John Templeton Foundation (www.templeton.org) promotes values such as freedom, creativity, love and forgiveness, and seeks to combine spiritual with scientific practice.

Clearly, and importantly, some readers may subscribe neither to any of the kinds of habit examined in this book, nor to those espoused by the John Templeton Foundation, and that is the point. Through multiple empirical case studies this book has raised critical questions, which are moral and political as much as pedagogical, about habit-intervention as a form of learning, but it has done so in ways that recognise considerable diversity beyond the kinds of intervention in the mainstream educational sector that have simultaneously raised so many hopes and so many fears. Similarly, just as Ecclestone and Hayes (2008) chart the rise of 'therapeutic education' across a range of mainstream settings (including primary schools and the workplace), and critique them for making children introspective and non-aspirational, there are some examples in this book of where therapeutic-style approaches (albeit not called that) *can* offer crucial, if short-term and specifically located measures that can turn around the life of a young person affected by bullying, for instance (Chapter Six). At the same time, several educators told me that these kinds of approaches did not work for all of the children they had worked with, and, again, that is the point. This, in the specific context of habit, is what I mean by *dissonance*: how the occasion to *compare* what happens at alternative learning spaces with other (if you like, mainstream) settings breeds both familiarity and unfamiliarity. Hence, dissonance is an important facet of autonomy, but autonomy may not always be the endgame. Rather, in some cases, it is my hope that in placing examples of autonomous learning spaces alongside one another and (in this chapter) alongside cognate mainstream examples, this book might also open up further *questions* about which kinds of habits and therapeutic education, and so on, might (in context) be desirable and which might not.

Non-human natures and life-itself

I argued in Chapter Eight for the careful consideration of how non-human natures are also constitutive of alternative learning spaces. Such natures may be represented by the dis/orderly materialities I accounted for in Chapter Five – skulls, twigs, glue, paper or glitter. Somewhat differently, those non-human natures might involve foodstuffs – the plants that children grow, tend, cook and eat at a care farm, or the manure that flows through a farmyard on a rainy day. I was particularly taken by Jane Bennett's careful interrogation of the phrase 'shit happens'. This phrase affords a microcosmic example of Bennett's entire project – to recognise the push of life-itself as one not entirely directed by human hands. In her understanding, material objects can have agency, but only inasmuch as they enter into contingent, often chance encounters with other agents (human and non-human). I have sought to tread a line between Bennett's theorisation of vibrant matter and a sense that to say that 'shit happens' in an educational setting is more than a little problematic. Educational settings are, quite rightly in many cases, some of the most contrived places – in part because of children's safety, and in part because educators work hard to provide a stimulating learning environment. Thus I have advocated a *'weak'* version of Actor-Network Theory that accounts for the agency of non-human agents, and that allows a far greater role for 'mess', but is equally concerned with the *extent* to which such forms of agency are allowed, admitted, and promoted in sometimes highly ordered, designed, alternative learning spaces. This varies considerably: some spaces are messier than others; some care farms look cleaner than others. The point is that many educators may to some extent allow for the excessiveness of non-human natures beyond their control, but always in certain circumstances, in certain spaces, and within particular parameters. Thus, as I have argued throughout this book, they are involved in a process of negotiation, albeit one that affords collaboration with non-human natures in *different* (but not necessarily more intensive or 'better') ways than those that take place in mainstream schools.

Ramifications, practical and political

Once again, the practical implications of these theoretical perspectives are quite profound, and relate to the versions of autonomy I have summarised thus far. I outlined these in some detail in Chapter Eight, but it is worth recapping them here. The first is that, in times of recession and austerity, some alternative educators (such as a care farm in East

Anglia), are gaining a creeping sensation that they may be called upon to help to preserve life-itself. Admittedly I have put this in a rather melodramatic way, but the point is that they see a potential extension of their role into providing a series of what are, in contemporary British society, viewed as *vital* services that may no longer be provided by the state. They are concerned that, if local communities (and especially children) are simply going to survive the difficult circumstances in which they are living, they may have to play a greater role. We could, then, say that theirs is a concern about the *endurance* of contemporary ways of life – albeit ways of life that, ironically, can cause multiple forms of oppression among the very groups they work with. The second implication is that some educators view their role as one in which they can prop up the seeds of quite subtle forms of dissonance among wider publics. For instance, while the impulse to lead the 'good life' – to grow one's own food – might be interpreted as a fashion statement or a drive to save money, it may be the case that individuals, families and schools are experimenting with lightly alternative ways of doing life-itself. This raises critical questions about what the role of care farms, for instance, might be. Do they offer technical advice? Do they offer an exemplary space (and role models) for inspiration and information? Should they offer support and outreach programmes to local schools or support 'Extended Services'-style engagements with local communities? Should they promote the 'good life'? Should they encourage people to do more – not only to grow a few carrots or look after a pig, but to engage in food cooperatives, to gradually stop buying supermarket food – to become more intensively involved in alternative forms of life? Should their work be supported by government funding, or by becoming a social enterprise company?

These are all questions about the level and type of dissonance that could be enacted among publics by alternative educators, and, in the end, about the level and type of dissonance required with mainstream governmental and financial systems. They are not simply questions about detaching from those systems and replacing them with totally *new* versions of life (hence why they are dissonant, and therefore autonomous). They do not merely impinge upon the work of care farms but could be reframed to encompass similar questions about the ways in which any alternative learning space might inspire or promote versions of life at some level of dissonance with neoliberal versions thereof. These are, then, questions for alternative educators as well as government ministers, and quite possibly they extend beyond the UK to other contexts in which state support for 'vital' social services is being rolled back.

I argued in Chapter Eight that all of this is not simply another way of falling back into the old adage that learning is inseparable from everyday life. I do happen to agree with this, as would every educator I interviewed. Instead, my argument has been that alternative learning spaces demand attention because they constitute – taken together or apart – a series of ways of envisioning life-itself that do not strictly conform to neoliberal versions thereof. They are just as important as the diverse economic practices witnessed by Gibson-Graham (2006) and the autonomous social centres depicted by Pickerill and Chatterton (2006). Indeed, I hope that an overall effect of reading this book has been to provoke thought, and hope, in the ways that these authors do (see Chapter Two). Of equal importance are the connections (which I have briefly charted) between some alternative learning spaces, other learning spaces, and the kinds of practices charted by Gibson-Graham: how alternative educators are connected up with other self-organising groups, such as eco-housing projects, local alternative energy solutions, food-growing cooperatives, Transition movements, and so much more. But of utmost importance is the impulse for connection with the mainstream – to forge sustainable, again often self-sufficient and enduring affiliations that exist *regardless* of definitions of 'alternative' or 'mainstream'. Thus, on the one hand, we can see alternative learning spaces as an embedded, but, I think, vital component in attempts to imagine and carry out life beyond neoliberalism. They are another piece of the puzzle so brilliantly laid out by Gibson-Graham and many others. On the other hand, alternative learning spaces offer some distinctive pieces for that puzzle, not least in the sense that they are *collaboratively* autonomous – that they enrol a great array of more-than-social processes within their versions of life-itself. My sense is that the same could probably be said for diverse economic and socially autonomous spaces, and I hope that the findings of this book recursively offer some theoretical purchase to studies of those spaces.

Finally, I hope that the value of a geographical perspective has become clear. This book shows just some of the many ways in which 'space' does not refer simply to the physical spaces in which learning happens, but to *spatialities* that combine materials, interpersonal relationships, feelings, habits, practicalities, policies and more-than-social processes. Clearly, there is much more to be done. This book has covered issues pertinent to my own interests and to the selection of alternative learning spaces I visited; moreover, it has not paid as much attention to the voices and experiences of children and young people as I would have liked (although it has done so more than most studies of alternative education). However, it has highlighted how a geographical perspective – informed by many other disciplinary insights – can help us to understand alternative learning spaces as *autonomous* spaces, constituted by all kinds of internal and external dis/connections with multiple 'mainstreams'. This book has also highlighted how, in quite specific times and places, autonomous learning spaces are 'scaled up': they attempt to be loving, outward looking and collaborative, extending beyond the social, and beyond learning, to envisage a role within collaboratively autonomous versions of life-itself. Whether or not they form (part of) dissonant versions of life-itself that will truly endure I cannot say. However, not least given the contemporary contexts surrounding state education in the UK, I remain convinced that the *geographies* of alternative education – of autonomous learning spaces – will continue to warrant the attention of academics, policy makers and practitioners for some time to come.

References

Adey, P. (2008) 'Airports, mobility, and the calculative architecture of affective control', *Geoforum*, vol 39, pp 438-51.

Adey, P. (2009) *Mobility*, London: Routledge.

Ahern, G. (2009) *Sun at midnight: the Rudolf Steiner movement and gnosis in the West*, Cambridge: James Clarke & Co.

Allin, L. and Humberstone, B. (2010) 'Introducing 'journey(s)' in adventure and outdoor learning research', *Journal of Adventure Education and Outdoor Learning*, vol 10, pp 71-5.

Allison, P., Carr, D. and Meldrum, D. (2012) 'Potential for excellence: interdisciplinary learning outdoors as a moral enterprise', *The Curriculum Journal*, vol 23, pp 43-58.

Amato, L. and Krasny, M. (2011) 'Outdoor adventure education: applying transformative learning theory to understanding instrumental learning and personal growth in environmental education', *Journal of Environmental Education*, vol 42, pp 237-54.

Amoore, L. and de Goede, M. (2008) 'Transactions after 9/11: The banal face of the preemptive strike', *Transactions of the Institute of British Geographers*, vol 33, pp 173-85.

Anderson, B. (2004) 'Time-stilled space-slowed: how boredom matters', *Geoforum*, vol 35, pp739-54.

Anderson, B. (2006) 'Becoming and being hopeful: towards a theory of affect', *Environment and Planning D: Society & Space*, vol 24, pp 733-52.

Anderson, B. (2010) 'Preemption, precaution, preparedness: anticipatory action and future geographies', *Progress in Human Geography*, vol 34, pp 777-98.

Anderson, B. (2012) 'Affect and biopower: towards a politics of life', *Transactions of the Institute of British Geographers*, vol 37, pp 28-43.

Anderson, B. and Harrison, P. (2010) *Taking-Place: non-representational theories and geography*, London: Ashgate.

Anderson, B. and Tolia-Kelly, D. (2004) 'Matter(s) in social and cultural geography', *Geoforum*, vol 35, pp669-74.

Anderson, K. and Smith, S. (2001) Editorial: emotional geographies, *Transactions of the Institute of British Geographers*, vol 26, pp 7-10.

Andrews, G., Kearns, R., Kontos, P. and Wilson, V. (2006) '"Their finest hour": older people, oral histories, and the historical geography of social life', *Social & Cultural Geography*, vol 7, pp 153-77.

Ansell, N. (2002) '"Of course we must be equal, but …": imagining gendered futures in two rural southern African secondary schools', *Geoforum*, vol 33, pp 179-94.

Ansell, N, (2009) 'Childhood and the politics of scale: descaling children's geographies?', *Progress in Human Geography*, vol 32, pp 190-209.

Arnot, J. (2002) *Reproducing gender? Essays on educational theory and feminist politics*, London: Routledge.

Arnot, M. and Reay, D. (2007) 'A sociology of pedagogic voice: power, inequality and pupil consultation, *Discourse: Studies in the Cultural Politics of Education*, vol 28, pp 311-25.

Backman, E. (2011) 'What controls the teaching of *friluftsliv*? Analysing the pedagogic discourse within Swedish physical education', *Journal of Adventure Education and Outdoor Learning*, vol 11, pp 51-65.

Ball, S. (2003) *Class strategies and the education market: the middle classes and social advantage*, London: Routledge.

Ball, S. (ed) (2004) *The RoutledgeFalmer reader in sociology of education*, London: Routledge.

Ball, S., Bowe, R. and Gewirtz, S. (1995) 'Circuits of schooling: a sociological exploration of parental choice of school in social class contexts', *Sociological Review*, vol 43, pp 52-78.

Barad, K. (2003) 'Posthumanist performativity: toward an understanding of how matter comes to matter', *Signs*, vol 28, pp 801-31.

Barnett, C. (2005) 'Ways of relating: hospitality and the acknowledgment of otherness', *Progress in Human Geography*, vol 29, pp 5-21.

Barrow, R. (2012 [1978]) *Radical education: a critique of freeschooling and deschooling*, London: Routledge.

Bartels, A. and Zeki, P. (2004) 'The neural correlates of maternal and romantic love', *NeuroImage*, vol 21, pp 1155-66.

Bauman, K. (2001). *Homeschooling in the United States: trends and characteristics; Working paper series*, Washington, DC: US Census Bureau Population Division.

Bauman, Z. (1990) *Modernity and ambivalence*, Cambridge: Polity Press.

Beck, U. and Beck-Gernsheim, E. (2002) *Individualization: institutionalized individualism and its social and political consequences*, London: SAGE.

Bennett, J. (2010) *Vibrant matter: a political ecology of things*, Durham, NC: Duke University Press.

Bennett, J. (2011) 'The solar judgment of Walt Whitman', in J. Seery (ed) *A political companion to Walt Whitman*, Lexington, KY: The University Press of Kentucky, pp 131-46.

Bennett, K. (2009) 'Challenging emotions', *Area*, vol 41, pp 244-52.

Bentley G. and Mace, R. (eds) 02009) *Substitute parents: alloparenting in human societies*, London: Berghahn Books.

Berget, B. and Braastad, B. (2008) 'Animal-assisted therapy with farm animals for persons with psychiatric disorders', *Annals Ist Super Sanita*, vol 47, pp 384-90.

Bielick, S., Chandler, K. and Broughman, S. (2001) *Homeschooling in the United States*, Washington DC: National Center for Education Statistics.

Biesta, G. (2005) 'Against learning: reclaiming a language for education in an age of learning', *Nordisk Pedagogik*, vol 25, pp 54-66.

Biesta, G. (2006) *Beyond learning: democratic education for a human future*, Boulder, CO: Paradigm Publishers.

Bilton, H. (2010) *Outdoor learning in the early years: management and innovation*, London: Routledge.

Bissell, D. (2007) 'Animating suspension: waiting for mobilities', *Mobilities*, vol 2, pp 277-98.

Bissell, D. (2012) 'Agitating the powers of habit: towards a volatile politics of thought', *Theory and Event*, vol 15, unpaginated, available at: http://muse.jhu.edu/, last accessed 11 June 2012.

Bondi, L. (1991) 'Attainment at primary schools: an analysis of variations between schools', *British Educational Research Journal*, vol 17, pp 203-17.

Bondi, L. (2005) 'Making connections and thinking through emotions: between geography and psychotherapy', *Transactions of the Institute of British Geographers*, vol 30, pp 433-48.

Bourdieu, P. and Passeron, J. (1977) *Reproduction in education, society and culture*, London: SAGE.

Braidotti, R. (2011) *Nomadic theory: the portable Rosi Braidotti*, New York: Columbia University Press.

Brent-Edwards, D. (2010) 'A comparison of local empowerment in education: Porto Alegre, Brazil and Chicago, USA', *Research in Comparative and International Education*, vol 5, pp 176-84.

Brooks, R. (2003) 'Young people's higher education choices: the role of family and friends', *British Journal of Sociology of Education*, vol 24, pp 283-97.

Brooks, R., Fuller, A. and Waters, J. (eds) (2012) *Changing spaces of education: new perspectives on the nature of learning*, London: Routledge.

Brown, G. (2007) 'Mutinous eruptions: autonomous spaces of radical queer activism', *Environment & Planning A*, vol 39, pp 2685-98.

Brown, G. (2009) 'Thinking beyond homonormativity: performative explorations of diverse gay economies', *Environment & Planning A*, vol 41, pp 1496-1510.

Bruce, T. (2011) *Learning through play: for babies, toddlers and young children*, Oxford: Oxford University Press.

Brunold-Conesa, C. (2010) 'International education: the international baccalaureate, Montessori and global citizenship', *Journal of Research in International Education*, vol 9, pp 259-72.

Bryant, R. and Goodman, M. (2004) 'Consuming narratives: the political ecology of "alternative" consumption', *Transactions of the Institute of British Geographers*, vol 29, pp 344-66.

Bunnell, T., Yea, S., Peake, L., Skelton, T. and Smith, M. (2011) 'Geographies of friendships', *Progress in Human Geography*, online early.

Burke, C. and Grosvenor, I. (2008) *Schools*, London, Reaktion.

Burls, A. (2008) 'Seeking nature: a contemporary therapeutic environment', *International Journal of Therapeutic Communities*, vol 29, pp 228-44.

Bussey, M. (2009) 'Education for liberation: a corner stone of Prout', in *Understanding Prout – essays on sustainability and transformation, volume 1*, Australia: Proutist Universal, pp 1-27.

Butler, J. (1990) *Gender trouble: feminism and the subversion of identity*, London: Psychology Press.

Butler, T. (2003) 'Living in the bubble: gentrification and its 'others' in north London', *Urban Studies*, vol 40, pp 2469-86.

Caddy, E. and Platts, D. (2004) *The Findhorn book of learning to love*, Findorn: Findhorn Press.

Calgren, F. (2008) *Education towards freedom: Rudolf Steiner education, a survey of the work of Waldorf schools throughout the world*, Edinburgh: Floris Books.

Callon, M. (1986) 'Some elements of a sociology of translation: domestication of the scallops and the fishermen of St Brieuc Bay', in J. Law (ed) *Power, action and belief: a new sociology of knowledge*, London: Routledge, pp 196-233.

Cameron, L. (2006) 'Science, nature and hatred: "finding out! at the Malting House Garden School, 1924-9', *Environment and Planning D: Society and Space*, vol 24, pp 851-72.

Carlisle, C. (2010) 'Between freedom and necessity: Félix Ravaisson on habit and the moral life', *Inquiry*, vol 53, pp 123-45.

Carnie, F. (2003) *Alternative approaches to education: a guide for parents and teachers*, London: Routledge.

Carr, W. and Kemmis, S. (1986) *Becoming critical: education, knowledge and action research*, Lewes: Falmer Press.

Cartwright, I. (2012) 'Informal education in compulsory schooling in the UK: humanising moments, utopian spaces?', in P. Kraftl, J. Horton and F. Tucker (eds) *Critical geographies of childhood and youth: contemporary policy and practice*, Bristol: The Policy Press, pp 151-68.

Castree, N. (1995) 'The nature of produced nature: materiality and knowledge construction in marxism, *Antipode*, vol 27, pp 12-48.

Chatterton, P. (2010) 'The urban impossible: a eulogy for the unfinished city', *City*, vol 14, pp 234-44.

Claxton, G. and Lucas, B. (2007) *The creative thinking plan: how to generate ideas and solve problems in your work and life*, London: BBC Books.

Collins, D. and Coleman, T. (2008) 'Social geographies of education: looking within, and beyond, school boundaries', *Geography Compass*, vol 2, pp 281-99.

Collom, E. and Mitchell, D. (2005) 'Homeschooling as a social movement: identifying the determinants of homeschoolers' perceptions', *Sociological Spectrum*, vol 25, pp 273-305.

Colls, R. and Hörschelmann, K. (2009) 'Editorial: Geographies of children's and young people's bodies', *Children's Geographies*, vol 7, pp 1-6.

Connolly, W. (2008) *Capitalism, American style*, Durham: Duke University Press.

Conroy, J. (2010) 'The state, parenting, and the populist energies of anxiety', *Educational Theory*, vol 60, pp 325-40.

Cook, I. et al (2004) 'Follow the thing: Papaya', *Antipode*, vol 36, pp 642-64.

Cook, V. and Hemming, P. (2011) 'Education spaces: embodied dimensions and dynamics', *Social and Cultural Geography*, vol 12, pp 1-8.

Cook-Sather, A. (2006) 'Production, cure, or translation? Rehumanizing education and the roles of teacher and student in US schools and universities', *FORUM*, vol 48, pp 329-36.

Coole, D. and Frost, S. (eds) (2010) *New materialisms: ontology, agency, and politics*, Durham, NC: Duke University Press.

Cooper, D. (2007) 'Opening up ownership: community belonging, belongings, and the collective life of property', *Law and Social Inquiry*, vol 32, pp 625-44.

Corsaro, W. and Eder, D. (1990) 'Children's peer cultures', *Annual Review of Sociology*, vol 16, pp 197-220.

Cossentino, J. (2006) 'Big work: goodness, vocation, and engagement in the Montessori method', *Curriculum Inquiry*, vol 36, pp 63-92.

Cox, M. and Rowlands, A. (2000) 'The effect of three different educational approaches on children's drawing ability: Steiner, Montessori and traditional', *British Journal of Educational Pscyhology*, vol 70, pp 485-503.

Cresswell, T. (2005) *Place: a short introduction*, Oxford: Blackwell.

Cruz, I., Stahel, A. and Max-Need, M. (2009) 'Towards a systemic development approach: building on the Human-Scale Development paradigm', *Ecological Economics*, vol 68, pp 2021-30.

Curren, R. (ed) (2007) *Philosophy of education: an anthology*, Oxford: Blackwell.

Dahlin, B. (2010) 'A state-independent education for citizenship? Comparing beliefs and values related to civic and moral issues among students in Swedish mainstream and Steiner Waldorf schools', *Journal of Beliefs and Values: Studies in Religion and Education*, vol 31, pp 165-80.

Davies, R. (2012) 'Places to go, things to do and people to see: space and activity in English youth work policy', in P. Kraftl, J. Horton and F. Tucker (eds) *Critical geographies of childhood and youth: contemporary policy and practice*, Bristol: The Policy Press, pp 79-95.

Den Besten, O., Horton, J., Adey, P. and Kraftl, P. (2011) 'Claiming events of school (re)design: materialising the promise of *Building schools for the future*', *Social and Cultural Geography*, vol 12, pp 9-26.

Dewsbury, J.-D. (2011) 'The Deleuze-Guatarrian assemblage: plastic habits', vol 43, pp 148-53.

DfE (Department for Education) (2012) *Education Bill*, London: HMSO.

DfES (UK Department for Education and Skills) (2003) *Building schools for the future: consultation on a new approach to capital investment*, London: DfES.

Dobozy, E. (2007) 'Effective learning of civic skills: democratic schools succeed in nurturing the critical capacities of students', *Educational Studies*, vol 33, pp 115-28.

Dodgshon, R. (2008) 'Geography's place in time', *GeografiskaAnnaler Series B*, vol 90, pp 1-15.

Dolan, P., Hallsworth, M., Halpern, D., King, D. and Vlaev, I. (2010) *MINDSPACE: influencing behaviour through public policy*, London: Institute for Government.

Ecccleston, K. and Hayes, D. (2008) *The dangerous rise in therapeutic education*, London: Routledge.

Erikson, R. and Goldthorpe, J. H. (1993) *The constant flux*, Oxford: Clarendon Press.

Escobar, A. (2010) 'Latin America at a crossroads', *Cultural Studies*, vol 24, pp 1-65.

Evans, B. (2006) '"Gluttony or sloth': critical geographies of bodies and morality in (anti)obesity policy', *Area*, vol 38, pp 259-67.

Evans, B. (2008) 'Geographies of youth/young people', *Geography Compass*, vol 2, pp 1659-80.

Evans, B. (2010) 'Anticipating fatness: childhood, affect and the pre-emptive 'war on obesity', *Transactions of the Institute of British Geographers*, vol 35, pp 21-38.

Evans, B. and Colls, R. (2009) 'Measuring fatness, governing bodies: the spatialities of the Body Mass Index (BMI) in anti-obesity politics', *Antipode*, vol 41, pp 1051-83.

Falk, J.H., Heimlich, J.E. and Foutz,S. (eds) (2009) *Free-choice learning and the environment*, Lanham, MD: AltaMira Press.

Ferguson, K. and Seddon, T. (2007) 'Decentred education: suggestions for framing a socio-spatial research agenda', *Critical Studies in Education*, vol 48, pp 111-29.

Fielding, M. and Moss, P. (2011) *Radical education and the common school: a democratic alternative*, London: Routledge.

Fournier, V. (2008) 'Escaping from the economy: the politics of degrowth', *International Journal of Sociology and Social Policy*, vol 28, pp 528-45.

Francesco, T. (2009) 'Cities at human scale: children's city', *Revista de Educacion*, pp 147-68.

Freire, P. (2008) [1974] *Education for critical consciousness*, London: Continuum.

Friedrich, D., Jaastad, B. and Popkewitz, T. (2010) 'Democratic education: an (im)possibility that yet remains to come', *Educational Philosophy and Theory*, vol 42, pp 571-87.

Gagen, E. (2004) 'Making America flesh: physicality and nationhood in early-twentieth century physical education reform', *Cultural Geographies*, vol 11, pp 417–42.

Gaither, M. (2009) 'Homeschooling in the USA: past, present and future', *Theory and Research in Education*, vol 7, pp 331-46.

Gardiner, M. (2004) 'Everyday utopianism: Lefebvre and his critics', *Cultural Studies*, vol 18, pp 228-54.

Gatto, J. (2009) *Weapons of mass instruction: a schoolteacher's journey through the dark world of compulsory schooling*, Canada: New Society.

Geertz, C. (1993) *The interpretation of cultures*, New York: Basic Books.

Gibson-Graham, J.K. (2006) *A postcapitalist politics*, Minneapolis, MN: University of Minnesota Press.

Gibson-Graham, J.K. (2008) 'Diverse economies: performative practices for "other worlds"', *Progress in Human Geography*, vol 32, pp 613-32.

Gill, T. (2007) *No fear,* Edinburgh: Calouste Gulbenkian Foundation.

Goffman, E. (1959) *The presentation of self in everyday life*, Harmondsworth: Penguin.

Golding, V. (2009) *Learning at the museum frontiers: identity, race and power*, London: Ashgate.

Grazzini, C, (1988) 'The four planes of development: a constructive rhythm of life', *Montessori Today*, vol 1, pp 7-8.

Greenberg, M. and Harris, A. (2011) 'Nurturing mindfulness in children and youth: current state of research', *Child Development Perspectives*, vol 6, pp 161-66.

Grimm, A., Mrosek, T., Martinsohn, A. and Schulte, A. (2011) 'Evaluation of the non-formal forest education sector in the state of North Rhine-Westphalia, Germany: organisations, programmes and framework conditions', *Environmental Education Research*, vol 17, pp 19-33.

Grimshaw, D. and Rubery, J. (2012)' The end of the UK's liberal-collectivist social model? The implications of the coalition government's policy during the austerity crisis', *Cambridge Journal of Economics*, vol 36, pp 105-26.

Guillen-Royo, M. (2010) 'Realising the "wellbeing dividend": an exploratory study using the Human Scale Development approach', *Ecological Economics*, vol 70, pp 384-93.

Gulson, K. and Symes, C. (2007) *Spatial theories of education: policy and geography matters*, London: Routledge.

Gustafsson, P., Szszepanski, A., Nelson, N. and Gustafsson, P. (2012) 'Effects of an outdoor education intervention on the mental health of schoolchildren', *Journal of Adventure Education and Outdoor Learning*, vol 12, pp 63-79.

Hainstock, E. (1997) *The essential Montessori: an introduction to the woman, the writings, the method, and the movement*, Harmondsworth: Penguin.

Hallman, B. (2010) *Family geographies: the spatiality of families and family life*, Oxford: Oxford University Press.

Halpin, D. (2003) *Hope and education: the role of the utopian imagination*, London: Routledge-Falmer.

Hammersley, M. (2006) 'Ethnography: problems and prospects', *Ethnography and Education*, vol 1, pp 3–14.

Hanson Thiem, C. (2007) 'The spatial politics of educational privatization: re-reading the US homeschooling movement', in K. Gulson and C. Symes (eds) *Spatial theories of education*, London: Routledge, pp 17-36.

Hanson Thiem, C. (2009) 'Thinking through education: the geographies of contemporary educational restructuring', *Progress in Human Geography*, vol 33, pp 154-73.

Harker, C. (2005) 'Playing and affective time-spaces', *Children's Geographies*, vol 3, pp 47-62.

Harland, J. and Mason, B. (2010) *Towards schools where people matter: a study of the Human Scale Schools project*, London: Calouste Gulbenkian Foundation.

Harrison, P. (2009) 'In the absence of practice', *Environment and Planning D: Society and Space*, vol 27, pp 987-1009.

Harrison, S. (2010) '"Why are we here?" Taking "place" into account in UK outdoor environmental education', *Journal of Adventure Education and Outdoor Learning*, vol 10, pp 3-18.

Hart, S. (2006) *The importance of attachment*, New York: Norton.

Harvey, D. (1991) *The condition of postmodernity: an inquiry into the origins of cultural change*, Oxford: Wiley-Blackwell.

Hassink, J., Elings, M., Zweekhorst, M., van den Nieuwenhuizen, N. and Smit, A. (2010) 'Care farms in the Netherlands: attractive empowerment-oriented and strengths-based practices in the community', *Health and Place*, vol 16, pp 423-30.

Hatcher, R. (2011) 'The Conservative-Liberal Democrat Coalition government's "freeschools" in England', *Educational Review*, vol 63, pp 485-503.

Haubenhofer, D., Elings, M., Hassink, J. and Hone, R. (2010) 'The development of green care in western European countries', *Explore*, vol 6, pp 106-11.

Hayes, R. and Herbert, C. (2011) *Rising above bullying: from despair to recovery*, London: Jessica Kingsley Publishers.

Hedeen, T. (2005) 'Dialogue and democracy, community and capacity: lessons for conflict resolution education from Montessori, Dewey, and Freire', *Conflict Resolution Quarterly*, vol 23, pp 185-202.

Hemming, P. (2007) 'Renegotiating the primary school: children's emotional geographies of sport, exercise and active play', *Children's Geographies*, vol 5, pp 353-71.

Herbst, P., Gruber-Fuchs, M. and Herbst, E. (2008) 'Some cycles of nature – applications of M. Montessori's cosmic education in a nursery school', *Journal of Geoscience Education*, vol 56, pp 220-24.

Hickey-Moody, A. and Crowley, V. (2010) Special issue of *Discourse: Studies in the Cultural Politics of Education*, vol 4.

Higgins, P. and Nicol, R. (2002) *Learning as adventure: theory for practice*, London: DfES.

Hine, R., Peacock, J. and Pretty, J. (2008) 'Care farming in the UK: contexts, benefits and links with therapeutic communities', *Therapeutic Communities*, vol 29, pp 245-60.

HMSO (Her Majesty's Stationery Office) (1988) *Education Reform Act*, London: HMSO.

HMSO (Her Majesty's Stationery Office) (1996) *Education Act*, London: HMSO.

HMSO (Her Majesty's Stationery Office) (2009) *House of Commons Select Committee on Education review of elective home education*, London: HMSO.

Holloway, J. (2010) *Change the world without taking power: the meaning of revolution today*, London: Pluto Press.

Holloway, S. (1998) 'Local childcare cultures: Moral geographies of mothering and the social organisation of pre-school education', *Gender, Place and Culture*, vol 5, pp 29-53.

Holloway, S. and Pimlott-Wilson, H. (2011) 'The politics of aspiration: neo-liberal education policy, "low" parental aspirations and primary school Extended Services in disadvantaged communities', *Children's Geographies*, vol 9, pp 79-94.

Holloway, S. and Valentine, G. (2000) *Children's geographies: playing, living, learning*, London: Routledge.

Holloway, S. and Valentine, G. (2001) '"It's only as stupid as you are": Children's and adults' negotiation of ICT competence at home and at school', *Social and Cultural Geography*, vol 2, pp 25-42.

Holloway, S., Brown, G. and Pimlott-Wilson, H. (2011) 'Editorial introduction: geographies of education and aspiration', *Children's Geographies*, vol 9, pp 1-5.

Holloway, S., Hubbard, P., Joens, H. and Pimlott-Wilson, H. (2010) 'Geographies of education and the significance of children, youth and families', *Progress in Human Geography*, vol 34, pp 583-600.

Holmes, M. (2006) 'Love lives at a distance: distance relationships over the lifecourse', *Sociological Research Online*, vol 11, unpaginated.

Holt, J. (2004) [1976] *Instead of education: ways to help people do things better*, Boulder, CO: Sentient.

Holt, L. (2007) 'Children's socio-spatial (re)production of disability in primary school playgrounds', *Environment and Planning D: Society and Space*, vol 25, pp 783-802.

hooks, b. (2003) *Teaching community: a pedagogy of hope*, London: Routledge.

Hopkins. P. and Pain R. (2007) 'Geographies of age: thinking relationally', *Area*, vol 39, pp 287-94.

Horton, J. and Kraftl, P. (2005) 'Editorial: For more-than-usefulness: six overlapping points about Children's geographies', *Children's Geographies*, vol 3, pp 131-43.

Horton, J. and Kraftl, P. (2006) 'What else? Some more ways of thinking about and doing children's geographies', *Children's Geographies*, vol 4, pp 69-95.

Horton, J. and Kraftl, P. (2009) 'Small acts, kindswords and "not too much fuss": implicit activisms', *Emotion, Space and Society*, vol 2, pp 14-23.

HSLDA (Homeschooling Legal Defence Association) (2012) *HSLDA FAQs* (available at http://www.hslda.org/docs/faqs/default.asp).

Illich, J. (2002 [1970]) *Deschooling society*, London: Marion Boyars.

Independent Schools Council (2012) 'About us'. Available at http://www.isc.co.uk, last accessed 8 June 2012.

Inoue, M. and Oishi, Y. (2010) 'Classifying the contents of the current system of education', *Journal of the Japanese Forestry Society*, vol 92, pp 79-87.

Jacobs, J. (2006) 'A geography of big things', *Cultural Geographies*, vol 13, pp 1-27.

Jacques, R. (2002) 'What is a crypto-utopia and why does it matter?', in M. Parker (ed) *Utopia and organization*, Oxford: Blackwell, pp 24-39.

James, A. and James, A. (2004) *Constructing childhood: theory, policy and practice*, Basingstoke: Palgrave Macmillan.

Jeffrey, C. (2010) 'Geographies of children and youth I: eroding maps of life', *Progress in Human Geography*, vol 39, pp 496-505.

Jeffs, T. and Smith, M. (2005) *Informal education*, London: Educational Heretics Press.

Johnston, R., Burgess, S., Harris, R. and Wilson, D. (2008) '"Sleepwalking towards segregation"? The changing ethnic composition of English schools, 1997-2003: an entry cohort analysis', *Transactions of the Institute of British Geographers*, vol 33, pp 73-90.

Jonas, A. (2006) 'Pro-scale: further reflections on the "scale debate" in human geography', *Transactions of the Institute of British Geographers*, vol 31, pp 299-406.

Jones, O. (2008) '"True geography [ ] quickly forgotten, giving away to an adult-imagined universe". Approaching the otherness of childhood', *Children's Geographies*, vol 6, pp 195-213.

Kai, K. (2009) 'The modification and adaptation of Montessori education in Japan', *International Journal of Learning*, vol 16, pp 667-76.

Kandel, E. (2005) *Psychiatry, psychoanalysis and the new biology of mind*, Washington DC: American Psychiatric Publishing.

Katz, C. (2008) 'Cultural Geographies lecture: Childhood as spectacle: relays of anxiety and the reconfiguration of the child', *Cultural Geographies*, vol 15, pp 5-17.

Kenway, J. and Youdell, D. (2011) 'The emotional geographies of education: beginning a conversation', *Emotion, Space and Society*, vol 4, pp 131-6.

Knight, S. (2009) *Forest schools and outdoor learning in the early years*, London: SAGE.

Knight, S. (ed) (2011) *Forest school for all*, London: SAGE.

Knowles, G. (2010) *Supporting inclusive practice*, London: Routledge.

Koinzer, T. and Leschinsky, A. (2009) 'Private schools in Germany', *Zeitschrift für Pädagogik*, vol 55, pp 669-85.

Koontz, C., Jue, D. and Bishop, B. (2009) 'Public library facility closure: an investigation of reasons for closure and effects on geographic market areas', *Library and Information Science Research*, vol 31, pp 84-91.

Kraftl, P. (2006a) 'Building an idea: the material construction of an ideal childhood', *Transactions of the Institute of British Geographers*, vol 31, pp 488-504.

Kraftl, P. (2006b) 'Ecological buildings as performed art: Nant-y-Cwm Steiner School, Pembrokeshire', *Social and Cultural Geography*, vol 7, pp 927-48.

Kraftl, P. (2007) 'Utopia, performativity and the unhomely', *Environment and Planning D: Society and Space*, vol 25, pp 120-43.

Kraftl, P. (2008) 'Young people, hope and childhood-hope', *Space and Culture*, vol 11, pp 81-92.

Kraftl, P. (2010) 'Architectural movements, utopian moments: (in)coherent renderings of the Hundertwasser-Haus, Vienna', *Geografiska Annaler Series B*, vol 92, pp 327-45.

Kraftl, P. (2012) 'Utopian promise or burdensome responsibility? A critical analysis of the UK Government's *Building schools for the future* policy', vol 44, pp 847-70.

Kraftl, P. (in press, 2013a) 'Moments of withdrawal', in A. Cameron, N. Smith and J. Dickinson (eds) *Body/state*, London: Ashgate.

Kraftl, P. (in press, 2013b) 'Towards geographies of alternative education: a case study of UK homeschooling', *Transactions of the Institute of British Geographers*, DOI 10.1111/j.1475-5661.2012.00536.x

Kraftl, P. and Adey, P. (2008) 'Architecture/affect/dwelling', *Annals of the Association of American Geographers*, vol 98, pp 213-31.

Kraftl, P. and Horton, J. (2007) '"The Health Event": everyday, affective politics of participation', *Geoforum*, vol 38, pp 1012-27.

Kraftl, P., Horton, J. and Tucker, F. (eds) (2012) *Critical geographies of childhood and youth: contemporary policy and practice*, Bristol: The Policy Press.

Kunzman, R. (2009) 'Understanding homeschooling: a better approach to regulation', *Theory and Research in Education*, vol 7, pp 311-30.

Lareau, A. (1987) 'Social class differences in family-school relationships', *Sociology of Education*, vol 60, pp 73-85.

Latour, B. (2005) *Reassembling the social: an introduction to Actor-Network Theory*, Oxford: Oxford University Press.

Law, J. (2004) *After method: mess in social science research*, London: Routledge.

Law, J. and Mol, A. (2001) 'Situating technoscience: an inquiry into spatialities', *Environment and Planning D: Society and Space*, vol 19, pp 609-21.

Lees, H. (2011) '"Transformed" by discovery at the modality level: schooling as one educational paradigm and elective home education as another …', Paper presented to PESGC Symposium, 2 April 2011.

Lees, L. (2001) 'Towards a critical geography of architecture: the case of an ersatz colosseum', *Ecumene*, vol 8, pp 51-86.

Le Tendre, G. (1999) 'Community-building activities in Japanese schools: alternative paradigms of the democratic school', *Comparative Education Review*, vol 43, pp 283-310.

Levitas, R. (2010) *The concept of utopia*, Berlin: Peter Lang.

Levy, G. and Massalha, M. (2010) 'Yaffa: a school of their choice?', *British Journal of Sociology of Education*, vol 31, pp 171-83.

Leyshon, A., Lee, R. and Williams, C. (eds) (2003) *Alternative economic spaces*, London: SAGE.

Lindemann-Matthies, P. and Knecht, S. (2011) 'Swiss elementary school teachers' attitudes toward forest education', *Journal of Environmental Education*, vol 42, pp 152-67.

Lois, J. (2009) 'Emotionally layered accounts: homeschoolers' justifications for maternal deviance', *Deviant Behavior*, vol 30, pp 201-34.

Longhurst, R. (2001) *Bodies: exploring fluid boundaries*, London: Routledge.

Lorimer, H. (2005) 'Cultural geography: the busyness of being "more-than-representational"', *Progress in Human Geography*, vol 29, pp 83–94.

Lorimer, H. (2007) 'Cultural geography: worldly shapes, differently arranged', *Progress in Human Geography*, vol 31, pp 89-100.

Lorimer, H. (2008) 'Cultural geography: nonrepresentational conditions and concerns', *Progress in Human Geography*, vol 32, pp 551-9.

Louv, R. (2005) *Last child in the woods*, Chapel Hill, NC: Algonquin Books.

Mabovula, N. (2009) 'Giving voice to the voiceless through deliberative democratic school governance', *South African Journal of Education*, vol 29, pp 219-33.

Manocha, R. (2011) 'Meditation, mindfulness and mind-emptiness', *Acta Neuropsychiatra*, vol 23, pp 46-7.

Marcus, G. (1995) 'Ethnography in/of the world system: The emergence of multi-sited ethnography', *Annual Review of Anthropology*, vol 24, pp 95-117.

Marston, S., Jones III, J. and Woodward, K. (2005) 'Human geography without scale', *Transactions of the Institute of British Geographers*, vol 30, pp 416-32.

Massey, D. (2005) *For space,* London: SAGE.

Matthews, H. (1998) 'The geography of children: some ethical and methodological considerations for project and dissertation work', *Journal of Geography in Higher Education*, vol 22, pp 311-24.

Matthews, H. and Limb, M. (1999) 'Defining *an* agenda for the geography of children', *Progress in Human Geography*, vol 23, pp 61-90.

Mayberry, M., Knowles, J., Ray, B. and Marlow, S. (1995) *Homeschooling: parents as educators,* Thousand Oaks, CA: Corwin Press.

Merry, M. and Howell, C. (2009) 'Can intimacy justify home education?', *Theory and Research in Education*, vol 7, pp 363-81.

Merton, B. et al (2004) *An evaluation of the impact of youth work in England,* Nottingham: DfES Publications.

Middleton, J. (2011) '"I'm on autopilot, I just follow the route": exploring the habits, routines and decision-making practices of everyday urban mobilities', *Environment and Planning A*, vol 43, pp 2857-77.

Mills, S. (2013) '"An instruction in good citizenship": Scouting and the historical geographies of citizenship education', *Transactions of the Institute of British Geographers*, vol 38, pp 120-34.

Mizen, P. (2003) 'The best days of your life? Youth, policy and Blair's UK government', *Critical Social Policy*, vol 23, pp 453-76.

Montessori, Maria (1992) *Education and peace,* Oxford: ANC-Clio.

Montessori, Mario (1966) *The human tendencies and Montessori education,* Amsterdam: Association Montessori Internationale.

Moore, R. (1996) 'Back to the future: the problem of change and the possibilities of advance in the sociology of education', *British Journal of Sociology of Education*, vol 17, pp 145-62.

Moore, R. (2004) *Education and society: issues and explanations in the sociology of education,* Cambridge: Polity.

Music, G. (2011) *Nurturing natures: attachment and children's emotional, sociocultural and brain development,* Hove: Psychology Press.

NCACS (2012) *National Coalition of Alternative Community Schools* website (available at http://www.ncacs.org/).

Neuman, A. and Aviram, A. (2003) 'Homeschooling as a fundamental change in lifestyle', *Evaluation and Research in Education*, vol 17, pp 132-43.

North, P. (2011) 'Geographies and utopias of Cameron's Big Society', *Social and Cultural Geography*, vol 12, pp 817-27.

Noyes, A. (2005) 'Pupil voice: purpose,power and the possibilities for democratic schooling', *British Educational Research Journal*, vol 31, pp 533-40.

O'Brien, E. (2009) 'Learning outdoors: the forest school approach', *Education 3-13*, vol 37, pp 45-60.

O'Brien, E. and Murray, R. (2006) *A marvellous opportunity for children to learn,* Forestry Commission and New Economics Foundation (available at www.forestry.gov.uk/pdf/...pdf/.../fr0112forestschoolsreport.pdf).

O'Brien, M., Ruskin, M. and Greenfield, J. (2000) 'Childhood, urban space and citizenship: child-sensitive urban regeneration', Children 5-16 Briefing Summary and End of Award Report, ESRC.

Oberski, I. (2011) 'Rudolf Steiner's philosophy of freedom as a basis for spiritual education?',*International Journal of Children's Spirituality*, vol 16, pp 5-17.

Ormerod, E. (2008) 'Companion animals and offender rehabilitation – experiences from a prison therapeutic community in Scotland', *International Journal of Therapeutic Communities*, vol 29, pp 285-96.

Pain, R. (2009) 'Globalized fear? Towards an emotional geopolitics', *Progress in Human Geography*, vol 33, pp 466-86.

Palmer, S. (2005) *Toxic childhood: how the modern world is damaging our children and what we can do about it*, London: Orion.

Papoulias, C. and Callard, F. (2010) 'Biology's gift: interrogating the turn to affect', *Body and Society*, vol 16, pp 29-56.

Pashby, K. (2011) 'Cultivating global citizens: planting new seeds or pruning the perennials? Looking for the citizen-subject in global citizenship education theory', *Globalisation, Societies and Education*, vol 9, pp 427-42.

Pickerill, J and Chatterton, P. (2006) 'Notes towards autonomous geographies: creation, resistance and self management as survival tactics', *Progress in Human Geography*, vol 30, pp 1-17.

Pickerill, J. and Maxey, L. (2009) 'Geographies of sustainability: Low Impact Developments and spaces of innovation', *Geography Compass*, vol 3, pp 1515-39.

Pierides, D. (2010) 'Multi-sited ethnography and the field of educational research', *Critical Studies in Education*, vol 51, pp 179-95.

Pike, J. (2008) 'Foucault, space and primary school dining rooms', *Children's Geographies*, vol 6, pp 413-22.

Pile, S. (2010) 'Emotions and affect in recent human geography' *Transactions of the Institute of British Geographers*, vol 35, pp 5-20.

Pile, S. and Keith, M. (eds) (1993) *Place and the politics of identity*, London: Routledge.

Ploszajska, T. (1996) 'Constructing the subject: geographical models in English schools, 1870–1944', *Journal of Historical Geography*, vol22, pp 388-98.

Popke, J. (2006) 'Geography and ethics: everyday mediations through care and consumption, *Progress in Human Geography*, vol 30, pp 504-12.

Probyn, E. (2005) 'Teaching bodies: affects in the classroom', *Body and Society*, vol 10, pp 21-43.

Prout, A. (2005) *The future of childhood*, London: Routledge.

Pykett, J. (2012) 'Making "youth publics" and "neuro-citizens": critical geographies of contemporary education practice in the UK', in P. Kraftl, J. Horton and F. Tucker (eds) *Critical geographies of childhood and youth: contemporary policy and practice*, Bristol: The Policy Press, pp 27-42.

Quirke, L. (2009) 'Legitimacy through alternate means: schools without professionals in the private sector', *British Journal of Sociology of Education*, vol 30, pp 621-34.

Ravaisson, F. (2008) *Of habit*, London: Continuum.

Rawson, M. and Richter, T. (2000) *The educational tasks and content of the Steiner Waldorf Curriculum*, Forest Row, Sussex: Steiner Waldorf Schools Fellowship.

Reay, D. (1998) 'Rethinking social class: Qualitative perspectives on gender and social class', *Sociology*, vol 32, pp 259-275.

Relph, E. (1976) *Place and placelessness*, London, Pion.

Richardson, L. and Wolfe, M. (2001) *Principles and practices of informal education: learning through life*, London: Routledge.

Ridgers, N., Knowles, Z. and Sayers, J. (2012) 'Encouraging play in the natural environment: a child-focussed case study of forest school', *Children's Geographies*, vol 10, pp 49-65.

Rivers, I. and Soutter, A. (1996) 'Bullying and the Steiner school ethos: a case study analysis of a group-centred educational philosophy', *School Psychology International*, vol 17, pp 359-77.

Rose, G. (1993) *Feminism and geography: the limits of geographical knowledge*, Cambridge: Polity Press.

Rose, G., Degen, M. and Basdas, B. (2010) 'More on "big things": building events and feelings', *Transactions of the Institute of British Geographers*, vol 35, pp 334-49.

Rose, N. (2007) *The politics of life-itself: biomedicine, power, and subjectivity in the twenty-first century*, Princeton, NJ: Princeton University Press.

Rothermel, P. (2003) 'Can we classify motives for home education?', *Evaluation and Research in Education*, vol 17, pp 74-89.

Rule, A. and Kyle, P. (2009) 'Community-building in a diverse setting', *Early Childhood Education Journal*, vol 36, pp 291-95.

Russell, W. (2012) '"I get such a feeling out of … those moments": playwork, passion, politics and space', *International Journal of Play*, vol 1, pp 1-13.

Sandseter, E. (2009) 'Characteristics of risky play', *Journal of Adventure Education and Outdoor Learning*, vol 9, pp 3-21.

Sargisson, L. (1996) *Contemporary feminist utopianism*, London: Routledge.

Sargisson, L. (2000) *Utopian bodies and the politics of transgression*, London: Routledge.

Saville, S. (2008) 'Playing with fear: Parkour and the mobility of emotion', *Social and Cultural Geography*, vol 9, pp 891-914.

Schonert-Reichl, K. and Lawlor, M. (2010) 'The effects of a mindfulness-based education program on pre- and early adolescents' well-being and social and emotional competence', *Mindfulness*, vol 1, pp 137-51.

Schumacher, E. (2011 [1973]) *Small is beautiful: a study of economics as if people mattered*, London: Vintage.

Schutz, A. (2001) 'John Dewey's conundrum: can democratic schools empower?', *Teachers College Record*, vol 103, pp 267-302.

Scraton, P. (ed) (1997) *Childhood 'in crisis'?*, London: University College London Press.

Sedgwick, E. (2003) *Touching feeling: affect, pedagogy, performativity*, Durham, NC: Duke University Press.

Sempik, J. and Aldridge, J. (2006) 'Care farms and care gardens: horticulture as therapy in the UK', in Hassink, J. and Van Dijk, M. (eds) *Farming for health: Green-Care farming across Europe and the United States of America*, Wageningen Ur Frontis series, Dordrecht: Springer, pp 147-61.

Sempik, J., Hine, R. and Wilcox, D. (eds) (2010) *Green care: a conceptual framework. A report of the Working Group on the Health Benefits of Green Care*, COST Action 866, Green Care in Agriculture, Loughborough: Centre for Child and Family Research, Loughborough University.

Seo, D. (2009) 'The profitable adventure of threatened middle-class families: an ethnographic study on homeschooling in South Korea', *Asia Pacific Education Review*, vol 10, pp 409-22.

Shankland, R. Genoli, C., França, L., Guelfi, J.-D. and Ionescu, S. (2010) 'Student adjustment to higher education: The role of alternative educational pathways in coping with the demands of student life', *Higher Education*, vol 59, pp 353-66.

Sharp, J. (2008) 'Geography and gender: what belongs to feminist geography? Emotion, power and change', *Progress in Human Geography*, vol 33, pp 74-80.

Sitrin, M. (2006) *Horizontalism: voices of popular power in Argentina.* Edinburgh: AK Press.

Sliwka, A. (2008) 'The contribution of alternative education', Chapter 4 in *Innovating to learn, learning to innovate*, OECD (Organisation for Economic Co-Operation and Development), available at: http://www.oecd-ilibrary.org/education/innovating-to-learn-learning-to-innovate_9789264047983-en;jsessionid=2iqj0etjq4gi7.epsilon, last accessed 8 June 2012.

Stehlik, T. (2008) 'Thinking, feeling, and willing: how Waldorf schools provide a critical pedagogy that nurtures and develops imagination, in T. Leonard and P. Willis (eds) *Pedagogies of the imagination: mythopoetic curriculum in educational practice*, Berlin: Springer, pp 231-43.

Stehlik, T. (2009) 'Waldorf schools as communities of practice for AVE and social sustainability', in P. Willis, S. McKenzie and R. Harris (eds) *Rethinking work and learning: adult and vocational education for social sustainability*, Berlin: Springer, pp 249-60.

Steiner, R. (1909) 'The education of the child in the light of anthroposophy', available at http://wn.elib.com/Steiner/Articles/EduChild/EduChild_note.html, last accessed 12 June 2012.

Steiner, R. (1919) 'An introduction to Waldorf education', available at http://www.elib.com/Steiner/Articles/, last accessed 12 June 2012.

Stevens, M. (2001) *Kingdom of children: culture and controversy in the homeschooling movement*, Princeton, NJ: Princeton University Press

Suissa, J. (2010) 'Should the state control education?', in R. Bailey (ed) *The philosophy of education: an introduction*, London: Continuum, pp 99-112.

Sutton-Smith, B. (2001) *The ambiguity of play*, Boston, MA: Harvard University Press.

Swarbrick, N., Eastwood, G. and Tutton, K. (2004) 'Self-esteem and successful interaction as part of the forest school project', *Support for Learning*, vol 19, pp 142-46.

Tannock, S. (2011) 'Review of *Radical Education and the Common School*', *British Journal of Sociology of Education*, vol 32, pp 939-52.

Taylor, A. (2011) 'Reconceptualizing the "nature" of childhood', *Childhood*, vol 18, pp 420-33.

Taylor, P. (1982) 'A materialist framework for political geography', *Transactions of the Institute of British Geographers*, vol 7, pp 15–34.

Thomas, M. (2005) '"I think it's just natural": the spatiality of racial segregation at a US high school', *Environment and Planning A*, vol 37, pp 1233-48.

Thrift, N. (2000) 'Afterwords', *Environment and Planning D: Society and Space*, vol 18, pp 213-55.

Thrift, N. (2004) 'Intensities of feeling: towards a spatial politics of affect', *Geografiska Annaler Series B*, vol 86, pp 57-78.

Thrift, N. (2007) *Nonrepresentational theory: space, politics, affect*, London: Routledge.

Turner, B. (1993) *Citizenship and social theory*, London: SAGE.

Turner, B. (2008) *The body and society: explorations in social theory*, London: SAGE.

Urry, J. (2007) *Mobilities*, Cambridge: Polity Press.

Valentine, G. (2000) 'Exploring children and young people's narratives of identity', *Geoforum*, vol 31, pp 257-67.

Valentine, G. (2008) 'The ties that bind: towards geographies of intimacy', *Geography Compass*, vol 2, pp 2097-2110.

Vaquera, E. and Kao, G. (2008) 'Do you like me as much as I like you? Friendship reciprocity and its effects on school outcomes among adolescents', *Social Science Research*, vol 37, pp 55-72.

Vecchi, V. (2010) *Art and creativity in Reggio Emilia: exploring the role and potential of ateliers in early childhood education*, London: Routledge.

Volckmar, N. (2008) 'Knowledge and solidarity: the Norwegian social-democratic school project in a period of change, 1945-2000', *Scandinavian Journal of Educational Research*, vol 52, pp 1-15.

Vrecko, S. (2010) 'Birth of a brain disease: science, the state and addiction neuropolitics' *History of the Human Sciences*, vol 23, pp 52-67.

Wainwright, E. and Marandet, E. (2011) 'Geographies of family learning and aspirations of belonging', *Children's Geographies*, vol 9, pp 95-110.

Walkerdine, V. (1988) *The mastery of reason: cognitive development and the production of rationality*, London: Routledge.

Wasburn-Moses, L. (2011) 'An investigation of alternative schools in one state: implications for students with disabilities', *Journal of Special Education*, vol 44, pp 247-55.

Waters, J. (2007) '"Roundabout routes and sanctuary schools": the role of situated practices and habitus in the creation of transnational professionals', *Global Networks*, vol 7, pp 477-97.

Whatmore, S. (1997) 'Dissecting the autonomous self: hybrid cartographies for a relational ethics', in G. Henderson and M. Waterstone (eds) *The geographical thought: a praxis perspective*, London: Routledge, pp 109-21.

Williams, S. (2001) *Emotions and social theory: corporeal reflections on the (ir)rational*, London: SAGE.

Willis, P. (1977) *Learning to labour: how working class kids get working class jobs*, Westmead: Saxon House.

Witten, K., Kearns, R., Lewis, N., Coster, H. and McCreanor, T. (2003) 'Educational restructuring from a community viewpoint: a case study of school closure in Invercargill, New Zealand', *Environment and Planning C: Government and Policy*, vol 21, pp 203-22.

Woods, G., O'Neill, M. and Woods, P. (1997) 'Spiritual values in education: lessons from Steiner?', *International Journal of Children's Spirituality*, vol 2, pp 25-40.

Woods, P. and Woods, G. (2006) 'In harmony with the child: the Steiner teacher as co-leader in a pedagogical community', *FORUM*, vol 48, pp 317-25.

Woods, P. and Woods, G. (eds) (2009) *Alternative education for the 21st century*, London: Palgrave.

Woods, P., Ashley, M. and Woods, G. (2005) *Steiner schools in England*, London: DfES.

Wooltorton, S. (2004) 'Local sustainability at school: a political reorientation', *Local Environment*, vol 9, pp 595-609.

Young, K. (2006) *The art of youth work*, Lyme Regis: Russell House.

Young, M. (1971) *Knowledge and control: new directions for the sociology of education*, Basingstoke: Collier-MacMillan.

Zembylas, M. (2007) 'Theory and methodology in research emotions in education', *International Journal of Research and Method in Education*, vol 30, pp 57-72.

Index

Note: The following abbreviations have been used – *f* = figure; *t* = table